URBAN YOUTH AND SCHOOLING

Education in an Urbanised Society

Series Editors: Gerald Grace, Meg Maguire and Ian Menter

Education continues to face a range of problems, crises, issues and challenges. Often, although not exclusively, those experiencing the most severe problems are working within an urban context. Such schools face very particular challenges – high ethnic minority intake, pupil underachievement, problems of teacher recruitment and retention, social deprivation and other factors. Teachers themselves need to be prepared for classes with a rapid turnover of pupils, pupils from homeless and refugee families, and pupils with English as an additional language.

This series is intended to help education professionals and academics gain a broader understanding of the challenges faced. It examines the problems facing teachers and learners working in challenging and difficult circumstances, with a view to overcoming disadvantage in contemporary education in the UK and Ireland. It explores social and educational developments and provides educational practitioners, academics and policymakers with focused analyses of key issues facing schools in an urban society, examining the interaction between theory and practice. It offers insights into the linkage between education development and wider social, cultural and economic needs and thus contributes to the achievement of social justice in and through education.

Current titles

Mel Ainscow and Mel West: *Improving Urban Schools*

Louise Archer, Sumi Hollingworth and Heather Mendick: *Urban Youth and Schooling*

Pat Broadhead, Chrissy Meleady and Marco A. Delgado: *Children Families and Communities*

Meg Maguire, Tim Woodridge and Simon Pratt-Adams: *The Urban Primary School*

Jill Rutter: *Refugee Children in the UK*

URBAN YOUTH AND SCHOOLING

The Experiences and Identities of
Educationally 'At Risk' Young People

LOUISE ARCHER
SUMI HOLLINGWORTH
HEATHER MENDICK

 Open University Press

Open University Press
McGraw-Hill Education
McGraw-Hill House
Shoppenhangers Road
Maidenhead
Berkshire
England
SL6 2QL

email: enquiries@openup.co.uk
world wide web: www.openup.co.uk

and Two Penn Plaza, New York, NY 10121-2289, USA

First published 2010
Copyright © The Authors, 2010

A catalogue record of this book is available from the British Library

ISBN 13: 978-0-33-522382-4 (pb)   978-0-33-522383-1 (hb)
ISBN 10: 0335223826 (pb)   0335223834 (hb)

Library of Congress Cataloging-in-Publication Data
CIP data applied for

Typeset by RefineCatch Limited, Bungay, Suffolk
Printed by Bell and Bain Ltd, Glasgow

Fictitious names of companies, products, people, characters and/or data that may be used herein (in case studies or in examples) are not intended to represent any real individual, company, product or event.

Mixed Sources
Product group from well-managed
forests and other controlled sources
www.fsc.org Cert no. TT-COC-002769
© 1996 Forest Stewardship Council

FSC

The *McGraw·Hill* Companies

CONTENTS

SERIES EDITORS' PREFACE

This is the fifth book in our series, 'Education in an Urbanised Society' and it is the first that deals specifically with urbanised youth and the transition (or not) between compulsory education and post-compulsory education and training. As the writers of this book explain, 'this book is about the experiences, identities and aspirations of 89 young Londoners identified by their urban schools as "at risk of dropping out or drifting away from education" and as "unlikely to progress into post 16 education" ' (p. 6). One of the difficulties in writing about these sorts of experiences and this cohort of young people is that in the desire to avoid pathologising or stigmatising these young people as 'problems' or 'failures' there can sometimes be a temptation to romanticise aspects of their situations and sideline the structural and material realities that shape their 'choice-making'. In this book, Louise Archer, Sumi Hollingworth and Heather Mendick have produced a sophisticated account that foregrounds the voices and perceptions of the young people that they spoke with, but in a way that recognises these accounts as starting points, and not the end, in generating new understandings and new explanations. It is also managed in a way that takes seriously the effects of material circumstances in shaping life chances.

As we are writing this introduction, there is a 'moral panic' in circulation about (some) young people. In the immediate aftermath of the credit crunch, as unemployment is steadily rising, grave concerns are being expressed about the lack of job opportunities that are currently available for those who have recently graduated from higher education. If the employment situation for this cohort of young adults is so difficult, what must it be like for those young people who have not participated in education and training beyond the compulsory phase? The realities and complexities of the situated lives of those young people who have not enjoyed school are not always well understood. Thus, there has sometimes been a tendency to 'blame' these young people themselves for being 'at risk' of becoming socially excluded. As this book illustrates, for those young people who have to navigate through complex and sometimes chaotic biographies, schooling may at best be a distraction or a place where they feel excluded, shamed or abandoned. In cases like this, choosing to extend this experience, by extending their formal education beyond the compulsory phase, would seem to be counter-intuitive.

As this book is placed in a series on 'urban' education, it is worthwhile commenting on the spatial issues that are significant in this particular volume. London is a global city with an enormous and diverse population and an extensive (low skill, low wage) service sector. Thus, while the 'chances' of securing work are that much greater in London, much of the work is of a particular type associated with the lowest wages, and some young people find themselves to be less employable than others. In the global city, surrounded by apparent opportunities and diversity, many young people readily believe that they will 'make it', that something will turn up and that with luck, they will be able to fulfil their aspirations. In the meantime, they have to search out immediate ways in which to make themselves feel valuable and worthwhile.

Many of the urban young people whose voices are detailed in this book are busy occupying multiple positions in relation to their diverse identities. One of the authors' important achievements here is the powerful way in which the lived identities of the young people are carefully, almost forensically, delineated. The data illustrate the ways in which the young people are caught up in complex identities that are situated between conventional and normalised versions that may simultaneously be in tension with the idealised version of the 'good' student. But always, and inevitably, even though they make up their identities in new ways and draw on their urban lives and urban worlds to do this, they are making up these identities in circumstances that are not of their own choosing (to paraphrase Marx).

The book also draws on the perspectives of teachers, parents and the young people themelves in relation to schooling. A significant consequence of what emerges is a requirement that schools, and urban policymakers, rethink the ways in which young urban students are shown 'respect' and that 'reciprocity' is extended in these schools – what we can see as a renewed contemporary version of critical pedagogy.

In this series of books, we are aiming to put together a collection that recognises the specificity of the urban, through recognising the theoretical, historical and cultural contexts, at the same time as grounding this in the realities of urban educational settings. This book fulfils these intentions admirably.

Gerald Grace, Ian Menter and Meg Maguire

ACKNOWLEDGEMENTS

There are many people who we want to thank for their help in producing this book.

Most of all we thank all those who participated in the research – the schools, teachers, parents and young people who gave their time and views so generously. We are very grateful to the Esmée Fairbairn Foundation (and particularly Hilary Hodgson), who provided funding for the original empirical study on which this book is based. We would like to thank the other researchers and administrators who worked on the funded study: particularly Anna Halsall who did such an excellent job of conducting much of the fieldwork with Sumi, and Alper Hulusi, RoseAnn Renée, Nathan Fretwell and Lindsay Melling.

We thank all our colleagues who provided support and assistance for the original study (conducted while we were all employed at the Institute for Policy Studies in Education at London Metropolitan University) and for the writing of the book (King's College London, London Metropolitan University and Goldsmiths, University of London).

Some of the data and discussions in the book are drawn from articles published in *Gender and Education, British Journal of Sociology of Education, Sociology* and *Urban Studies*. We thank the publishers (Taylor & Francis and Sage) for giving us permission to reproduce material. We are grateful to Open University Press and the series editors for giving us the opportunity to write this book and for their patience during the delay in the book's production while Louise was on maternity leave.

Louise would like to thank Diane Reay for her help with the project and for her (always) useful feedback on analyses and draft papers. She also thanks Matt for his invaluable love and support and Martha and Jamie for their always welcome affection and distraction.

Heather would like to thank her co-authors for generously involving her in this book although she joined the original research project towards the end; Jocey Quinn for feedback on a draft chapter; and the many people with whom she has had conversations related to this book, including Anna Carlile, Anna Llewellyn, Kim Allen, Rosalyn George and Nicola Rollock. She also thanks Ruth, Graham and Sue for their love and friendship.

Sumi would like to thank Anna Halsall for sharing the joys and frustrations of fieldwork and for being a great colleague. She would also like to thank Helen Lucey for her support as her ESRC-TLRP Meeting of Minds Mentor, who has helped immensely with her academic writing. She would also like to thank her ever-supportive family.

SOCIAL EXCLUSION, RISK AND URBAN SCHOOLS

Urban areas and urban schools

This book is about the experiences, identities and aspirations of 89 young Londoners identified by their urban schools as 'at risk of dropping out or drifting away from education' and as 'unlikely to progress into post-16 education'.

In popular imagination, urban schools, and the landscapes in which they sit, are represented as risky, dangerous spaces haunted by the spectre of drugs, poverty, crime and the threat of violence, always about to erupt. We can see this as Michelle Pfeiffer's White teacher inspires Black and Hispanic students in *Dangerous Minds*, accompanied by Coolio rapping 'been spending most my life living in a gangster's paradise' and as Hilary Swank's White teacher challenges her multicultural high school students by comparing the Holocaust to gang warfare in *Freedom Writers*. These images are racialised, in North American popular culture particularly, as White teachers are positioned as 'saviours' and White students are largely absent from representations of urban schools. When they are present, they are constructed as being outside of the orbit of the gangs, drugs and violence and/or as capable of redemption (Chennault, 2006): the lone White student in *Freedom Writers* is the only member of the class who has not been shot at. In UK films, urban spaces are marked by a crosscutting of class and 'race'/ethnicity as either the site of multi-ethnic working-class gang warfare and drug-taking, as in London-based *Kiddulthood*, or as a site of nostalgia for a lost industrial, Northern and mostly White working-class, past, as in Sheffield-based *The Full Monty*. Recently, in Manchester-based *Looking for Eric*, these two combine with a twist, as the multi-ethnic younger generation are redeemed by the solidarity of their White working-class 'fathers'.

Such fictional accounts blur into factual ones as reality TV presents a daily diet of inner-city drunkenness, violence and crime replayed in gritty verité through CCTV footage, and rolling 24 hour news coverage of 'public concern' about this. Indeed incidents of youth gun and knife crime are now major news stories. In 2008, the cover of the international edition of *Time* magazine carried a picture of the face of a young man in a 'hoodie' emblazoned across a Union Jack with the headline: 'Unhappy, Unloved and Out of Control – An epidemic of violence, crime and drunkenness has made Britain scared of its young' (Mayer, 2008). While in the mid-1990s references to gangs in national British daily newspapers *The Sun*, *The Daily Mail* and *The Guardian* hovered at around two or three per year, by 2001 this had scaled up to 111, 234 and 1451 respectively. This explosion of discourse has continued and in 2008 *The Sun* chalked up 1074 items mentioning gangs, *The Daily Mail* 1244 and *The Guardian* a vast 2501, averaging eight references in every single issue of the newspaper. This media-fuelled outbreak of concern about 'gang culture' has resonances with the 1970s 'moral panic' around mugging (Hall et al., 1978). The contemporary panic around gangs is associated with youth, with particular cities, notably London, Manchester and Birmingham, and with particular urban locales within these cities that are coded as working class and minority ethnic. It is the latest development in an ongoing history of the pathologisation of urban spaces, in which they are constructed by the dominant imagination as 'rubbish' and 'shit', as dumping grounds (Lucey and Reay, 2002) that contain the socially excluded, 'unfit' and undesirable. As we explore in Chapter 2, these labels transfer from urban spaces to urban schools and infect the identity work of their young students.

It is thus unsurprising that UK urban areas, and the young people who live there, have long been the focus of specific social and educational policies. In the 1960s Educational Priority Areas were set up in areas of disadvantage in London, Liverpool, Birmingham and West Yorkshire. Area-based initiatives came back into fashion in 1997, when the election of a New Labour government 'marked a sharp swing back to neighbourhood projects . . . now seen as the answer to the geography of disadvantage described by the newly established Social Exclusion Unit' (Smith et al., 2007: 143). There were several such schemes in the field of education:

> Education action zones (and to start off with, these were mainly urban), Excellence in Cities (initially in six large conurbations and their adjoining areas – inner London, Birmingham, Leeds/Bradford, Liverpool/Knowsley, Manchester/Salford and Sheffield/Rotherham) and Fresh Start, which would close and reopen 'failing schools', were all set up to 'rescue' urban schools.
>
> (Maguire et al., 2006: 111)

London Challenge, launched in 2003, contains many elements typical of education area-based initiatives and is being exported to other urban areas (initially the Black Country and Greater Manchester). The scheme attempts to bring about a cultural change in some of London's most deprived areas.

> London educates approximately a sixth of all pupils in England. It faces a unique combination of inner city challenges and south east costs. London is placed in a uniquely complex context: a large number of small local

authorities (LAs), high levels of deprivation and low achievement, a highly diverse and mobile population, and high costs of living which affect recruitment and retention of teachers. These are not seen in such sharp relief anywhere else in the country. The London Challenge will provide some challenges and opportunities for schools and local authorities in London putting them at the leading edge of education nationally and internationally which can be replicated elsewhere.

(http://www.dfes.gov.uk/londonchallenge/faqs.shtml)

London Challenge involves a range of measures that encourage schools to work together such as creating families of similar schools that share best practice, and the London Performance Collaborative, a group of secondary schools who work together with an advisor to improve their examination results. It also incorporates initiatives aimed at particular groups of students: those classified as gifted and talented (G&T), as having English as an Additional Language (EAL) and as 'at risk'. Other activities include: summer universities which offer a diverse range of learning activities to young people during their 'holidays'; opening new schools, particularly in neighbourhoods where many young people go outside of the area for their education; incentives for teachers to take part in continuing professional development, including the possibility of becoming specialised in teaching in London; and a 'Leadership Incentive Grant'.

We see such policies as constitutive of the identities of people and places not as external to them (Ball, 1994). The London Challenge constructs London as a specific space that requires 'targeted' initiatives, ways of working, teaching skills and educational leadership. It is typical of New Labour policy in its attempts to combine collective approaches to tackling social injustice with a focus on developing individual talent and ability, selecting and marking out particular students for attention (Ball, 2007). It attempts to raise aspirations without questioning who decides what acceptable aspirations are (see Chapter 5), and whose aspirations are being normalised and whose pathologised.

It also shares with other New Labour education policy an unhelpful focus on, or obsession with, 'achievement', in a way that is 'extraordinarily narrowly conceived ... as exclusively reflected by credentials from performance in examinations' (Francis and Skelton, 2005: 2). Instead we feel it is more fruitful to look broadly at young people's educational engagement, encompassing their sense of themselves as learners and their experiences of the formal educational system and of learning in informal settings, in the context of exploring their wider identities. This is our task in this book. The questions that orient us are: How can we understand the identities and educational engagement of urban, working-class London young people? What are the powers and possibilities of schooling and broader educational policies in these processes? And, what are the social justice implications? In this opening chapter, we set out the policy, social justice and research contexts. We look first at the tropes of social exclusion and risk in education policy, then at issues relating to social class, 'race'/ethnicity and gender in education. Finally, we describe the schools and people who participated in the research discussed in this book.

Social exclusion and education

Social exclusion is a recurring motif in New Labour policies, such as the area-based initiatives discussed above, where it figures as a problem to be fixed by intervention; a static term that can be used to label particular individuals. Within such policies, social inclusion is signalled by (lifelong) participation in education or work with training. This construction renders the socially excluded as those who cannot or, increasingly, will not be part of the economic and educational 'mainstream'. In contrast, we 'see social exclusion as a dynamic, multifaceted process, encompassing both material deprivation and an inability to participate in the ordinary social and political activities of everyday life. Of particular significance are its spatial manifestations, with growing evidence of areas of spatial segregation across the cities of industrial societies' (Warrington, 2005: 797). Thus, we would argue that policy needs to be understood as integral to the processes through which social exclusion and social inclusion are constructed, rather than as merely a response or solution to social exclusion that stands externally to the 'problems' in question.

Shifting economic conditions, in particular the decline of the UK manufacturing industry, mean that few young people can now expect to find regular paid employment on leaving school at 16 as their parents' generation might have done. Further education has instead 'become the dominant structure through which post-16 transitions are made' (MacDonald, 1997: 21). The Conservative governments of Margaret Thatcher and John Major focused on creating a low-skill low-wage workforce. However, when he became prime minister in 1997 New Labour's Tony Blair stressed that his incoming government's three priorities were 'education, education, education'. This was part of an attempt to move to a high-skill high-wage workforce, as part of a knowledge economy (Brown and Lauder, 2004). Within this, the issues of post-compulsory participation and social inclusion/exclusion are ongoing concerns. The UK government 2001 White Paper states that 'too many young people still gain low or no qualifications and leave learning for good at 16' (DfES, 2001: 8). More recently, the Department for Education and Skills drew attention to findings that: 'Nearly half of young people still do not achieve five good GCSEs [General Certificate of Secondary Education] at school. More still do not reach that standard in English and mathematics. And one in twenty leaves without a single GCSE pass' (DfES, 2003b: 6). As Figure 1.1 shows, the levels of participation in post-compulsory education in the United Kingdom have dipped in recent years and fallen below the average for Central and Eastern Europe and more than 10 percentage points below the average for North America and Western Europe.

As we argue in detail in Chapter 7, interventions addressing this have contained a contradictory mix of carrots and sticks. Carrots come in the form of the Education Maintenance Allowance (EMA), payments of up to £30 per week to students from less affluent backgrounds who stay on in post-16 education and training (http://ema.direct.gov.uk/), and the Connexions service which provides both general careers education and targeted support to disaffected young people, offering them a personal advisor who can work with them and their parents and carers on a one-to-one basis. Sticks include the plan to raise the

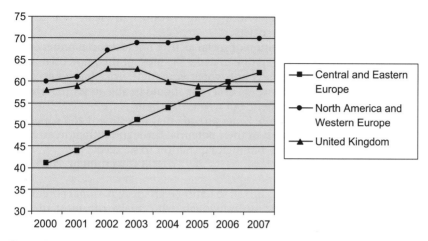

Figure 1.1 Participation in tertiary education (as percentages of total cohort).

Source: http://stats.uis.unesco.org/unesco/ReportFolders/ReportFolders.aspx

compulsory education age from 16 to 17 by 2013 and to 18 by 2015 (DCSF, 2009b) and targets, notably the government's goal to widen participation in higher education (HE) to 50 per cent of 18 to 30-year-olds by 2010. These schemes 'target' young people who do not fit the normalised educational pathways and attempt to bring them into the mainstream – although whether those concerned embrace or resist such attempts is a moot point. As Furlong and Cartmel (1997: 17) note, 'the sharp decline in opportunities for minimum-aged school-leavers in many areas has produced an army of reluctant conscripts to post-compulsory education'.

There are notable silences and gaps within New Labour's education policies: for example, they largely ignore those members of the elite who opt out of the mainstream in various ways, such as through private schooling (Ball, 2003), and those middle/upper-class school-leavers who are not in education, employment or training, for example being on gap years, but who are not reliant on state support due to their possession of other resources and forms of privilege. There are also some inherent contradictions, notably where policy's championing of parental 'choice' results in the exacerbation of social class and race segregation in London schooling (Gewirtz et al., 1995), as middle-class parents are facilitated in opting out of state education and/or forsaking less well performing schools in favour of the 'better' or 'best' options available (Ball, 2006).

The recent global economic downturn has fed into the government's emphasis on educational participation as a route to national economic competitiveness *and* social justice. This is evident in Prime Minister Gordon Brown's introduction to the 2009 White Paper where educational 'investment for tomorrow' is set alongside measures to prevent the collapse of the banking sector as a way of 'creating real hope for the future':

> If Britain can seize the opportunities of this new global age, our future is full of potential. Our country will be richer in the years to come. But the

ultimate prize will be greater still: the opportunity to create not just a richer country, but a fairer society.

This is the modern definition of social justice: not just social protection but real opportunity for everyone to make the most of their potential in a Britain where what counts is not where you come from but what you aspire to become, a Britain where everyone should be able to say that their destiny is not written for them, but written by them. . . .

The measures in this White Paper provide that investment and support for people to make the most of their potential throughout their lives: not just one chance at 11 or 16, but lifelong chances to succeed.

(HM Government, 2009: 1)

Here individual progression is linked to national progress; national potential is realised through self-actualizing individuals who 'make the most of their potential throughout their lives'. For within a knowledge economy, education is necessary for the nation's economic competitiveness. This a world defined by a neoliberal political framework where choices are more than acts of consumption; they are also a means of making one's self. 'Individuals are to become, as it were, entrepreneurs of themselves, shaping their own lives through the choices they make among the forms of life available to them' (Rose, 1999: 230). So, from a neoliberal perspective, people who opt out of education or training, or those who are 'at risk' of doing so, 'appear to be unable – or worse, unwilling – to fit themselves into the meritocratic educational system which produces the achievement vital for the economic success of the individual concerned and of the nation' (Francis, 2006: 193).

Despite the self-conscious appeal to notions of social justice and equity alongside economic concerns ('the opportunity to create not just a richer country, but a fairer society'), it is notable that social justice concerns remain secondary to the overarching economic imperative. Therefore, such policy excludes despite its rhetoric of inclusion and its talk of 'all Britons', for it defines people in terms of 'what you aspire to become' while simultaneously constructing some aspirations as valued and others as valueless. As we discuss later these constructions are classed, racialised and gendered. Moreover, social justice is configured deliberately and explicitly as a 'modern' form (Bauman, 1998), signalled by Brown's talk of a shift from the 'social protection' of the collectivist welfare state to a meritocratic society in which there is 'real opportunity for everyone to make the most of their potential'. Each individual must take responsibility for their own talents, gifts and abilities. Those who fail to do so are thus held responsible for that failure. Self-construction is both the goal and the means to that goal for 'everyone should be able to say that their destiny is not written for them, but written by them'.

Thus, educational policy is about the future as well as the present. It is directed not just at those who are currently socially excluded but also at those 'at risk' of social exclusion, 'at risk' of ending up not in education, employment or training (NEET). Annaliese Dodds (forthcoming) traces a change in emphasis within social policy between previous concerns with identifying and acting upon those who are socially excluded to current interest in identifying and acting upon those who are 'at risk' of social exclusion: 'This new approach uses "risk" as an organizing concept, maintaining that the most important task of social policy is to quickly identify "the most at-risk households, individuals and children so that interventions can be targeted more effectively at those at risk – to themselves or to others" (Her Majesty's Government, 2006)'. Failure in education is taken as a key 'risk factor' in predicting future social exclusion.

Risky business

In educational policy and practice, the categorisation of 'at risk' has become common parlance to denote the sorts of young people that we interviewed for our study, that is, urban youth from working-class backgrounds with complicated or fractured relationships to education. This terminology is prevalent not just in the UK but also in Australia and North America: 'Youth "at risk" is the currently favoured label used in Australian policy for youth whose educational outcomes are considered too low, with an emphasis on the risk of not completing senior secondary education' (te Riele, 2006b: 129). Te Riele (2006b) critically questions the underlying policy assumption of a normative majority versus a problematic 'at risk' minority and the assumed dichotomy between these two, arguing that the relationship is far from clear cut. In particular, 'the dominant conceptualization of youth "at risk" draws attention to what is wrong with these youth, rather than to what may be wrong with schooling' (te Riele, 2006b: 129). Te Riele proposes the alternative term 'marginalised' youth, as a means for capturing (and drawing the focus of attention to) these young people's relationships to schooling and societal institutions. However, we feel this still constructs a dichotomy between a normative majority and a marginalised minority and so we use 'at risk', the inverted commas signalling it as problematic.

'Risk' not only occupies a central position within educational policy and practice but has been proposed as the defining feature of the 'New Times' of contemporary social life (Beck, 1992; Giddens, 1990). Although not entirely new given mid-twentieth-century ideas that 'degeneracy could be nipped in the bud, by regulating the development of children in order to ensure their fitness as adults' (Walkerdine, 1984: 165), increasingly social policy is organised around not just managing present dangers but controlling future dangers. In place of a language of certainty, government policy speaks a language of 'risk'. Risk colonises much of contemporary life – including crime, physical and mental health, violence, drugs and, our focus in this book, education – and it compels action. Its reach continues to grow: the term 'at risk' has recently started being applied to schools by the Training and Development Agency for Schools.

In this sense there are parallels with the precrime system in Philip K. Dick's science fiction short story *Minority Report*. The precrime system is a crime-free society, so-called because people are arrested *before* they commit a crime. This works through the use of a group of three precog mutants with the power to predict and report on the future. Here, as in our own society, desires for certainty and control (Walkerdine, 1988) sit alongside fears of risk and danger, as is evident in the following discussion of precrime:

'With the aid of your precog mutants, you've boldly and successfully abolished the postcrime punitive system of jails and fines. As we all realize, punishment was never much of a deterrent, and could scarcely have afforded comfort to a victim already dead.'

... 'You've probably grasped the basic legalistic drawback to precrime methodology. We're taking in individuals who have broken no law.'

'But they surely will,' ...

'Happily they *don't* – because we get them first, before they can commit an act of violence. So the commission of the crime itself is absolute metaphysics. We claim they're culpable. They, on the other hand, eternally claim they're innocent. And, in a sense, they *are* innocent.'

(Dick, 2000: 72, original emphasis)

As the story continues, the head of precrime, John Anderton, is identified in the reports of two of the three precogs as a future murderer. He should be captured and punished but uses his position to effect an escape. Upon investigation he finds out that the third precog produced a different reading of the future in which he was innocent; this is the 'minority report' in distinction from the 'majority report' of the two other precogs. This report is out of time phase with the other two, being slightly ahead of them, and so the prediction it contains is based on more data and crucially on the fact of Anderton seeing the majority report that identifies him as a murderer. At one point in the story John Anderton discusses this with his wife Lisa who also works in precrime:

'I wonder,' she said . . ., 'how many times this has happened before.'

'A minority report? A great many times.'

'I mean, one precog misphased. Using the report of the others as data – superseding them.' Her eyes dark and serious, she added, 'Perhaps a lot of the people in the [prison] camps are like you.'

'No,' Anderton insisted. But he was beginning to feel uneasy about it, too. 'I was in a position to see the card, to get a look at the report. That's what did it.'

'But –' Lisa gestured significantly. 'Perhaps all of them would have reacted that way. We could have told them the truth.'

'It would have been too great a risk.'

(Dick, 2000: 89)

Here Dick captures both the productive power of labels, as Anderton's knowledge of his criminality sets him onto an alternative crime-free path, and the ways that people, particularly those involved in making and implementing policies, are invested in reading risk as certainty. They, like Anderton, cannot imagine the possibility that those acted upon by the state may not need such action or that the actions of the state itself may create that need.

In contemporary England we share this desire to know the future, or at least what it would be were we not to intervene. However, we have nothing that gives us the (illusion of) assurance about what the future holds for particular individuals that the precog mutants give within the society that Dick imagines. Although all societies have systems for controlling risk, the specific processes of risk selection and management found within a particular society are central to how we define ourselves in distinction from others, to how we experience and relate to our bodies, money, work and so on and to how we make choices in relation to these. 'Those phenomena that we single out and identify as "risks", therefore, have an important ontological status in our understandings of selfhood and the social and material worlds' (Lupton, 1999: 14). In particular, there has been an intensification and individualisation of risk within neoliberalism, which is demanding that individuals become more risk conscious and holds them responsible for failing to do this, positioning them as architects of their own failure (Walkerdine, 2003). As Kemshall (2002: 1) argues, 'risk, particularly an individualized and responsibilized risk, is replacing need as the core principle of social policy formation and welfare delivery'.

With the shift to 'risk' in social policy the emphasis on young people has intensified in line with the twin beliefs that they 'are being socialised into the deviant cultures of their economically sidelined parents' (MacDonald, 1997: 19) and that they are open to other influences and so to other futures. However, this risk culture has uneven effects (Francis, 2006). In contrast to dominant policy approaches that focus on 'managing' risk, we would argue that risk can be more usefully conceptualised as the product of sociocultural processes and must be understood in relation to social identities and inequalities. In the next section we look at how neoliberalism, social exclusion and risk interact with urban young people's identities and with differences of social class, 'race'/ethnicity and gender.

Identities and differences: social class, 'race'/ethnicity and gender

As discussed above, within contemporary neoliberal society, identity takes work for 'each individual must render his or her life meaningful as if it were the outcome of individual choices made in furtherance of a biographical project of self-realization' (Rose, 1999: ix). In this context of consumer individualism it has become popular to proclaim the end of the 'old' categories of social class, 'race'/ethnicity and gender, to argue that these are no longer useful concepts (Beck, 1992; Giddens, 1990). However, research, including this book, shows that social class, gender and 'race'/ethnicity are not disappearing. Instead their effects are becoming more obscure, as young people, like those in research by Ball, Maguire and Macrae (2000: 4), come to 'see themselves as individuals in a meritocratic society, not as classed or gendered members of an unequal society'. Writing about young people's transitions to adulthood, Furlong and Cartmel (1997: 6) trace ongoing inequalities and call the idea that social divisions are no longer important 'the epistemological fallacy of late modernity'. While subsequent chapters detail our theorisations of the role of social class (Chapter 2), 'race'/ethnicity (Chapter 3) and gender (Chapter 4) in urban young people's lives and education, in this section we briefly outline key policy issues in relation to each of these and situate our own approach to these three dimensions of inequality.

In doing this, we try to avoid commonsense understandings, for example, we reject the idea that gender or ethnic differences in attainment and choices are due to biological factors, seeing them instead as socially constructed categories. 'Common sense consists of a number of social meanings and the particular ways of understanding the world which guarantee them. These meanings, which inevitably favour the interests of particular social groups, become fixed and widely accepted as true irrespective of sectional interests' (Weedon, 1997: 77). We use the term discourses to refer to these collections of meanings that are enacted in the ways that we talk and behave (Foucault, 1972; MacLure, 2003). They define objects into being and set limits on what we can think, feel and be. It is discourses that provide the resources for, and so constraints on, identity construction; we make ourselves but not in conditions of our own choosing (Epstein and Johnson, 1998). We are concerned to understand the assumptions within these discourses and the patterns of logic that hold them together, so that we can take them apart and make possible new meanings and ways of being.

Social class

In policy, class is often masked (Skeggs, 2004): it is common for (working-)-class, particularly in inner-city areas, to be synonymous with 'social exclusion' and 'disadvantage' (Archer and Yamashita, 2003b; Gewirtz, 2001). We will argue that these are loaded terms that conceptualise middle-class experience as normative, and depict the working classes as deficient in some way (Colley and Hodkinson, 2001; Gillies, 2005). To develop this point we begin with our notion of social class.

Social class is a widely available but highly contested concept; 'although most people have some understanding of the "class system" there is no single scale upon which everyone is agreed' (Gillborn and Gipps, 1996: 17). Much policy and quantitative research in education uses eligibility for free school meals as a marker of class, but, this is problematic since not all those eligible for these take them up and although class and poverty are linked, they are not synonymous. Policy and common usage often focuses on employment-based divisions, such as 'manual' or 'professional' occupational groupings (for example, the NS-SEC, the most recent official classificatory system in England). The vast majority of the young people in this book are from families that would be seen as 'working class' in terms of these indicators. However, we take the view that 'economic conditions constitute just one aspect of class rather than providing us with a comprehensive picture' (Reay, 2004b: 140). For, with a widening gulf between rich and poor in the UK, while class may be disappearing in discourse in the public realm, it is ever present in people's lived experiences (Holt and Griffin, 2005; Reay, 2004b). Thus, we use an understanding of class as both economic and cultural, an approach which we develop further in Chapter 2. This approach explores how economic advantages can transfer into cultural ones and vice versa, for example via private tuition (research shows that 43 per cent of 11–16-year-olds in London have private tuition Sutton Trust, 2009).

Research consistently shows large differences in attainment by social class that are much greater than those by 'race'/ethnicity or gender (DfES, 2006). However, the main policy focus has been on increasing working-class participation in further education (FE) and higher education (HE). Data from two longitudinal studies of large samples of 17-year-olds in England show that whereas only 3 per cent of young people with parents holding 'professional' occupations were classified as NEET, this applied to 9 per cent of young people whose parents had 'lower supervisory' jobs and 14 per cent of those whose parents carried out 'routine' work (DCSF, 2009a). Using a more cultural measure, only 3 per cent of those young people whose parents had degrees were NEET, compared with 11 per cent of those whose parents had only GCSE-equivalent qualifications or lower. The data also show that whether measured by parents' economic position or their educational capital, the time spent in the NEET category increases as you go down the social class hierarchy. Similarly, these young people's intentions to apply to HE are differentiated by social class. It is very difficult to obtain complete and up-to-date statistics of university entry by any measure of social class, which says something of the elusiveness of this category. However, all previous studies have shown marked differences, whatever measure has been used (Archer et al., 2003; Greater London Authority, 2007; Reay et al., 2005). Indeed HE participation is now more dependent on family background than it was before 1997 (Hills and Stuart, 2005).

Policy addresses this classed pattern of participation in post-compulsory education both financially and culturally. Financially it offers residual grants and hardship funds for young people from families on low incomes. Culturally it provides a range of initiatives to 'raise' aspirations and increase knowledge about HE among under-represented communities. The Aim Higher programme (www.aimhigher.ac.uk) was set up to work with young people from neighbourhoods with lower than average HE participation, from working-class backgrounds, and from families with no previous experience of HE. It is one of a number of programmes attempting to raise working-class aspirations and hence university participation through a range of interventions including university visits, study support and summer schools.

Within such programmes aspirations not involving educational progression, and those holding them, are implicitly constructed as deficient and wrong. However, as we elaborate in Chapters 4 and 5, the decision by a working-class young person to aspire to employment rather than university study at 18 can easily be understood as responsible and rational given their needs and the risks of HE. HE risks are greater for working-class people in terms of their investment of time and money, their relationships with family and friends and their sense of self. Simultaneously the potential benefits of HE are fewer because they are more likely to go to lower status institutions and to get lower paid jobs afterwards (Archer et al., 2003). So policy attempts to 'raise' aspirations, as if these were individual asocial traits, are problematic because they normalise remaining on the educational conveyor belt and do not acknowledge the role of policy in creating the 'problem' of 'low' aspirations. Thus, the blame, and hence responsibility for action, is located with the individual student or family concerned, something which is common to the policy treatment of ethnic minority students and education.

'Race'/ethnicity

Urban schools contain a significant and growing number of minority ethnic children and young people:

> In 2006 around 17% of secondary school students (aged between 11 and 16) and 21% of primary students (age 5–10) were classified as being of minority ethnic heritage (DfES 2006a: 3). In the cities of London, Birmingham and Leicester it is projected that by the end of this decade no group will account for 50% or more of the population
> (Gillborn and Rollock, 2009)

Minority ethnic attainment and participation have been perennial policy concerns. However, there are important differences between ethnic minorities, with Chinese and Indian students remaining the 'model minorities' in terms of their high attainment and Black Caribbean young people generally constructed through discourses of failure, with Black Caribbean boys being consistently over-represented in school exclusions by a ratio of three to one in comparison to their White peers (Gillborn and Rollock, forthcoming). Moreover, there are important differences within ethnic minority groups, notably by social class and gender (Gillborn and Mirza, 2000); although such differences also vary across groups with, for example, social class differences being greater among White than Chinese young people (Archer and Francis, 2007).

There have been various shifts in emphasis within educational policy over the years in relation to issues of 'race'/ethnicity. In the 1960s, minority ethnic students were predominantly viewed as 'problems', as deficient learners whose various lacks in language, skills, abilities, and so on, needed to be compensated for. Over the 1980s, multicultural and antiracist movements meant respective shifts in focus to the 'celebration' of cultural differences, and the impact of racism on students' experiences and achievement (Griffiths and Troyna, 1995). The publication of the Macpherson Report in 1999 marked a key point in public sector policy with regard to race, heralding in the notion of institutional racism and, through the Race Relations Amendment Act (2000), placing a duty on schools to promote good race relations and specifically to record and report on racist incidents and on permanent exclusions by race. However, as Rollock (2009) argues these moves have had little success due partly to the failure of Ofsted to engage with race equality in inspections.

Indeed, issues of 'race'/ethnicity have become silent of late within New Labour government policy and, rather than flagging up the potential role of structural or wider social issues in the creation of racialised patterns of achievement, current policy approaches predominantly locate the 'problem' within minority ethnic families, communities and individuals. For example, the high-profile Aiming High scheme (DfES, 2003a) focuses on tackling minority ethnic underachievement and under-participation in post-compulsory education, using some of the same approaches as in Aim Higher but with a greater emphasis on learning mentors. It reflects the individualistic focus on 'fixing' low aspirations, poor parenting and lack of role models (see critique in: Archer and Francis, 2007), that is supported by media coverage of minority ethnic young people (for example, *Daily Mail*, 2009). As discussed earlier, this transfer of responsibility for 'failure' to the individual has been identified as a feature of neoliberalism which enables the state to absolve itself of any responsibility for the re/production of disadvantage.

However, in contrast with working-class young people, most minority ethnic groups' participation in HE is proportionally higher than among White people. That the participation rate for young people in HE has seen the highest growth in London can be attributed partially to growth among members of ethnic minorities (HEFCE, 2005). Within neoliberal individualistic framing, this is viewed as evidence that the problem has been solved. Thus, remaining structural inequalities are left unaddressed, including: the on average lower grades that minority ethnic students obtain at university, the position within the universities hierarchy of the institutions they attend, and their employment prospects on leaving (Ball et al., 2002a). Instead, eyes turn to who is now lowest in the league tables and to ways to fix them; as we explore in the next section, the new disadvantaged are White, working-class boys.

Gender

In media and policy discourses, girls are no longer a problem. Indeed, young women seem to represent the ideal, flexible, neoliberal subject (McRobbie, 2008). Working-class boys by contrast: 'are usually from broken homes, unlikely to work, will descend into crime or drugs and pass on that fate to their children. Three-quarters of low achievers in Britain's deprived areas are working-class, white and male' (Wark, 2007). Penny Wark's newspaper article calls for a fight against the 'cycle of despair' that she (like many media and policy commentators) fears is currently afflicting White working-class boys in the UK. Indeed, for many, these boys constitute an 'underclass', a ticking time bomb of social ills that requires urgent action and intervention.

Drawing on the work of Epstein et al. (1998), Francis and Skelton (2005) have identified four contemporary dominant discourses that are predominantly drawn upon within academic, media and policy debates about boys' underachievement. As they point out, all these discourses are in popular usage but all are, to some extent, problematic in the ways that they conceptualise masculinity and the 'problem' of underachievement. The first, termed the *poor boys* discourse derives from the men's rights movement and argues that boys' underachievement is the product of over zealous feminist agendas that have victimised boys and led to their educational disadvantage. In contrast, the *boys will be boys* discourse posits that boys are 'naturally' (biologically, psychologically) different to girls and hence need teaching approaches that are more in tune with their different learning styles. The *at risk boys* discourse is well illustrated by Wark's views above, arguing that boys' underachievement stems from their social exclusion and the resultant low self-esteem and alienation that are passed through families, from father to son. Finally, the *problem boys* discourse draws attention to the ways that 'bad' male practices and cultures, notably 'laddishness' and antisocial peer cultures, produce underachievement. As Francis and Skelton explain, these dominant discourses are not mutually exclusive and may be drawn on in various combinations. While proffering a range of sites of 'blame' (and by implication, intervention) for the issue of boys' under-achievement, they share two problems: they uncritically accept the 'fact' of boys' underachievement and are based on rigid and under-theorised notions of masculinity. The end result is that working-class boys are individualised and held accountable for their failure. For while some of these discourses, notably 'poor boys' are: 'applied to boys generally, these neo-liberal policy drives are beginning to position some boys differently, with an increasingly sour note developing in the policy documents on "failing boys" ' (Francis, 2006: 191).

In comparison to boys, girls are largely ignored within current research and policy and little attention has been given to the experiences of those girls who are failing, or being failed by, the educational system. Research by Osler and Vincent (2003) suggest that many schools neither notice nor meet the needs of such young women. They ascribe this to both the policy focus on boys and girls' less visible forms of disengagement, including truanting and parentally condoned absence. Hence many girls do not receive the support they need, an issue that can become crucial within post-school transitions:

> [B]oys who leave school early are better able to access work and training than are girls . . . it is vital to note that leaving school early is almost always problematic for girls. Girls find it more difficult to access paid work than their male peers and they tend to be significantly over-represented in the 'out of the labour market' figures.
>
> (Osler and Vincent, 2003: ix)

Additionally, there are many other issues around gender apart from attain-ment such as the persistence of gender inequalities in patterns of educational and employment choice (Beck et al., 2006; Mendick, 2006), the anxiety experienced by girls around education, often associated with self harm and eating disorders (Evans et al., 2008; Walkerdine et al., 2001), and experiences of sexual harassment and sexual violence within schooling (Carlile, 2009). In Chapter 4, we highlight the struggles for young women in doing femininity, in relation to appearance and heterosexuality, and the tensions this creates with success at school.

For all young people, constructing a viable identity takes work. The available discourses of the 'good pupil', 'at risk teen', 'Muslim girl', 'White working-class boy', and so on, constrain as much as more obvious factors, such as poverty. Our identities are made up of multiple positionings in, often contradictory, discourses. There are unconscious factors – desires, anxieties, fantasies, projec-tions, defences – as well as conscious ones at play when people do identity work and take up positions within discourses. 'Our sense of ourselves . . . may be at times contradictory and precarious but only a conscious awareness of [its] contradictory nature . . . can introduce the possibility of political choice between modes of [identity] in different situations and between the discourses in which they have their meaning' (Weedon, 1997: 87). So, it is only by under-standing the complexity of the discourses in which we live, and our own positionings in relation to them, that we can open up other possibilities. For social structures and policies are not deterministic:

Schools also produce forms of resistance. Children and their teachers have always been able to interrupt and subvert (to an extent) some of the intentions of educational policymakers. And, in part, it is this resistance that has contributed to the demonization of the urban school as a place of disruption, difficulty and distress.

(Maguire et al., 2006: 10)

Thus to understand urban schools, we need to look at what happens there and at the ways of being of the people in them.

Researching educationally 'at risk' urban youth

In this book we report on data collected as part of a longitudinal study between July 2003 and June 2005, funded by the Esmée Fairbairn Foundation (the project was directed by Louise and Sumi and Heather were members of the larger project team). Overall, 89 young people in six schools took part, together with five of their parents and 19 school staff members. We used a mixture of qualitative methods to tap into these young people's views and experiences, including individual interviews with students, staff members and parents, student discussion groups and photo-diaries. All the interviews were conducted by one of four interviewers: two White women, one Black Caribbean woman and one Turkish man.

Urban schools

We recruited young people to take part in the study through six schools. The six schools are geographically spread across London (three in North London, one in East London, two in West London) and had, at the time of selection, results below the national average at GCSE. **Blackwell Street** is a mixed comprehensive that had been undersubscribed for several years preceding the research. The school has an ethnically diverse student population, with a large proportion of Turkish and Kurdish students. **Cowick** is a fully subscribed ethnically diverse all-girls comprehensive that attracts students from across the borough. **Littleton** is an oversubscribed ethnically diverse all-boys comprehensive school that attracts students from both the local housing estates and the neighbouring boroughs. **Riverway** is a mixed comprehensive school with particularly low results and low rates of progression into post-compulsory education. The school predominantly serves local estates, is nearly entirely working-class and has two main student ethnic groups: White and Bangladeshi. **Hillside Park** is a mixed comprehensive that is currently oversubscribed. It serves a relatively small catchment area, consisting largely of one, predominantly White working-class, estate. **Eastleigh Central** is a large ethnically diverse mixed comprehensive school that mostly serves local estates.

Table 1.1 compares these schools in terms of the proportions of students:

- from different ethnicities (White UK, and ethnic minorities making up more than 5 per cent of the school population are shown)

Table 1.1 The participating schools

Type of school	Littleton All boys	Cowick All girls	Blackwell Mixed	Eastleigh Mixed	Hillside Mixed	Riverway Mixed
Ethnicity						
White UK	37	8	1	5	79	44
White other	7	14	31	12		6
Indian	10	5	8	18		31
Bangladeshi	8	6	19	7		
Black Caribbean	14	15		14		
Black African		15				
EAL	37	53	72	81	15	46
SEN						
With statements	3	2	2	3	3	7
Without statements	24	12	33	18	35	16
FSM	44	37	18	29	34	32
KS 3 attainment						
English – level 5+	51	65	28	72	48	45
Maths – level 5+	67	66	32	48	49	52
KS4 attainment (5+ A*–C grades)						
2003: national: 53	51	49	27	26	20	25
2004: national: 54	62	54	36	27	26	31
2005: national: 57	52	49	17	27	46	35

Sources: London Challenge website; DCSF website.

- with English as an Additional Language (EAL)
- with Special Educational Needs (SEN)
- who are eligible for Free School Meals (FSM)
- who attained the national 'benchmark' of National Curriculum level 5 or above in maths and English at Key Stage 3 (KS3, aged 14)
- who attained the national 'benchmark' of 5 of more GCSEs at A*–C grades at Key Stage 4 (KS4, aged 16)

The data covers 2005, the final year of the study, in all cases except the GCSE attainment data which covers 2003–2005, the entire period of the study; as you can see, there was a great deal of variation in results during this time.

All of these schools are 'urban', both geographically and in the sense that they are 'schools that serve "deprived areas" and excluded communities' (Maguire et al., 2006: 17). They reflect a range within this, from schools that 'have several other key characteristics, most notably greater proportions of children from a minority ethnic background and children for whom English is an additional language' to those that 'serve a more homogeneous working-class community' (Maguire et al., 2006: 17). Urban schools also generally have other 'challenges' compared to non-urban schools such as a higher number of students with special educational needs, a higher staff turnover and more problems recruiting teachers.

London is a very specific urban location. However, all places and spaces have their own specificities and we would suggest that there are points of generalisation from London to other urban areas, such as: the diversity of London's population (Maylor et al., 2007), the increasing segregation in schooling and housing by 'race'/ethnicity and social class (Warrington, 2005), the coming together of the local and the global (Hall, 1991a), the intensification in levels of risk (Beck, 1992), and the neoliberal policy context (Sofer, 2007). Many of these are indeed 'specific to global cities like London, but may well be reflected, perhaps on a smaller-scale, in many other Western urban settings' (Ball et al., 2000: 21). Thus, we hope that insights from our particular study might be of use and relevance to those working and living in other contexts.

Urban youth

At the centre of the research are a series of semi-structured interviews with 53 young people in the final years of compulsory schooling, Years 10 and 11 (14 to 16 years old). We asked the six participating schools to identify students in this age bracket who they felt fitted the criteria of 'at risk of dropping out of education' and 'unlikely to progress into post-16 education'. We then sought parental consent to take part for those identified. We wanted to recruit young people who were still 'hanging on' in mainstream education but who were 'at risk' of 'dropping out' and/or not continuing, so we chose to access them via schools rather than, for instance, sites of alternative educational provision, such as Pupil Referral Units (PRUs).

Each student was tracked over the course of the two year project and, wherever possible, interviewed three (and in some cases four) times. While all initial interviews were conducted within one of the six participating schools, later interviews varied in their location as the young people's circumstances changed. For instance, some young people moved into PRUs and were interviewed in these sites whereas others had left school, so their follow up interviews were conducted in places such as local cafés. All participants were from ostensibly 'working-class' backgrounds. Table 1.2 shows their chosen pseudonyms organised by school and year group; girls are shown in bold and boys in plain text. In terms of gender and 'race'/ethnicity, the sample comprised 23 girls and 30 boys, of whom 26 were White UK, 11 Black African/Caribbean, 6 mixed heritage, 4 Asian, 3 Middle East and 3 White Other. Twenty-six students were in Year 11 at the start of the project and 27 were in Year 10. More detailed demographic information about the participants is given in Appendix 1.

In the individual interviews, participants were asked about: their educational histories, their current experiences of school, their aspirations and future plans, their educational choices and the influences on these, their knowledge and feelings about university and about government policies. We also asked about their identities, for example, by exploring their interests, how they described themselves and their activities outside of school. We followed

Table 1.2 The participating young people

	Littleton	Cowick	Blackwell	Eastleigh	Hillside	Riverway
Year 10	Darrell	**Jade**	David	**Helal**	**Jane**	Babu
	James	**Kay**	**Hapsa**	**Nadira**	Mark	Dan
	John	**Kemisha**	**Jermina**	Robert	Mike	**Lacie**
	Max	**Leah**	**Nadia**		**Natalie**	Lee
	Mike	**Yesim**			Nick	**Michelle**
	Roger					
Year 11	Darren	**Amanda**	Germaine	Bob	Ben	Bob
	David	**Analisa**	**Jordan**	**Melissa**	David	Jay
	Jason	**Charlene**	Mike	Peter	**Janine**	**Lucy**
	Mark	**Kyle**		**Sarah**		Verona
	Tyson	**Latoya**		Steven		

Note: Girls are shown in bold and boys in plain text.

up these issues with a small number of participants using photographic diaries (alongside a fourth interview) and parental interviews.

Eight students completed photographic diaries: Jane, Tim, Nathan, Nadia, Melissa, Babu, Lacie and Lee. They were given a disposable camera and asked to take photographs representing 'a day in my life' over an agreed 24-hour period. They were told that they could take photographs of whatever they liked or felt to be important, inside or outside of school. A researcher met the student the next day to collect the camera. These students were provided with their own set of photographs and interviewed about their diary. We asked them to discuss each photograph in turn, about who or what they had *not* taken pictures of and why, and what they would perhaps have liked to do. Semi-structured individual interviews were conducted with a small group of five parents. This group comprised four White UK mothers, of John, Lee, Lacie and Mike (Hillside Park), and Babu's Bangladeshi mother who was interviewed in Bengali with a translator. Mothers were asked about: their aspirations, hopes and expectations for their children, their experience of the school as a parent, their child's learning and achievement and issues such as careers advice.

The data from the core group of students was supplemented by interviews with 18 staff members and eight discussion groups involving an additional 36 young people. Staff members included Deputy Headteachers, Heads of Year, subject teachers, Inclusion Managers, Learning Mentors and Connexions Advisors (see Appendix 2 for a complete list). The professionals interviewed consisted of eleven women and eight men, of whom 12 identified as White UK, three as Black African/Caribbean, two as Turkish and one as White Other (with information missing from one). They were asked: to provide a general context to their own work and to their school, unit or service; to identify key issues from their perspective; and about their views of factors affecting students' engagement and progression, including government policies. The student discussion groups comprised 22 boys and 14 girls: 20 White UK,

8 Black African/Caribbean, 4 mixed heritage, 2 Asian, 2 Middle East and 1 White Other. These groups were used to explore particular issues arising from the ongoing analysis. Six of the discussion groups focused on aspirations and two focused on experiences of vocational education and its impact on their choices and aspirations.

We took care regarding how students were invited to participate in the study, so as not to negatively affect their confidence and sense of self by naming them as 'drop-out' students or as 'at risk'. The study aims were explained as focusing on aspirations, identities and post-16 choices and students were informed that they were selected on the basis that they were in Year 10 or 11. However, inevitably the study impacted on the destinations and aspirations of the participants. Due to the repeat interview format, they perhaps thought more about their aspirations than they would have otherwise. The repeat interviews also generated rapport between interviewers and students, with a few young people asking for advice or information both during and after the fieldwork period. In these circumstances, the research team provided appropriate information or support and encouraged the young person to take the issue further with a relevant service, such as Connexions. Thus, our research was also, in small ways, constitutive of these young people's identities and there is a possibility that, for a few, the process of taking part in the study actually increased their likelihood of continuing in education.

Listening to 'at risk' young people

Young people, such as those who feature in the pages of this book, who 'drop out' of education are a hard-to-reach group; they remain marginalised within mainstream schooling and policy. Importantly, the views of these young people are usually absent from discussions around policy and practice, even though 'what students say about teaching, learning and schooling is not only worth listening to but provides an important – perhaps the most important – foundation for thinking about ways of improving schools' (Rudduck et al., 1996: 1). Lack of consultation with young people is a great difficulty with the many policies discussed earlier that claim to be addressing their 'needs' without taking into account their 'constructions of self and their social positioning . . . their "needs" are frequently decided with very little reference to their own view' (Phoenix, 2000: 95). Excluding young people from consultations about their schooling is founded on views of childhood and adolescence which construct these as developmental phases in which people are less capable of making decisions about their lives and in which their views have less value than those of people who are chronologically older (Epp and Watkinson, 1996). When young people are given space to speak, the voices heard usually belong to those who are educationally successful. However, 'it is the less effective learners who are most likely to be able to explore aspects of the system that constrain commitment and progress; these are the voices least likely to be heard and most important to be heard' (Ruddock et al., 1996: 177).

Thus, in this study we foreground urban students' 'voices' on the policies and strategies of which they are 'targets', bringing their views into the policy arenas from which they are usually excluded, and setting their voices alongside those of teachers and parents. Voice is a popular metaphor among education-alists concerned with youth issues (Hadfield and Haw, 2000), and one that informs our analysis. The authority of voice derives from the way that it speaks someone's lived experience. However, experience is not, in any simple way 'lived'; it is always already constructed by the available discourses. There is no simple connection between someone's position – as an 'at risk' young person or as anything else – and the 'truth' or 'value' of what they say. As Stuart Hall (1991b: 58) reminds us: 'There is absolutely no political guarantee already inscribed in an identity. There is no reason on God's earth why the film is good because a Black person made it. There is absolutely no guarantee that all the politics will be right because a woman does it'. However, while there are no guarantees, when one group's perspectives are systematically excluded from a field of knowledge, using this group's views as a starting point can provide a basis for developing alternative knowledges about these processes of exclusion (Hughes, 2002). We believe that the disjunctions between the views expressed by the young people in this book and those expressed by their teachers and by policymakers build a strong case for this kind of approach. In this way of working, voices and the experiences they speak into existence are 'not the origin of our explanation, but that which we want to explain' (Scott, 1992: 38).

Thus, the student (and other) 'voices' in the rest of this book must be treated with care; they are ventriloquised through the three of us; they tell of the conscious and unconscious identity work of the participants and also of the constitutive power of schooling, policy and other aspects of the social. Before we begin this ventriloquism, we outline how we have organised the material in the rest of the book.

Outline of the book

In Chapters 2, 3 and 4 we explore the interrelated inequalities of social class, 'race'/ethnicity and gender introduced in this chapter. In Chapter 2, we focus on the role of social class, poverty and space in the dis/engagement and non/progression into post-16 education of urban young people. We analyse stu-dents', parents' and education professionals' constructions of 'the street' and 'the estate' as key factors affecting educational engagement and look at how young people adopt 'branded' identities as a source of value and esteem. We argue that poverty and social class within the contemporary urban context can be understood in terms of the generation and negotiation of vulnerability and risk by urban young people and their families and that urban schools are con-tradictorily positioned within this, between their working-class locale and the middle-class world of academia.

In Chapter 3, we turn to the increasingly complex and entangled ethnicities of urban youth, as they occupy multiple positions in relation to culture, nationality, residency, parentage, 'race', language and religion. These multiple and shifting ethnicities create multiple and shifting racisms. We explore these from the point of view of staff and of White and minority ethnic students in urban schools. Finally we analyse the experiences of refugee young people and those having English as an Additional Language.

In Chapter 4 we build on the previous chapters to examine participants' classed and racialised masculinities and femininities. We look at what leads some of them to want to follow alternative pathways to further and higher education. In particular, we suggest that young men's desires to become responsible wage-earners and young women's desires to enter into conventional heterosexual femininity (through having a boyfriend and concerns for their appearance) are in tension with educational engagement and the holding of 'high' aspirations. We also look at how young women are coming into conflict with schools by 'speaking my mind', which does not fit with images of the 'ideal female pupil'.

In Chapter 5, we suggest that education policy and practice would benefit from more complex understandings of urban young people's aspirations. We use data to illustrate how many urban working-class young people do not hold a single or consistent aspiration, instead, for example, several 'conflicting' ideas may be held at once and these often change over time. We show how their aspirations and views of their future lives are formed in relation to known and familiar trajectories. We also discuss how many young people in the study deferred their aspirations – preferring to 'wait and see' until after GCSE results before making decisions about their futures. We argue that this strategy can be understood as pragmatic and grounded within the young people's 'risky' lives, but can also seriously disadvantage them. Our discussion also focuses on those students (mostly girls) within the study who expressed 'high' aspirations, and we examine the complexities of these and the structural barriers to their realisation.

In Chapter 6, we explore what teachers, students and parents had to say about teaching and learning in urban schools, looking in turn at pedagogy, assessment and curriculum. Drawing on data and related studies we suggest that teacher-student relationships are critical to the educational engagement of young people. We explore how to build relationships of 'respect', and 'reciprocity' between teachers and students in urban schools, and at some of the structural constraints that make this difficult. In particular, we argue against assessment-driven systems of dividing students into 'ability' sets (called tracking in the US) and into 'academic' vs. 'practical'/'vocational' groupings.

In Chapter 7, we explore the views of young people, parents and educational professionals on a range of policies and initiatives aimed at increasing educational engagement and post-16 participation among urban young people. We look first at how these interventions aim to remake the selves of the targeted young person, in the image of the ideal neoliberal (White, middle-class) subject. We then discuss the ways that these interventions are a contradictory mixture of choice and coercion, for, in neoliberal terms, people have to be persuaded (or even compelled) to participate in their own self-realisation. In the final chapter, we review the key themes emerging from the book and outline their implications for educational research, policy and practice.

Summary

In this chapter we have introduced our research study looking at the identities of urban young people whose schools classified them as educationally 'at risk'. We have taken a critical look at discourses around urban education, social exclusion and risk both within social policy and more broadly in society. In relation to social class, 'race'/ethnicity and gender we have suggested that these discourses contribute to a process whereby the effects of structural inequalities are attributed to individual failings and failures. Finally we argued for the importance of listening to 'at risk' young people and their views on their schooling.

'THE STREET', 'THE ESTATE' AND 'MY TRAINERS': SOCIAL CLASS AND URBAN EDUCATION

It has become relatively commonplace within education policy documents and reports for notions such as *cultures of poverty* and *poverty of aspirations* to be identified as key factors that are creating and sustaining working-class under-achievement and disengagement from education (for example, DCSF, 2008; DfES, 2004, 2005b; Panel on Fair Access to the Professions, 2009). Inherent within such notions is the idea that working-class families do not always value education sufficiently, often due to parents' negative experiences of education and/or family histories of unemployment. This assumption was set out by the Social Exclusion Unit Report (1999), suggesting that parents who are poor, unemployed and who have 'little or no history of work' have a negative influence on young people's participation in structured learning (Colley and Hodkinson, 2001: 48). As Colley and Hodkinson (2001) note, the Social Exclusion Unit (1999) report is peppered by a litany of 'lacks' and 'needs', in which working-class (or 'socially excluded') families are framed as deficient or dysfunctional in some way. Such notions were taken up enthusiastically by government ministers, for example David Blunkett (1999, cited in Gewirtz, 2001: 365) claimed 'we need parents who are prepared to take *responsibility* for supporting their child's education and we need a *culture* which *values* educa-tion and demands the best'. As Gewirtz points out, this rhetoric implicitly sets out that there are (problematic – read as 'working-class') parents within society who do not currently take responsibility for their child's education and whose 'culture' does not value education. The policy concern with raising working-class aspirations is still very evident – in his foreword to the publication of the 2009 report of the Panel on Fair Access to the Professions (the title of which alone speaks volumes, *Unleashing Aspiration*), Alan Milburn MP states: 'We have to enter what is new territory for public policy and find new ways of systematically raising the aspirations of those youngsters and families who simply do not believe that they will ever progress' (Panel on Fair Access to the Professions, 2009: 7).

Within academic work, a sustained critique has developed to challenge the prevalence of the *poverty of aspirations* discourse, pointing out how it can pathologise and blame working-class families for their 'failure' while hiding the role of wider structural inequalities and barriers (in relation to HE, see Archer et al., 2003). However, as evidenced above, it remains a popular public discourse and is often drawn on within media commentaries on class and education issues.

Unsurprisingly, elements of a 'cultures of poverty' and 'poverty of aspiration' discourse were found within some of the professionals' talk ('the parents often have a really negative view of education and schooling and don't see the worth of it', Connexions Advisor, Littleton), although often these were mediated and balanced with other discourses. For instance, some educators were concerned that particular families do not push children to attend school, either because education is not seen as a priority in these families or because other family needs are considered more pressing (such as caring for siblings). The source of 'not valuing education' was recognised as not simply a 'working-class value' but as rooted within a range of other social problems and issues such as drug or alcohol problems.

Teachers struggled to make sense of the issues that they encountered (for example, where 'parental control is sadly lacking', and families where children 'basically fend for themselves') without recourse to the pathologising and blaming inherent within dominant policy discourses. As Hillside Park's deputy headteacher explained, he felt uncomfortable blaming families but seemed not to have access to an alternative discourse: 'I am certainly not trying to blame families for everything, but I think that there is an issue there . . . I don't think they are able to parent their children very well'.

While 'cultural factors' can be 'part of the explanation for the persistence of poverty' (Atkinson and Kintrea, 2004: 452), this understanding of poverty fails to take into account structural factors (MacDonald et al., 2005). It fundamentally rests on the notion of meritocracy, assuming there is equality of opportunity, which by inference places the onus of responsibility on individuals while failing to recognise how people live within conditions of inequality (see Byrne, 1999). It is important to find other languages to engage with the issues. As Colley and Hodkinson (2001: 341) argue, discourse 'becomes an important element of social practice', such that deficit constructions of the poor are drawn from popular myths which appeal to dominant moral codes but this 'restricts the space for policy debate and legitimates certain policy interventions'.

One teacher (Hillside Park's Head of Year 10) framed the issue as a 'lack of respect' for school and education among certain communities. As McDowell (2007: 276) has argued, the notion that the working classes are 'disrespectful' has a long history (see Skeggs, 1997), and efforts to render them more 'respectful'/'respecting' are still evident within contemporary policies, such as the New Labour government's so-called 'respect agenda', epitomised by Anti Social Behaviour Orders (ASBOs) (see for example, Home Office, 2003). Indeed, Skeggs (1997) argues, the notion of 'respectability' has been appropriated by the middle classes to such an extent that it is seen as synonymous with middle-class identity and as antithetical to (particularly White) working-class identities (Haylett, 2001).

As such commentators note, the White working classes have long been iden-tified as constituting a particular social 'problem', although McDowell (2007) also points to an increase in negative attitudes among the more affluent sec-tions of society towards the working classes and their (assumed) attitudes, exemplified in the rise of popular disgust against 'chavs' (Tyler, 2006). In our study, teachers tended to identify the problems affecting the White working classes as a lack of ambition – which was seen as a deep-seated and gener-ational issue in many cases:

In my experience, from my year groups, it's certainly the White working-class students who are not ambitious, who do not have that possibly background desire to go on to further education.

(Head of Year 10, Littleton)

They are unambitious I would say. A lot of our community is unemployed, a lot of our parents are working-class and a lot of them would have what people would probably call in a sense racist attitudes.

(Head of Year 11, Riverway)

As illustrated by the latter of the two quotes above, in some cases a notion of problematic values and attitudes was evoked. For instance, some staff worried that the young people had the 'wrong' sorts of aspirations and attitudes – a discourse that is reinforced in policy rhetoric around the need to 'raise' and 'change' some young people's aspirations. For example: 'this one will just get married and have children basically and be quite happy with that' (Head of Year 10, Riverway), 'what they see as really important is instant cash rather than looking to the long term prospects' (Head of Year 10, Littleton). Further and higher education are increasingly positioned within education policy as the only legitimate ambitions for young school-leavers (see Watts and Bridges, 2006), such that other aspirations or life choices (for example, to get married, start work, have a family) are rendered illegitimate or 'risky'.

While policy tends to work with relatively simple models of cause and effect (problem-solution), we found that the education professionals in our study grappled and wrangled with ways of trying to make sense of the urban young people's lives. There was a feeling that 'low aspirations' and disengagement from education were complexly related to a range of social, cultural, structural and economic factors – although participants did not necessarily have a ready language or conceptual model to explain these. As one Head of Year put it, 'it's the whole cultural package – it's the family package, it's the peer pressure package'. There was a recognition that factors such as high unemployment in local areas and a lack of material resources played a part, but at the same time participants struggled to balance these with the role of individual agency, and indeed the role of schools and themselves as teachers.

As Reay (2006: 292) has highlighted, teachers are increasingly invested with 'impossible powers of transforming educational failure into success without any of the knowledge and understanding that is necessary before they can even begin to make small headway into an enormous problem'. In this chapter, we attempt to develop a counterpoint to dominant policy discourses in terms of providing an understanding of the issues associated with working-class educational engagement that encompasses structural, social and individual levels of analysis. We begin by considering teachers', young people's and parents' constructions of the role of 'the street' and 'the estate' within the young people's aspirations and engagement with schooling. We then consider urban young people's vulnerability/susceptibility to risks and their contradictory experiences of education as simultaneously both a 'middle-class' space and their urban schools as stigmatised 'worthless' (working-class) places. Finally we look at ways in which the young people attempted to generate alternative forms of value and worth through their investment in 'Nike' identities.

In doing so we work with a notion of social class as grounded within, and produced through, identities and cultural practices, rather than just reflecting occupational backgrounds or economic earning power. As Reay (2004b: 151) has argued '[c]lass is a complicated mixture of the material, the discursive, psychological predispositions, and sociological dispositions'. Moreover, we recognise that classed identities are patterned but not fixed; they are relational constructs that are produced through social and individual practices and processes, the meanings of which are constantly contested (Skeggs, 2004).

'The pull of the street'

Education professionals, parents and students alike drew on 'the street' as a key symbolic resource within their discussions about identity and engagement with schooling. In particular, 'the pull of the street' was a term used to signify the danger posed to urban young people's educational engagement and achievement by their local environments. 'The street' represented an intermingling of geographical, social and cultural factors – it was both a 'place' (the surrounding urban locale) and a cultural space (spanning youth cultural practices, peer group cultures, identities, ways of being/talking/thinking). It was overwhelmingly associated with danger: notably with fears of crime, drugs and violence. In all its formations, 'the street' was constructed as the antithesis of 'school' and as an oppositional pull to education.

> The pull of the street is also a genuine pull around here.
> (Deputy Headteacher, Hillside Park)

> You are tending to kind of battle against street culture, if that's the correct way of putting it, you know? That's how you feel at the time when you receive classes, that you're trying to get them to put away the street culture.
> (Head of Year 10, Hillside Park)

The language of struggle ('battle', 'pull') is evident within the above teachers' accounts. The street is imbued with power – it competes with schools for control of the hearts and minds of the young people in question. Against this powerful source of influence, working-class parents were seen as having little control or ability to counter the 'pull' of the street. Indeed, teachers tended to describe parents as 'fearful' and 'scared' of the street.

Young people also constructed 'the street' as playing a powerful role in shaping their everyday lives and subjectivities. As exemplified by the following quote from Dan (Riverway), themes of crime, risk, urban decay, violence and drugs were commonplace. Dan described his local area as a 'tip' (waste/refuse site), saying it is: 'Not good anymore . . . Everything gets broken. Too many killings around that area so I want to move out . . . Too many like fights and druggies around that area and stuff like that. Too many, like, police driving around now, it is, like, not safe anymore'.

The impoverished material and physical environment was linked with an impoverished social environment, characterised by danger and violence. Others described similar landscapes of violent crime and vandalism, 'drugs', 'graffiti' and 'burnt out cars' in which they felt unsafe. In line with other research, a number of young women, particularly, explained how they were not allowed to go out after dark (Evans, 2006; Reay and Lucey, 2000b). As Back and Keith (2004: 59) argue, young people are often taken to personify the risks of the city, but speaking to young Londoners themselves reveals how they are equally fearful, and statistics would suggest, are just as likely to be victims of crime. As Giddens (1998, cited in Back and Keith, 2004: 58) has claimed: 'The degeneration of local communities is usually marked not only by general dilapidation, but by the disappearance of safe public space – streets, squares, parks and other areas where people can feel secure'.

Nevertheless, the restriction and surveillance of public spaces that often arises as a response to high levels of crime did not appear to alleviate fear of danger. Some schools had installed CCTV cameras and an internal swipe card system. But Lee (Riverway) felt that this made his school feel 'like a prison'. The security measures were constructed as not merely protecting the school buildings, pupils and staff from the external dangers of 'the street' and the high crime in the local area, but as also managing the risk posed to the 'outside' by particular pupils, like Babu (Riverway): 'They don't let me go out cos I'm too naughty in school . . . they know I'm going to come back but they just don't trust me. I might do something wrong outside.' Thus the school's physical environment operated as both a product and a mediator of the 'dangerous' and risky urban environment, which is experienced and represented as both fortress and prison by those contained within it.

'The estate'

Bound up with notions of 'the street' and 'street culture', was the spectre of 'the estate', which constituted a prominent feature within the discourse of a number of members of staff. This was felt particularly in the three schools that served highly localised catchment areas (Eastleigh Central, Hillside Park, Riverway), compared to the schools that served a wider catchment area (Blackwell Street, Cowick, Littleton). The problems of poverty on 'the estate' were not issues 'out there' but were brought into schools with the young people:

> But all this comes from what is going on out in the streets and they just
> bring it back here . . . You can't separate it, because all, the majority of kids
> come, are from the [name] Estate and the majority of them live there and
> everything that goes on there comes back in here . . . If you go and look,

it's just miserable. I think that has a big effect on these kids coming to school because living where they do it's not nice. What goes on there, drug dealings, to people fighting, to the crack situation, it does have a major effect because a lot of my kids live on an estate. All my kids that I work with live on estates. I don't have one child that lives in a house.

(Learning Mentor, Eastleigh Central)

Described as 'miserable' and 'not nice', 'the estate' is posed as something inherently problematic. These constructions of the street and the estate stand in contrast to middle-class spaces which tend to be described as 'nice', 'positive' home environments (see Comber, 1998; Williams and Hollingworth, 2006). A boundary is constructed in which learning has 'its place' (Creswell, 1996; Sibley, 1995) in the school and in the middle-class home – whereas 'the street' and 'the estate' (conflated in the Learning Mentor's account) is not conceived as somewhere that learning (or the right kind of learning) can take place.

'The estate' operated as a risky space – contained to some extent within physical/geographical boundaries but also extending beyond these perimeters into the school as its effects (including poverty and crime) and cultures (encompassing values and attitudes) become written on the bodies and minds of the young people who live there. It was a profoundly alien space for many teachers (a point discussed later in the chapter) and was constructed as at odds with 'school culture'.

The estates that the young people lived on were often located nearby or adjoining to more affluent areas of the city. As Maguire and colleagues (2006: 6) highlight, 'in demographic and geographic terms, most cities include both the most and least privileged and powerfully demonstrate the stark polarization between access to and exclusion from cultural/social patterns of consumption'. Similarly, Watson's (2006) research with London children underlined the contrast between gentrified areas of the city, which are better resourced, and the bleak landscapes of some of the poorer working-class areas. Indeed, researcher fieldnotes describe the area surrounding Riverway as poor and 'run down' but with very wealthy areas located in close proximity – creating an intense juxtaposition of poverty/wealth. As David (Littleton) noted of his local area in West London, 'some areas are quite quiet and peaceful, other areas are quite violent'. Yasser (Littleton discussion group) also observed that life chances are shaped by 'how you're brung up and in what environment', underlining the powerful role of social locations and structures of inequality within young people's lives: 'the place I was brought up because there's a lot of like crime going on there, like in the estates and stuff like that, but children who live a bit North of London like [name of area] they don't have estates there, they have like pleasant neighbourhoods, and they've got like the three grammar schools and stuff like that.'

Maguire et al (2006: 119) emphasise that 'urban children learn from their contextualised setting'. Contrary to the young people in MacDonald and colleagues (2005) work in Teesside, who 'did not really know how their contemporaries in more prosperous locales fared', because of this juxtaposition of poverty and wealth, young Londoners in this research tended to be very aware of this disparity. From Yasser's articulation, it is clear that he recognised that 'other' children, in the surrounding suburbs, have very different experiences and opportunities that are not inflected by crime and the associated fears and risks. Yasser even made the connection between 'pleasant neighbourhoods' and an abundance of 'better' schools. These descriptions of the young people's experiences of their local urban area contrast starkly with other studies' accounts of the 'emancipatory' city (see Lees, 2004) in which middle-class young Londoners describe an exciting, bustling, cosmopolitan multicultural urban environment (Byrne, 2006; Reay et al., 2007).

A significant number of the young people in this study moved away over the course of the project, but only a few moved out of the city. Others had ambitions to escape. Analisa (Cowick) dreamed of moving away, claiming 'if you keep growing up in "Fairwick" you are going to grow up with, like, not a good [chance]' and Dan (Riverway) had ambitions to 'escape' and leave the local area via 'Army College' and by the end of the study had secured a place (in fact, several saw army as their way out). Steven (Eastleigh Central), who described his local area as 'horrible' with 'dead cockroaches and rats', subsequently moved to Scotland to live with his dad. He told us: 'Well up in Scotland it's like peaceful up there and there ain't much, like, bother because where I live as I've got a big family down here it's too noisy and where my father lives it's nice and quiet so it'll help me with all my studying and everything.'

Concurring with findings of other authors researching young people living in deprived or 'socially excluded' local areas (for example, Reay and Lucey, 2000b) many of these young Londoners expressed a resignation about their local areas claiming that they are 'used to' it and wouldn't want something different. Indeed, as Mark (Littleton) put it: 'It is normal because, like, I grew up with it'. MacDonald and colleagues (2005: 879) highlighted that '[f]amiliarity with these places was key to understanding why most wished to stay', and as Matthews and Limb (1999: 65, emphasis added) emphasise, 'local places *matter* to individuals . . . affording personal identity through attachment'.

Vulnerability and susceptibility: poverty, risk and working-class engagement with education

We have so far discussed how 'the street' and 'the estate' operate as popular cultural signifiers of poverty, risk and danger, and later we discuss how urban schools become similarly marked as 'sink' institutions, attempting to contain the problems of such communities. Obviously we hope to contest such discourses and challenge their symbolic power in terms of how they are used to negatively define urban young people's identities and engagements with schooling through notions of deficit and lack. Yet at the same time, we want to underline that the young people in our study were living within conditions of inequality and poverty that had powerful, negative and all too 'real' effects on their lives.

Young people told stories of unstable or difficult home lives, 'family problems' such as divorce and alcoholism, dangerous or abusive elements, health problems, bereavement and teenage pregnancy alongside the fears and risks of crime discussed earlier in the context of 'the street' and 'the estate'. As Beck

(1992) writes, risk adheres inversely to class structures – with the privileged able to purchase safety from risk while those at the bottom are exposed to the highest levels of risk.

Various pupils felt that their engagement at school had been negatively affected by issues within their home and family lives. For example, Jason (Littleton) said he had 'a lot of family problems' in Year 11 which impacted on his GCSE performance. Similarly Nadira (Eastleigh Central) explained in her Phase two interview, 'there's a lot of like family problems going on. Not necessarily directly to do with me but there is a lot of family things, a lot's going wrong in my family at the moment. But, it's like that's kind of stressing me out a bit.' She reflected back later: 'I think the reason why like I fell behind in Year 10 was because of things that were happening outside school. There was a lot of family stuff happening. There were family problems and so that was important.'

A number of the students had very poor attendance records which inevitably impacted on their achievement. Leah (Cowick) had been strongly affected after her father was attacked and stabbed while working as a mini cab driver. She described being scared to leave her family and come to school. She told us: 'Sometimes I take off quite a few weeks [when] it gets really bad for me. I like cry a lot and don't want to go ... I am just all the time worrying about things ... I just always think something is going to happen to my mum and dad after my dad had the accident.' Understandably, concern for her family's safety affected Leah's attendance and her ability to concentrate when she did attend school. Yet she did not tell her teachers and those we interviewed seemed puzzled by her poor attendance and distraction in class (see also Chapter 4).

The effects of poverty on the young people also meant that they were susceptible to health problems, and a number of pupils talked about the effects of family ill health on their engagement and attendance. Changes to family relations and bereavements were also mentioned. For example Nadia, Hapsa and Jermina (all at Blackwell Street) had all lost a parent. Around the time of the first interview, James's (Littleton) father had just come back into his life and his grandmother (who had been his primary carer until this point) suggested that his father's reappearance had caused a degree of upset and turmoil in James's life. Over one third of pupils were from lone parent families or had experienced their parents going through difficult separations. For example, Verona (Riverway) lived with his father since his mother had left them when he was aged 4 to go to live with a new partner in America. Verona was still very much upset and affected by these events, maintaining that his mum's boyfriend 'took my mum away and destroyed our family'. One young woman, Jordan (Blackwell Street), fell pregnant over the course of the project and did not return to school once she had her baby.

A few young people experienced dangerous or abusive elements in their home lives that could cause them to miss or experience problems at school, for example, in relation to anger management or mental health issues. Jermina (Blackwell Street) and Amanda (Cowick) both suffered physically violent parents over the course of the study. Amanda's attendance at school dropped dramatically and Jermina ran away from home to stay with an older boyfriend, and did not come to school. Later she told us that she had been persuaded by phone calls from friends and teachers to return home and to school: 'The teachers were like phoning on my mobile telling me to come to school, "we all miss you" and my friends even rung me and they were like "come to school" and so I decided to come back'. But her attendance remained erratic.

Drawing on the sociology of Pierre Bourdieu (1977, 1984; Bourdieu and Passeron, 1990), we can understand the young people in our study as being disadvantaged by their lack of dominant forms of *capital* – that is, they did not enjoy high levels of economic capital (wealth) so their families were unable to purchase safety from risk (as might the middle classes), for instance, by being able to afford to access better healthcare and support services or move house, area and/or school. Their families did not possess dominant forms of cultural capital, that is, they did not enjoy the taken-for-granted knowledge and ability to understand and navigate the education system that characterises many middle-class families' engagement with education. Their social networks tended to be restricted to urban, working-class environments rather than enabling them to access more privileged social and cultural spaces – although some were able to use social capital (i.e. value generated by their networks of social relations) to 'escape' elsewhere, as noted earlier and/or to access jobs (see Chapter 5). In other words, the capitals that these working-class families did possess were not symbolically valued in society and predominantly did not translate across social fields. That is, they were not able to create advantage in different social spheres for the families concerned, as middle-class forms of capital are often able to do. In the following sections we move on to employ Bourdieu's notion of *habitus* to help understand urban young people's educational experiences and their constructions of alternative sources of value. The utility of habitus as a concept lies in its ability to link the 'macro' structural relations in society with the 'micro' level of the individual. It refers to how dispositions and ways of thinking, feeling and being in the world are developed within individuals in ways that are constituted and shaped by their structural contexts and locations. As we discuss below, we try to use the concept of habitus to help explain how young people are simultaneously unique individuals with agency *and* subjects who are produced by their structural locations in the sense that their ways of thinking about and engaging with the world are strongly inflected by identities and inequalities of 'race', social class and gender.

Between the street, the estate and middle-class culture: the urban school as a contradictory space

Within this impoverished local landscape, students at some of the schools constructed their school in similarly bleak terms, deriding its physical, but also social, condition. This occurred particularly at Riverway School, where the young people's photo-diaries and researcher fieldnotes comment on the poor physical state of the locale. Pupils at Riverway talked about the physical state of the school as a 'shit hole' with 'rats running around'. The location of the school (rubbing up against highly affluent areas of the city) no doubt intensified such perceptions. These perceptions were not solely restricted to students, but reflected wider popular discourses in which particular schools are 'known' as 'good' or 'bad'. As we argue here, these wider constructions can be powerful, being implicated in how young people at such schools feel about not only the school, but also themselves and their own learning. Indeed, we noted a tendency for pupils at Riverway to be particularly negative about education and learning. Lucy claimed 'I just don't like it . . . I just don't like coming' and Lee was adamant that 'people hate school in this area'. The way in which (some) urban schools are discursively constructed as 'bad' and 'crap' can have profound effects on the students there and their learning (Hollingworth and Archer, forthcoming; Reay, 2004b). As Young (1999: 213) argues: 'Families with high enough incomes to afford alternatives avoid the state secondary schools in most inner London boroughs precisely because many of the pupils in such schools are from families who would, on any criteria, be classified as being among the excluded.'

Reay (2004a) and Reay and Lucey (2000a) argue that many urban working-class areas and schools are pathologised spaces, associated with images of expelled waste and detritus (as 'crap', 'shit', 'rubbish'). Waquant (1996: 239) refers to this as 'territorial stigmatisation' – the labels stick because those who are located within such demonised spaces have no power to reject them. This positioning requires those subsumed within such spaces to engage in psychic negotiations to attempt to reconcile and deal with these negative connotations. In our study, young people and parents were clearly aware of these pathologising discourses. Lee's mother, for example, argued strongly against the popular local view of Riverway school being 'crap': 'Five years ago Lee couldn't read and write and now he is sitting GCSEs . . . that is how much that school has brought him up. . . . It does wind me up when I hear people saying that [the school is crap] because they don't even know the school they don't know kids what go to this school and so why drag the school down?'. Lee's mother was clearly angry and frustrated by the local discourses of derision aimed against Riverway School, especially since she felt the school had been such a positive influence on Lee, particularly with regard to his literacy ('5 years ago Lee couldn't read and write and now he is sitting GCSEs'). As she goes on to argue, many proponents of this negative view of the school have no real knowledge or contact with the school and do not have to live with the consequences of these discourses, as do Lee and the other students and their families. As Waquant (1996: 238–9) noted in his study of low income, socially excluded urban areas in Paris and Chicago: 'To dwell in a . . . low-income estate means to be confined to a branded space, to a blemished setting experienced as a "trap" '. Similarly Harvey's (1973: 82) observation still rings true here: 'Those with the capacity to transcend space . . . command it as a resource. Those who lack such skill are likely to be trapped by space.' The middle classes in the inner city are able to transcend these disparaged or defamed spaces – they have access to 'more pleasant' parts of the city; they live in 'nicer' houses, not 'miserable' estates; and they have the economic or cultural resources to enable them to reject 'sink' inner-city comprehensive schools. Although a few like Steven (Eastleigh Central) were 'fortunate' enough to have the opportunity to leave the local area, this is not an option for many. It is evident that the school choice agenda in the UK has exacerbated the middle-class 'chatter' around schools and their reputations, with academic league tables formalising and solidifying these hierarchies of reputation. As skilled – even expert – 'choosers' (Ball, 2003), the middle classes are centrally implicated within the reproduction of these hierarchies – yet as Lee's mother's quote hints at, they seldom have to live with the effects of a disparaged school's reputation (cf. Reay et al., 2008).

However, while urban schools, such as Riverway, are often constructed in classed terms (as disparaged working-class spaces/sites), and indeed were recognised as such by students, parents, teachers and local popular discourse, they were also experienced as contradictory spaces by the young people with whom we spoke. In particular, while the school population (its students and their families) and its material state (its buildings and locale) were clearly signalled as 'working-class', its culture and ethos (its institutional *habitus*, the taken-for-granted ways of being and understanding that are expected and normalised) were experienced by students and their families as middle-class.

A jarring between working-class students' habitus and the middle-class culture and ethos of the school was recognised by one or two members of staff. Indeed, one Head of Year 10 (Hillside Park) explicitly described the struggle to enforce a 'middle-class way': 'you're constantly reinforcing the middle-class way if you like, you know, I mean: "put your hand up" '. As Reay (2004c: 435) explains, an individual's habitus can be understood as constituting 'a complex internalized core from which everyday experiences emanate'. It provides the framework for action, shaping what is considered im/possible and un/desirable. It is an amalgam of past and present, of the individual and their social location: 'a person's individual history is constitutive of habitus, but so also is the whole collective history of family and class that the individual is a member of' (Reay, 2004c: 434). Thus working-class students (constituted by their specific 'habitus') may experience the middle-class ethos and social world (or 'field') of education as an alien and unfamiliar place with different 'rules of the game'. To use Bourdieu and Wacquant's (1992: 127) well-known metaphor, unlike the middle-class student whose habitus means they can understand and move easily within the school environment, as a 'fish in water', the working-class student is more likely to feel the weight of the water.

Some Connexions Advisors and Learning Mentors reflected on how differences in social class between (mostly middle-class) teachers and (working-class) students can mean that some teachers do not have a good understanding of the problems and issues faced by the young urban working-class people who they teach: 'Because on the whole, it's middle-class people teaching working-class people and although, I'm not undermining their compassion, I'm not undermining their understanding of the issues, but their experiences may be, you know they may have had experiences obviously with alcoholic parents, drug using parents' (Connexions Advisor, Littleton). As a Learning Mentor agreed, a lack of shared experience and understanding on the part of White, middle-class staff can sometimes mean they may not fully understand the young people or be able to relate to them and their urban, working-class lives:

In this school, yeah, because if you bring, we've got obviously loads of Iraqis, Kurds, Muslims, Hindus, loads of Asians and if you bring, no offence, a White middle-class [teacher] from Dorset it's not going to work because: one, the kids are not going to relate to you. . . . You've got to know what the kids like, you've got to know their lingo and understand what they're saying to you, I mean, the dress sense and everything, it does make a difference . . . Being aware of what's going on, London life, what's going on in the estates. But if you're say from Dorset, from a nice part, you won't have a clue what these kids go home to.

(Learning Mentor, Eastleigh Central)

As we discuss in Chapter 4, a number of girls in our study described how their ways of behaving, such as 'speaking my mind', brought them into conflict with middle-class school cultures and gendered expectations of how 'nice' girls should behave. In the final following section of this chapter we also examine how the young men and women's performances of urban style (and their espousal of 'Nike' identities) were read negatively within schools. Some of the young people gave examples of how they felt their interests and cultural reference points were not valued – or were viewed as illegitimate within schools. Mark (Hillside Park) recounted how within a particular art class he had been reprimanded for a piece of work that he had done in a 'graffiti style' – which his teacher had sanctioned, but which had outraged the Head of Art. What upset Mark the most was the way in which he had been chastised in a patronising manner for this transgression.

Issues of accent and language were also raised. For example, a discussion group of young women at Cowick School worried that their teachers judged their answers and ability in class differently because they did not express themselves in a valued linguistic style. As one of them put it:

If there's a class going on and teacher's talking or whatever and you're all answering a question and let's say you're saying it a sort of different way to someone else, the teacher could be like 'yes you're right, but no, no, you're not quite there'. She's sort of like thinking 'okay well she said the same thing but the way she presented it was different' and because of that you're like 'no, sorry you're wrong'.

This experience, they explained, also impacted on their confidence in relation to applying to further and higher education, where they felt that in order to be 'educationally successful' they would effectively need to change themselves and the way they talked and presented themselves, to be 'many different people in one person'. They described this strategy as 'twisting' or 'changing up'. As sociologists of education point out, working-class identities are often associated with problematic and difficult relationships to education – while education may be associated with a process of 'finding yourself' for the middle classes, the middle-class educational environment is more likely to be experienced as a process of 'losing yourself' for the working classes (Hey, 2003; Mahony and Zmroczek, 1997; Reay, 2001b). The girls imagined that these issues would extend into the workplace, and were concerned that people like themselves (with 'street' accents) are less likely to be employed in white-collar jobs ('people think "sorry, you're not capable of working in an office" '), compared to more middle-class people who 'have a wider range of vocabulary'.

Other young people in the study also felt excluded from particular (middle-class) professions because of their own less privileged backgrounds, with Max (Littleton) describing how he walked out on his work experience placement in an expensive London hotel because it was so 'posh' he felt uncomfortable. As Archer and colleagues (2003) and Reay and colleagues (2005) have noted in relation to working-class access to HE, many of the young people in this study felt uncomfortable and unable to access 'posh' or middle-class spaces and institutions, which were seen as 'not for us'. Geoff Whitty (2001: 287) thus argues that 'instead of seeing failure as the result of a deficit in working-class homes materially and culturally' we should entertain the notion that 'working-class failure [is] a relational outcome of middle-class power to define what counts as knowledge and achievement'.

Creating alternative spaces and places of value: 'My Trainers', 'My Nike'

In addition to recognising their own disadvantaged social locations, many of the young people we interviewed were also painfully aware that they were 'looked down on' by society. This symbolic violence (i.e. the psychological and representational injury/injustice inflicted by unequal social relations), unsurprisingly, prompted the young people to engage in various attempts to generate self (class) worth and value through alternative means. As noted within other research (Cohen, 1972; Hall and Jefferson, 1976; Watt and Stenson, 1998), young people can construct status and meaningful identities for themselves through notions of belonging, investment in peer cultures and via relationships with 'territory' and spaces outside school. In this respect, we might argue that the young people's investments in peer cultures and the 'cultures of the street' (as discussed earlier) might be understood not as simple *causes* of educational disengagement, but as more complexly related, as simultaneously a response to, a product of, and a contributory factor to educational marginalisation.

The young people's investments in spaces and activities outside of school were not merely confined to hanging around the street. For example many of the boys spoke about their passion for football and several belonged to local clubs. Other pastimes included Babu's (Riverway) rather enterprising hobby of buying up old cars, renovating them and selling them on. Mark (Hillside Park) spent his weekends helping his father build an extension on their home. Several of the young people also had part-time jobs and were developing skills, experience and networks through these.

Fashion and appearance constituted a prime interest for the majority of young people in our study. They heavily invested in 'style', as symbolised in particular by branded clothing. As discussed elsewhere (Archer et al., 2007b), we read these investments as attempts to generate capital and to claim value and recognition through alternative means within schools. As Kenway and Bullen (2001) describe, class identities are increasingly becoming organised around patterns of consumption. For all the young people in the study, their appearance was a highly important project and considerable value was placed upon having the 'right' symbols of style. When asked what is important in life, Jenni (Cowick discussion group) explained: 'Like my valuable stuff like for example my clothes. [Interviewer: Your clothes?] Yeah my trainers and my jewellery'.

A strong attachment to, and valuing of, 'my trainers and my jewellery' was voiced across gender and ethnic boundaries. Collective identities were constructed through consumption which was symbolised and conveyed by branding and the ability to perform, read and manipulate branded styles. For the young people in this study, there was a conflation of sportswear brands, but particularly Nike, with their own identities. Indeed, respondents often positioned the Nike brand as synonymous with their own class identity/location – or as Sean (Littleton discussion group) put it, 'we're Nike': 'In a way what we wear – like what I just said yeah – you wouldn't really expect [upper-class] people to come out in Nike tracksuits and stuff, we expect them to have that Gucci designer stuff. But people like us they're just: we're Nike.'

Identification with and loyalty to particular brands, such as Nike, became a means through which identity was not only performed on the body but etched on the psyche. Brands like Nike were implicated in young people's personal identity constructions, it was a way of 'being me'. Indeed, as Roxanne and Laetitia suggested in a Cowick discussion group, without wearing the Nike brand they would feel 'uncomfortable', inauthentic and 'not me'. However, this desire to 'be me' by wearing branded clothing and trainers was also heavily policed by peer groups (non-conformity being 'social suicide'). Thus successful performances of style generated currency and status within peer groups and afforded 'safety' from bullying and marginalisation.

The importance that young people placed on their appearance frequently brought them into conflict with their schools over issues of uniform. For example, Max (Littleton) would often get sent home for wearing trainers to school. Yesim (Cowick) frequently got told off for wearing a Nike vest top (often hidden under her other clothes) at her school (where there is no uniform as such, but logos are prohibited). Jane (Hillside Park) would also frequently come into conflict with teachers over her hair colour, earrings and appearance. Similarly Jordan (Blackwell Street) complained 'I don't like my shoes, I'd rather be in my trainers' and explained how she often got told off because 'my earrings are too big and my chains are too long and there's too many of them'.

We would suggest that the young people's struggles to establish a sense of self-worth are heightened due to their location within an education system and wider social field in which working-class identities are derided and un/devalued. Sayer (2002: 1.4) suggests that class identities are highly charged because they are associated with 'injustice and moral evaluation' and those living stigmatised class identities will work to produce themselves as having worth. Indeed, he argues that people's resentment about social or symbolic (class) stigmatisation is often stronger than their resentment over lack of material wealth.

The young people's performances of 'style' and consumption can thus be read as taking place within struggles for recognition. Whereas their consumption of 'Nike style' may be positioned by the middle classes as negative, tasteless and as even signifying danger or threat (for example, hoodies are banned by several large UK shopping malls), the young people themselves used it as a site for generating value and worth. In other words, they used appearance as a means for generating capital.

The young people's performances of 'Nike style' were also (partially) implicated in their positioning of HE as unrealistic and undesirable. This resistance was grounded in the feeling that 'people like us' do not go to university. In line with other studies, young people perceived HE as being for 'posher' and 'cleverer' people and for 'people with money' (Archer et al., 2003). However, the point we would like to draw out here is that they *also* constructed HE as not fitting with their own investments in, and performances of, fashionable or desirable identities. For instance, not only was HE participation regarded as generally unaffordable and a risky investment for working-class families, but the prospect of student debt (and the decline in earning power associated with being a university student) was felt to prevent young people from performing fashionable identities. As Jordan (Blackwell Street) put it, the prospect of university did not fit with her (desire for) performance of a desirable 'Nike' femininity: 'I don't see that [university] as a path for me. . . . Living on them grants. I like to have new Nike trainers and Nike tops and a new chain every month so I don't think the grant would suit me.' Here, Jordan positions HE as an unthinkable lifestyle option, and one that is alien to her *habitus* – it would not 'suit' her. As Reay (2004c) argues, habitus is profoundly embodied: the body does not just exist in the social world, the social world is also written on the body.

Finally, we should note that while the young people's constructions of 'Nike identities' can undoubtedly be viewed as creative youth cultural forms, they also contain a certain irony in that they are using a form of capitalist leisure consumption to escape/resist the effects and inequalities of capitalism (Willis, 1990). The problematic nature of these Nike identities is not solely that they bring the young people into difficult and conflictual relationships with education, but that they are also contributing to the sustenance of global corporations who have been critiqued for being parasitic upon urban youth in particular (Klein, 2000).

Summary

This chapter has discussed the role of social class (as an identity and form of inequality) within urban young people's relationships to education and schooling. We have examined the symbolic work done by notions of 'the street' and 'the estate', the impact of poverty and risk in young people's lives and have considered the ways in which the urban school is an ambiguous site. That is, it may be coded both as a working-class (often disparaged) space in public discourse while also being experienced by its students as having a middle-class institutional habitus. Finally we looked at some of the ways in which the urban, working-class young people in our study attempted to generate alternative forms of value and worth for themselves, notably through performances of style and 'Nike' identities. However, these identities can bring young people into conflict with schools and can, in some cases, be implicated in their resistance to post-compulsory education.

ENTANGLED IDENTITIES: 'RACE', ETHNICITY AND SCHOOLING

Introduction

As outlined in Chapter 1, minority ethnic achievement remains a perennial educational policy issue, as evidenced by the range of policies and initiatives designed to 'tackle' it. Attention has long been directed at the lower rates of recorded achievement and higher rates of exclusion among African Caribbean pupils, and to a lesser extent attention is also now being given to achievement and progression among pupils from Muslim backgrounds. But since the 1990s, particular concerns have been raised in relation to White (working-class) boys who are increasingly being touted within the media as the 'new' class of underachievers. While severe concerns have been raised in relation to the achievement and educational needs and experiences of 'new' racialised groups such as refugee children, they have tended to be eclipsed by this 'boys' under-achievement' debate.

In this chapter we explore some of the ways in which issues of 'race' and ethnicity impacted on young people's aspirations and engagement with education. We examine students' ethnic identity constructions and their under-standings of racism, and outline some of the barriers faced by refugee students and those for whom English is not their mother tongue.

The chapter begins by examining the complex, 'culturally entangled' (Hesse, 2000) ways in which young people constructed racialised identities within the multi-ethnic urban setting. We discuss how their ethnic/racialised identities were rarely straightforward or clear-cut, but were complex and shaped by numerous experiences and influences. We discuss the use and limitations of notions of 'hybridity' for understanding these identities before moving on to consider teachers' constructions of issues of 'race'/ethnicity and achievement.

Young people's constructions of multi-ethnic, entangled urban identities

During the interviews, we asked young people to self-define what they considered to be their ethnic identity. The sample reflected the 'multicultural-scape' (Hesse, 2000) of contemporary urban settings, comprising pupils from a range of ethnic backgrounds. Table 3.1 groups these self-definitions into some broad categories that give a sense of the range of ethnicities among our participants (see Appendix 1 for the self-defined ethnicities of those we interviewed individually).

Pupils are often grouped into standardised ethnic categories in order to measure differences in achievement, and so on. While useful up to a point, these standardised ethnic categories do not really capture the richness and the complexity of contemporary urban young people's ethnic identities and the ways in which they construct and live out multifaceted, racialised identities in their daily lives. In this section we ask, how might we better understand the ethnic/racialised identities of urban young people?

As Hesse (2000: 2, original emphasis) argues, young people's ethnic identities can be conceptualised as complex 'cultural entanglements': 'commonplace forms of *creolization, hybridity, syncretism* [that] represent a profound challenge to the idea that national and social forms are logically coherent, unitary or tidy'. The young people we tracked did not simply or straightforwardly claim or perform racialised identities as, for instance, 'Black', 'Asian' or 'White'. Rather, they drew on a whole mix of racialised symbols and themes in their identity constructions. These identities were expressed and embodied

Table 3.1 Classification of students' ethnic backgrounds

Broad category	Self-definition	Number of students	
'White'	White UK	46	*(50)*
	Irish	3	
	Polish	1	
'Black'	Black African	10	*(19)*
	Black Caribbean	7	
	'Black'	2	
'Asian'	Indian Sikh	1	*(5)*
	Bangladeshi	3	
	Pakistani	1	
'Mixed'	'Mixed'	6	*(10)*
	Mixed Mauritian/English	1	
	Mixed Danish/Lebanese	1	
	Mixed Turkish/White	1	
	Mixed Pakistani/Trinidadian	1	
'Other'	Turkish	2	*(5)*
	Iraqi	1	
	Moroccan	1	

through a variety of forms of speech, accent, language, style, appearance, dress, walk, 'attitude', and so on.

For instance, Melissa (Eastleigh Central) constructed her identity as firmly embedded within 'Turkishness'. She described how her whole social life revolved around her Turkish friends and family and she closely aligned herself with a notion of 'loud' Turkish femininity. However, her photographic diary also contained various other cultural markers, indicating a more culturally entangled construction of identity. For instance, the photograph shown in Figure 3.1 from Melissa's photo-diary depicts one of the posters on her bedroom wall of Black US rapper Tupac. In describing why she took and included this photograph, Melissa explained, 'these are like my all ten favourite things, like singer, rapper, actor as well so, just my all time favourites . . . mostly rap, hiphop, you know, them sort of things'. Melissa was in no way unusual among the young people in the study, most of whom expressed an interest in rap and hiphop. Nor was this interest restricted to merely enjoying particular types of music. Students from across the diversity of ethnic backgrounds also styled their bodies and appearance in ways associated with 'Black' street culture. For instance, Leah (Cowick) is an Indian Sikh girl (who was born in the UK) whose hair, make-up and jewellery adopts a distinctly 'Black' (Caribbean-influenced) style. Bangladeshi boy Babu's (Riverway) white padded Prada jacket worn over a Nike sweater (both of which were worn over his school jumper) also referenced 'bling' culture, with its emphasis on labels and extravagance (symbolically evoking a US Black 'gangster' look).

Many young people, from both 'Black' and a whole range of other ethnic backgrounds, engaged in embodied performances of 'Blackness' through, for

Figure 3.1   Melissa's photo of her poster of Tupac Shakur.

instance, their clothes, hairstyles, speech and even ways of walking (termed bopping, see Majors and Billson, 1992; Sewell, 1997). In the case of White and other minority ethnic young people this was more than simply, as Back (1996) discusses, a case of 'non-Black' young people 'acting Black' and aping Black male styles because they are fashionable. Rather, these young people's identity constructions reflect the culturally entangled contexts within which they grow up. These contexts are both at a global scale, whereby globalisation enables discourses around 'coolness' to operate across international boundaries thanks to the speed and extent of access to the internet, media and transnational marketing, and at a local level, as a product of the young people's immediate multicultural urban context.

But why were these young people so attracted to 'Black' (North American) styles in particular? We would suggest that this is because performances of 'Black' urban styles are often coded as 'cool' and attractive within popular culture due to their symbolic associations with notions of 'hardness' and (hyper)heterosexuality. These identities are linked with 'tough' styles of music, such as rap and hiphop, and derive status/power from their associations with the glamorous-yet-dangerous fantasy of 'bling' and 'gangster' lifestyles. Notions of 'Black cool' may also draw potency from a discourse of 'slackness', which Noble (2000: 154) discusses as deriving from working-class Caribbean cultures and as a 'potential politics of subversion': 'Slackness represents "backward", "rude" folk/ghetto culture, vying for recognition and value within official Jamaican national identity.' In other words, stylised performances of 'Black cool' may be read as desirable and attractive due to their associations with notions of subversion, counter-culture and resistance to the 'mainstream'.

It is important to remember, however, that in discussing young people's *performances* of clusters of behaviours, appearance and so on, and in reading these as 'Black cool', we are not seeking to essentialise or reify 'Blackness' (or 'Black cool'). While these discourses are strongly racialised, gendered and classed, and have been produced through particular racialised social and geographical histories, we would refute any reading of them as indicative of 'biological' race. At the same time, this is not to say that we refute any notion of 'culture' – indeed, we would read these as profoundly cultural discourses – albeit not in any straightforward sense of being mere reflections of some homogenous or coherent entity that might be termed 'Black culture'. Rather, we would argue that an important feature of these discourses is the way that they have been shaped by dominant racist constructions of Blackness, notably the construction of Black masculinity as an object of both fear and desire within the White imagination (Fanon, 1986) and constructions of Black femininity as loud, 'vulgar' and highly sexualised (Mama, 1995).

Hence, we would argue, young people's constructions of 'Black cool' identities and styles can be read as complex and ambiguous performances. On the one hand, successful performances may be experienced as powerful by the young people themselves, conferring value and status, for the reasons outlined above. On the other hand, they are linked with particular, narrow (racist) constructions of 'Blackness' and thus may feed in to racist discourses. Moreover, while the specific racialised aspect of these performances provides the source of their power, it also means that they are often read negatively by others (notably dominant others), as signifying criminality, violence, excessive/pathological sexuality, and so forth.

While we have so far focused upon some of the common elements within the young people's performances of 'Black cool', it is also important to understand that the young people were not simply mindlessly reproducing or mimicking set cultural styles. Rather, they actively and creatively mixed elements of popular versions of 'Black cool' with a range of local inflections, combining 'traces of various social, historical, geographical and cultural elements' (Archer and Yamashita, 2003a: 118). These identities were distinctly geographically situated within local areas and even to the level of local ward or borough. For instance, Jordan (Blackwell Street) is a White British girl who drew on aspects of 'Black cool' in her construction of self (such as her 'bling' jewellery) while also identifying strongly with her local area. When asked to elaborate on her ethnicity, she replied: 'I was born in North London, I am a North London girl, I love London'. For Jordan, her 'ethnicity' was more than just being 'White' or 'British'; it was also grounded within being 'a North London girl' and adopting a particular form of culturally entangled, urban style.

Complex ethnic backgrounds

The pupils' constructions of racialised and ethnic identities were additionally complex due to many of the young people's histories of displacement and/or their emotional links with other parts of the globe. While the majority of pupils in the study were British nationals, their ethnic and national allegiances and feelings of 'belonging' were far more intricate than being a mere matter of their passport or their ethnic/cultural heritage. Quite a few young people maintained a sense of belonging with their countries of origin, often reinforced by continuing close links. For instance Germaine (Blackwell Street) had come to the UK from Jamaica when he was 8 years old and his father and younger brother still live in Jamaica. Germaine had not been back to Jamaica since he left (although he was hoping to visit soon) but spoke regularly to his father and brother on the phone.

These shifting ethnic identities were profoundly emotional in nature; they were not mere translations of the 'facts' of their familial origins or nationality. Jermina (Blackwell Street), for example, had come to the UK from Sierra Leone, as a French-speaking Black African national. She described her ethnicity in her initial interview as Black African, but in later interviews she started to talk about her Jamaican roots. She talked particularly about wanting to go back to 'her country' ('When I've finished at university I want to go back to my country'), although she had never actually been to Jamaica. She explained that her older brother also now describes himself as Jamaican: 'He would definitely say Jamaican because like he's . . . I don't like – he's [not] strictly Jamaican [but] he's got all friends like Jamaicans, he's got like, he dress like them and now he'll almost look like them as well, so he would say he is.' As discussed above, popular performances of 'Black cool' are specifically linked to Caribbean (as opposed to African) cultures, and hence Jermina's account of her brother's identification with Jamaican friends and style of dress could be read in this light. However, Jermina's shift towards a Jamaican identity was also grounded within the emotional terrain of her daily family relations, coinciding in particular with her increasing estrangement from her African step-father and her increasing desire to align herself with the nationality of her 'real' (biological) father (who was Jamaican). 'I am half Jamaican and half African and so I am going back to Jamaica soon . . . my real dad is Jamaican my stepdad is African, from the same country as my mum.' In other words, ethnic identification can be strongly emotionally inflected, as exemplified by Jermina's shifting sense of identification in relation to her relationships with her parents and step-parent.

For young people with parents and families from different ethnic and/or national backgrounds, it was also clear that their ethnic identifications were more complex than simply claiming a 'mixed' identity. For instance, Nadia's (Blackwell Street) ethnicity is recorded as White European. She was born to a White Danish mother and a Lebanese father and lived in Denmark until she was about 14. She moved to England with her father following the death of her mother (although her brother, who is disabled, remains in care in Denmark). 'My mum is Danish and my dad is Arabic. I live with my dad. My mum is dead. She died last year. I've got a brother, he lives in Denmark'. However, when asked about how she defines her own ethnic identity, she claimed an 'English' identity: 'I would say I am English. Because you live in England and you've got English passport and stuff and that is the thing that counts.' Yet, at the same time, she felt that she does not necessarily 'belong' or feel comfortable in England, and described finding it quite different from Denmark ('there are a lot of rude people [here]. There aren't rude people in Denmark'). Nadia described desperately wanting to return to Denmark to see her brother ('my first wish would be to go back to Denmark and see my brother'), something for which her father was anxiously saving.

The complexity of young people's ethnic identifications was not restricted to those from minority ethnic backgrounds but also applied to young people from ostensibly 'White British' backgrounds. Sometimes, the descriptor hid other aspects of their racialised identities, for instance, Janine (Hillside Park) self-identified as English and fitted the 'White UK' category, but her family were historically travellers. Janine's parents had currently settled as pub landlords and the family did not now identify themselves as travellers. However, during the course of the study, Janine left school and went to work on a travelling fairground.

Ben attended Hillside Park, a mainly White school, and his ethnicity was officially recorded as White UK. However, in his interview he constructed his own personal sense of ethnicity as 'from England, but I've got a bit of West Indian in me' due to Trinidadian connections (which he termed 'blood') on his father's side of the family. Ben also talked about how he and his friend (who is 'part Trinidadian') dream of going to the Caribbean to live and set up a business together: 'Well because we're both from the same country and both got the same blood in us, from Trinidad . . . I would say I'm from England, but I've got a bit of West Indian in me, that's what I'd say.'

Often White pupils were unable to conceive of their Whiteness as an ethnicity, reflecting the dominance and hegemony of Whiteness, such that it is perceived by those subsumed within it as being 'the norm' and 'outside' of 'race'/ethnicity (Fine et al., 1997). For instance, Lee (Riverway) initially did not fill in the section of the short demographic information sheet used at the start of the study to record participants' background information. When asked to complete the missing section, Lee replied incredulously 'I haven't got an ethnic, I was born in the UK.'

Like Jordan's (Blackwell Street) identification of herself as a 'North London girl', a number of White pupils conceptualised their ethnic identity in specific- ally localised, geographic terms (see Nayak, 2003). For instance, Verona (Riverway) identified himself as 'White English', but elaborated further in the interview: 'I'm London cockney. That is what I'd be . . . If you live between the bells up near St Paul's if you can hear the bells ring, you are a cockney.' How- ever, not all pupils constructed multi-layered identities. Mark (Hillside Park), whose views we discuss in detail below, expressed popular racist and national- istic opinions about 'Englishness', arguing that it should only encompass White people and complaining that he dislikes it when people from minority ethnic backgrounds 'claim' to be English. Such views indicate the relationality of dominant identities, such as Whiteness – yet also their precariousness, as Mark's comments suggest that he feels the need to defend and police the boundaries of 'Englishness'.

Hybridised identities?

Within the academic literature, it has been suggested that the complexity of contemporary ethnic identities might be encapsulated by the notion of 'hybridity' (Bhabha, 1996). Hybrid identities draw on two or more different cultural 'stocks', blending together different cultural elements to create new cultural forms and possibilities. These ideas are also taken up in the notion of hyphenated identities (Modood, 1992), such as 'Black-British' and 'British- Asian'. Again, these are seen as identities that create new cultural forms through a blending of different cultural sources.

This conceptualisation of hybrid or hyphenated identities undoubtedly provides a useful shorthand to capture the complex cultural entanglement of many urban young people's ethnic identities, as illustrated above. However, at a conceptual level, caution is required when employing these concepts. First, the biological origins of the term 'hybrid' can risk implying that the 'cultures' in question are somehow fixed, discrete and 'real' entities (Yuval-Davis, 1997) or 'pure' identities (Ahmed, 1999) that are simply grafted together. Rather, we would argue that the cultures in question are better conceptualised as shifting, complex and continuously shaped (and reshaped) by relations of power. Thus, as Anthias (2001: 619) argues, the terminology of hybridity may 'unintention- ally provide a gloss over existing cultural hierarchies and hegemonic practices' within 'cultures'.

Secondly, it has been argued that the idea of hybridity, in itself, is not *neces- sarily* liberatory or progressive. This argument is staked against Bhabha's (2001) eulogisation of hybridity as constituting a 'third space' (of liminality) in which the hybrid subject can obtain a 'double perspective' as 'the voice that speaks from two places at once and inhabits neither' (Anthias, 2001: 628) by virtue of their intercultural location. Bhabha was primarily theorising the creative possibilities explored by artists, poets and other cosmopolitan subjects who migrate across national and cultural boundaries. As such, he emphasises the progressive, creative and emancipatory potential of hybridised identities and the new cultural forms associated with them. While we would undoubtedly agree that the identities of the young people in our study might also be read as constructive, agentic and creative, fusing different cultural elements into exciting new forms, we feel that this view must be tempered. Hybridity is not necessarily progressive and 'may be tied to violence and alienation . . . Through migration and diasporization, the opposite to hybridity can occur: a ghettoization and enclavization process' (Anthias, 2001: 628). In other words, we must not forget the structural relations (and inequalities) within which young people are forming their 'hybrid' identities. Thus, in the next sections we discuss the wider contexts and racialised relations within which this 'identity work' happens.

Teachers' constructions of 'race'/ethnicity and achievement

When asked about the most pressing issues facing their schools in relation to issues of 'race'/ethnicity and achievement, one of the most common responses across many of the teacher interviews was a concern with White working-class underachievement. Many teachers described an approximate ethnic hierarchy of attainment and engagement, in which White working-class pupils (but particularly boys) were located at or near the bottom, followed by complex layerings of other minority ethnic group pupils. For example, Riverway's Head of Year 11 said, 'it would probably be White boys who are seen to be underachieving quite often. So those in my mind, it would probably be the most high percentage of White boys are not achieving as they should be achieving, according to the data'. As indicated in this quote, schools are increasingly obliged to monitor pupil achievement through the collation and return of quantitative data. Teachers are also encouraged to do this by the ongoing government fascination with testing and examination league tables, which have exacerbated competition between schools via 'choice' policies and the promotion of educational markets.

It is unsurprising that so many teachers identified White working-class male underachievement as a key concern given the pervasiveness of the boys' underachievement debate. As discussed in Chapter 2, the perceived reasons for White working-class (male) underachievement were predominantly framed as a 'cultural' (class) issue and, as we discuss in Chapter 4, we found a distinct group of boys within our sample who did not want to go on to FE and who expressed a clear preference for leaving education as soon as possible to find work. However, these were not only White boys and, as various writers suggest, we need to be alert to the pathologisation of White working-class cultures within everyday parlance (Reay and Lucey, 2000b; Reay, 2002).

Teachers recognised that their views were only impressionistic from their own experience, but generally felt that minority ethnic families were more likely to value education as a means for achieving social mobility. This is an interesting point, and encouraging to the extent that it suggests a positive shift away from the dominant educational (policy) discourse that positions minority ethnic families as having low aspirations. Indeed, minority ethnic students were often seen as being highly motivated and strategic in their aspirations and as valuing education as a means for escaping poverty:

> English Second Language speaking families would probably be the ones where education is seen as one way of getting out of things, you know? The vehicle for attainment, performance, achieving things.
>
> (Head of Year 11, Riverway)

> From my experience . . . a few tend not to go onto post–16 and mainly actually indigenous White, which is a curious thing because a lot of the Turkish Kurdish kids [and] Somalian kids, they leave school [but] they go onto something else – they want to learn, they want to get their competency, they want to get into a field. But you know, White kids tend to go for a job. . . . I don't think they value post–16 education as much maybe, I don't know, I'm not sure.
>
> (Assistant Headteacher, Blackwell Street)

The importance of the aspirations that teachers hold for their students has been widely documented within educational research, and particular attention has been given over the years to the ways in which institutional structures, practices and narrow or stereotypical teacher attitudes can all impact negatively on minority ethnic students. For instance, in the 1980s the spotlight was directed in particular at relations between Black students and White teachers (Wright, 1987a, 1987b). Since the late 1990s, research highlighted the ways in which some teachers tend to hold lower expectations of minority ethnic young people (Basit, 1997a, 1997b; Blair and Bourne, 1998; Blair, 2001a, 2001b; Connolly, 1998). However, as the above extracts suggest, teachers who work within urban, highly multicultural settings, may be operating with quite intricate differentiations in relation to a range of ethnic backgrounds.

While most teachers felt that the families of students from minority ethnic backgrounds were, on the whole, more aspirational and supportive of the value of education than their White peers, some concerns were also raised regarding their perceived increased propensity to exhibit attendance issues. For instance, concerns were raised about the frequency with which some young people were absent from school where family members relied on their children for help with translation and/or where families made extended trips back to their countries of origin (see Rutter, 1999). As Blackwell Street's Assistant Headteacher put it: 'translation is a big issue for us and we have to really impress on parents the importance of making appointments outside of school times'.

Despite the promising recognition that minority ethnic families are not necessarily or inherently suffering from 'low aspirations' or a lack of role models, the degree of generalisation and stereotyping of 'ethnic groups' within some respondents' talk does indicate the continued seduction and prevalence of ethnic stereotyping. Of course, we must remember that interviews were being conducted at a level of generality (teachers were not asked just to comment on particular individuals, but were questioned about their general views and experiences). Bearing this point in mind, however, we would still like to raise a note of caution regarding the tendency to homogenise pupils from particular backgrounds. This is illustrated within the following extract from an interview with a Learning Mentor.

> The Asians, with the Asian girls, they're very low key, keep to themselves and they just get in and 'yeah, I want to go to university, whatever'. I think that maybe comes down to parents as well, because the Asian mums say 'go to school, keep on going' or whatever. I would say White Irish, I'm working with a couple of girls, White Irish, lovely girls, they crack me up, they'll just leave school and work, that's their attitude. 'Mum did it and I'm going to do it'. Oh yeah, 'my mum worked for Marks and Spencer's [a highstreet chain] for four years and now she's a manager'. That's the type of attitude they have and they all want to have quick money as well so they get jobs to buy their trainers and go out. It's more about enjoying themselves than struggling going to university for four years. They say, 'oh Miss that's too long, I'm not going to do that'. Whereas the Iraqi boys, their attitude is, they're either going to work for dad or be self-employed. They're like, 'I'm not going to have an education. Why? Because I can work for someone or have my own business'. So they're more focussed on working straight after school, earning a bit of money, saving up and opening their own business, becoming self-employed.
>
> (Learning Mentor, Eastleigh Central)

While recognising diversity between groups of students, the learning mentor falls into the trap of reproducing a range of dominant stereotypes. For instance, the stereotype of 'Asian girls' as 'quiet' and driven to educational achievement by their families has been extensively discussed and critiqued (Archer, 2002; Basit, 1997a; Shain, 2003). Moreover, research has argued that even seemingly positive stereotypes (for example, of Chinese pupils as hard-working, high achievers) can be experienced as problematic and oppressive by the diversity of people subsumed within them (Archer and Francis, 2007). Indeed, the problem with any stereotypes is that they work to homogenise and reify, stifling the diversity within young people's experiences and aspirations and potentially preventing professionals from holding high (or broad) expectations for them. As Hayes and colleagues (2006) argue, it is vitally important for educators to hold (and transmit) high aspirations for all students, irrespective of their imagined abilities or likely progression routes.

Racism: views and experiences of minority ethnic students

In contrast to the government policy identification of low aspirations and a lack of role models as holding back the achievement of minority ethnic students, it was notable that young people themselves identified racism as a key factor affecting their success. Among the most vocal and frequently articulated experiences of racism were voiced by Black (African and Caribbean) young people.

Across the study sample, Black students expressed a clear and consistent view that racism in society might hold them back from achieving their aspirations. Several discussed how they imagined that they would need to battle hard to overcome these barriers. Young Black women seemed particularly aware of these issues, with one discussion group of Cowick students describing how their decisions about continuing into FE were strongly influenced by their perceptions of the ethnically segregated nature of different FE colleges. Like the minority ethnic students in Reay and colleagues' (2005) study, the young women discussed the tensions arising from trying to choose a college where they might 'fit in'. They were concerned that the 'better' colleges would reject them, imagining that staff there would be thinking 'you're Black, what are you doing at my college?' and 'why are you going to that college? It's full of, *you know*', with the girls' latter comment in particular highlighting the unspeakable (and painful), yet always known, dimension of negotiations around 'race'/ethnicity.

Black students also reported feeling constrained by wider societal assumptions and racist stereotypes, such as the view that Black people are only destined for menial positions (to 'sweep floors' or 'somebody who, like, cleans toilets something like that') and by the imagined future boss who 'only hires White people'. As one Black African boy, Kwame, put it:

> [T]here are some people look down on you. As in – my dad is like, he's a Black businessman yeah, and where he's concerned you don't really see a lot of Black businessmen in his position and people sometimes are surprised at him. And even his friends turn on him saying 'oh why are you still doing this, you're not like capable of doing this' and my dad's lost friends because of that because my friends think that 'oh, Black people are just supposed to live in the gutter' and stuff.
>
> (Kwame, Littleton discussion group)

While for some, this recognition acted as a source of motivation to 'prove myself', others expressed a sense of resignation ('no matter where you go there's always going to be people that's going to look down on you no matter what coloured skin [or] race you are'). As Chanel, a Black young woman in a Cowick discussion group, put it: 'It depends on how strong the person is, if the person has a very strong character then the person would just be like: "okay, I don't really care". But if the person is, like, gives in to what everyone says then obviously the person wouldn't have the encouragement to do it'. Racisms were not only seen as an issue affecting their future lives 'out there' in society, but were also identified as operating within schools. For instance, Charlene (Cowick) described the pain she felt when other students mocked her African accent.

Black students' fears about racism did not go wholly unnoticed by the educational professionals in their schools. Although as the following quote from a learning mentor illustrates, the issue of how to work with these fears is complex:

> The other day I had four Black students and I said, 'guys you're not going to get far if you continue like this and you don't improve, I'm here to

support you whatever.' And one of them said, 'who's going to give me a job anyway? The other day a woman looked at me on the bus and just turned away because I'm Black'. I said 'no it's not. If you go with that attitude, you are not getting a job or you're not going to achieve anything'. I said [name of Connexions advisor] is Black and he's got a job and [name], I said 'she's Black'.

(Learning Mentor, Eastleigh Central)

In this extract, the learning mentor describes her attempts to get the four boys in question not to give up hope. Her obvious concern is that the boys are 'giving up', lacking the motivation and ambition to achieve due to their fears about the prevalence and inevitability of racism, which they imagine will stop them getting jobs in the future. The Learning Mentor's tactic in response is to highlight the importance of their own 'attitude' as a factor in their achievement and future job success, and she names two concrete examples of Black people, known to the boys, who have jobs. This is obviously done with a highly laudable aim in mind, but we would suggest that a focus on changing 'attitudes' alone may be limited. An emphasis on individual agency can appear to be a seductive answer for 'overcoming' structural inequalities, but it can place a considerable burden on individuals to prove themselves to be remarkable and resourceful in the face of inequalities. It may be more productive to acknowledge and work with the conditions of inequality, not least because this does not preclude recognising their existence. The technique of identifying 'role models' is also a common strategy for inspiring young people. But as research points out, these will need to be people to whom young people can relate as 'like me' in more complex ways than simply sharing a particular gender or racial background (see Archer and Yamashita, 2003a; Skelton, 2001). As we discuss further in Chapter 6, educators are caught within the same social structures and inequalities as the young people they work with, and hence the ways they are able to deal with such instances will be shaped and constrained by the available discourses and resources. Currently, dominant education policy and media coverage of educational issues tends towards an individualistic model that does not fully engage with or recognise the role of structural constraints – a situation that we feel might be usefully rethought.

Racism: views and experiences of White pupils

While considerable advances have been made with respect to the embedding of anti-racist and racial equality values within the formal and informal practices and structures of schools in the UK, it would be naïve to imagine that this translates unproblematically into a lack of racism within British schools (Gaine, 1995). On the whole, the vast majority of young people did *not* express racially prejudiced views of any kind – although there were a few exceptions. For instance, Kay (Cowick) talked about her eagerness to move out of London to the home counties, which she felt were 'nicer' because 'there are less coloured people'.

There were also a few examples of White young people at Riverway School reacting against the multicultural, anti-racist ethos, its relatively substantial number of Asian teachers and their own positioning as a numerical minority within the school's student population. These feelings of resentment were expressed in accusations of 'racism' – namely that White pupils were somehow discriminated against due to being in a minority. For example, Lucy complained that Riverway School favoured 'Asian' students ('they'd rather listen to the Asians'), calling it a 'racist school' and referring to particular members of staff as a 'racist' or 'bigot' – although she also admitted to being loud and disruptive in class and hence attracting disapproval and reprimands for her behaviour. As other studies have noted, these feelings of 'being hard done by' are not uncommon among White students when exposed to anti-racist teaching practices and when faced with the (novel) position of being part of a minority, as opposed to the 'normal' ethnic majority, group (Gaine, 2000).

Perhaps unsurprisingly, these views (that Asian students receive favouritism and White students experience 'racism') were not shared by 'Asian' students at the school. For instance, Babu (Bangladeshi), made a very similar claim, albeit complaining this time that the school discriminated against Asian students, saying 'the teachers are racist'. Babu's complaints seemed to stem from one particular subject class, in which he happened to be the only Asian student and appeared to feel isolated (he was highly complimentary of a different class and teacher, for instance).

What is striking is the way in which both Lucy and Babu drew on the accusation of 'racism' (and in particular the notion of 'teachers as racist') as a means for articulating and venting their frustrations with particular experiences of learning. Indeed, it was notable that neither identified any actual examples of being discriminated against in any way. Rather, they used the accusation of racism as a catch-all term to express dissatisfaction at their relations with particular teachers or classes. These examples illustrate the difficulty of investigating issues of racism within schools, the contested nature of definitions of racism and indeed the ways in which it can be used as a general discourse to challenge and complain about perceived biases and notions of favouritism at school and to explain pupils' own educational disengagement or disadvantage. This is not, of course, to deny the ongoing prevalence or impact of racism on pupils (as discussed in sections above and below), nor is it to disregard the maxim that 'if someone perceives something as racist, then it must be treated as such'. Rather, our aim in including these more 'difficult' (less clear-cut) examples is to underline the messy, complicated and contradictory nature of racialised relations within schools and students' varied reactions and interpretations of what racism 'is'.

A contrasting example is provided by Mark, a White boy who attends Hillside Park, a school with a predominantly White pupil population. Mark expressed what we would interpret as racist constructions of 'Englishness' and immigration. However, he denied that his views were racist. For instance, he complained that he 'hates this country' and 'hates Tony Blair' because he 'lets all the Kosovans in', but added:

It's not racist just because you don't want poncers coming into the country . . . That's why I don't like it here: all of them are just taking over

. . . I don't mind if they are actually working for a living and [if] they are working like just as hard as my mum and dad do, then that is fair enough . . . it's just the fact that when they come over and they don't want to pay for nothing and they know that England is an easy ride.

In line with previous studies that have flagged up the complexity of racism (for example, Billig et al., 1988; Wetherell and Potter, 1992), Mark suggested that he did not extend his views to individual refugee students at his school, and although he personally knew refugee students whom he felt were 'alright', these interpersonal relations did not compromise his views on the wider issue: 'they are alright to speak to if you know them. . . . But just to let them in to ponce off you, I just think that is sad.'

Again, the point that we emphasise here is the complexity of racism. On the one hand, Mark seems to suggest that he bears no interpersonal animosity to refugee pupils at his school. On the other hand, these 'positive' personal relationships and interactions do not appear to lessen his vehement views about refugees in general (as 'poncers'). While 'denying' that his views are racist, Mark actually articulates a well-established racist discourse that constructs refugees as 'leech-like' and work-shy and threatening to the 'respectable', hard-working (White) people of Britain (Archer et al., 2005).

Of course Mark's comments are not unique, for instance, Reay (2004a) describes how refugee children are frequently constructed in negative and pejorative terms, as 'rubbish' and hence their schools are seen as 'dumping grounds'. Mark's comments also highlight the inadequacy of traditional multicultural strategies (see Rattansi, 1992) for promoting intercultural understanding and awareness (for example, through teaching and learning about other cultures) and even interpersonal contact. Hence we would argue that attempting to work with Mark's views requires complex and sensitive approaches that engage with the contradictory elements and the underlying emotional attachments (such as, themes around identity, belonging and nationhood) that are all combined within his articulation. As the following section also discusses, the issue is particularly pertinent for refugee young people themselves, who continue to experience the effects of this prejudice.

The struggle to fit in: EAL and migrant pupils

We have so far discussed issues of 'race', racism and ethnicity in relation to minority ethnic and White majority young people within our study. Of course this does not reflect the whole extent of 'racialised' experiences and issues and in this section we consider some of the additional, specific problems that minority ethnic young people from migrant and refugee/asylum-seeker backgrounds may encounter in relation to schooling. We focus on two main themes that characterise these students' descriptions of their struggles to fit in – namely the effects of displacement and of language.

While there are no definitive statistics, Jill Rutter (1999: 4) suggests that 'at least 60,000 "refugee" children of compulsory school age [are] residing in the UK. In Greater London some 6.5 per cent of all school children are asylum-seekers, refugees or other groups of forced migrants.' In her comprehensive book on *Refugee Children in the UK*, Rutter (1999) discusses how many refugee and asylum-seeker children experience considerable difficulties adjusting to new schools and making friends. As she explains, the overwhelming focus and concern of policy and research in this area has been on how experiences of trauma impact on children's physical, emotional and educational well-being and progress. Indeed, the impact of trauma was evident among our study participants (see below). However, Rutter argues that its dominance of research and policy agendas actually prevents analysis of other factors (both pre- and post-migration) that can impact on children's progress. She thus argues that it is crucially important not to homogenise refugee children.

A number of young people in the study were refugees or recent migrants. Their refugee status impacted on their experiences of learning and school in a number of ways. For instance, their previous experiences of migration often impacted negatively on their level and extent of education. Hapsa (Blackwell Street), a refugee from Somalia, did not get the chance to go to school until she arrived at secondary school in the UK. Jermina (Blackwell Street), a refugee from Sierra Leone, also revealed that she did not go to school until she came to the UK aged 12. The young people's experiences of forced migration often entailed difficult family circumstances and disruptions. Jermina, for instance, described the hardship that her mother had been through in trying to get the family out of Sierra Leone and how her mother's career and education had suffered in order to provide for her children. The process of migration had entailed Jermina being separated from her mother for long periods of time, during which she was looked after by an aunt. Experiences of displacement and often traumatic previous events in their lives made it difficult for the young people to settle down at school straight away. Jermina, like other refugee young people, continued to feel traumatised by the life events she experienced in her previous country ('when I think of it my stomach aches because they [pause] . . . I don't like it'). Even those young people whose families were voluntary, as opposed to forced, migrants described the process of uprooting and arriving in a new country as 'scary'.

It was not solely experiences of trauma, however, that shaped the extent to which young people were able to 'slot' into the school system and progress. How far families possessed relevant knowledge, expectations and understandings about the UK education system also played a part. Many families lacked the necessary cultural capital (see Chapter 2) to understand and make sense of the system – that is, the taken-for-granted knowledge of 'how things work' and an instinctive feel for the unspoken 'rules of the game'. As Hapsa (Blackwell Street) explained, she and her mother had no knowledge of the education system ('my mum doesn't know about anything about school') and no one at home could help her make subject choices or assist with homework and learning ('it is bad, because your parents should know something'). Consequently she experienced schooling as an alien and confusing place. She had to learn not only a new language and subject matter, but also the tiny everyday micropractices of 'how things are done', such as how to behave in the classroom: 'I never used to know what to do in the classroom, I used to just sit down there

. . . In Year 8 I used to like sit in the classroom and do nothing, now I know it'. Nadia (Blackwell Street) similarly reflected on how she had to learn a new set of 'rules of the game' on coming to school in the UK, including differing cultural norms and practices, such as wearing a uniform, standing up when a teacher enters the room and the practice of detention. While she had now picked these up, she still felt disadvantaged by having so little knowledge about post-16 routes due to her family's unfamiliarity with the system: '[my dad] doesn't know much about college as well . . . I think because I'm from another country'.

Language

The young people's prior experiences of trauma and their lack of cultural capital in a new country and educational system were compounded by issues of language. Indeed, language was the most commonly raised theme by migrant and refugee pupils in relation to problems they experienced in education. These issues comprised not only the practical problems posed by not being proficient in English but also experiences of being stigmatised, marginalised and bullied due to language differences.

Eight pupils did not speak English as their first language and these young people recounted the considerable difficulties they encountered at school as a result. A further six pupils were bi- or tri-lingual – although some had difficulty explaining their 'mother-tongue'. For example, Germaine's (Blackwell Street) first language is recorded on the school records as 'Jamaican Patois' and Jermina (Blackwell Street) described her 'native language' as 'broken English . . . I don't know' – although she had come from a French-speaking country and did not know any English on her arrival in the UK. Not being able to speak English on arrival made school a scary and confusing place, as Jermina recalled:

> It was hard, because I didn't have a clue what they were doing in the classroom and I was sitting there and I couldn't do the work because I couldn't understand it because I couldn't read it and I couldn't speak English either. . . . I never used to understand and then when I stayed in this school for a year I started picking up the English then.

David (Littleton) similarly experienced problems reading and writing because he did not speak English fluently. These problems spanned a whole range of subjects, not just 'language-based' lessons. For instance, David found science and geography very hard and Hapsa (Blackwell Street) said that she even had trouble with maths because she did not understand the instructions. Both Hapsa and Jermina agonised over science lessons because they could not understand the language being used, while Charlene (Cowick) found modern foreign languages difficult. However, as they became more proficient in English, so the young people's happiness and confidence in school grew: 'because I understand what teachers are saying now, explaining to me' (Hapsa).

As the following teacher explained, schools recognise that EAL students are often 'at risk' due to their lack of English and as a result provide them with additional language support. However, as the teacher also suggests, beyond this the students are expected to fit in with the mainstream lessons and curriculum and the onus falls on teachers to accommodate them:

> When we have a casual admission who has no English and has never been to school before and that child is at serious risk of leaving here in two terms time with no exam results . . . What we do is the child is assessed when they come in . . . What we do is we look at the curriculum, they are given induction, they are given nine hours of induction and as one of their options they're given something called option support, which is an extra three hours a week but quite frankly, for the rest of the timetable they are expected to be in lessons and the teachers are expected to differentiate and provide something for that student to do, whether they can communicate with them or not.
>
> (Head of Year 11, Blackwell Street)

The issue of bilingual education and the manner in which it is (and might be) undertaken is a topic of heated debate (Baker, 2006; Garcia and Baker, 2007), especially in the United States (Rethinking Schools Online, 2002/2003). Research suggests, however, that rather than viewing these children and young people's 'other' languages as a 'problem' to be overcome, it can be incredibly fruitful if schools can develop ways of working with multiple languages in the classroom (for example, Gregory, 1996; Martin, 2003; Sneddon, 2000). For instance, the work of Kenner (2000, 2004) demonstrates how minority ethnic children benefit from their bilingualism and can actively combine languages in developing English literacy. She also suggests that children may experience their different linguistic and cultural worlds as more coherent and simultaneous than many educators imagine and that this can be harnessed to positive effect through integrating minority and majority languages within the UK classroom.

Alongside the practical issues around learning and understanding English, almost all the students for whom English was not a mother tongue talked about their experiences of being marginalised or bullied on account of their language differences. This seems to be a common experience, as many of the refugee pupils in Rutter's (1999) research similarly recounted being teased by other pupils for not knowing English. Within our participants, Charlene (who started primary school in Year 6, less than a year before moving to Cowick) described experiencing racist bullying on account of her accent and African heritage: 'I was very quiet . . . Because I had an African accent, people take the piss and stuff.' The fear of this bullying led her to truant from school. Nadia (who entered Blackwell Street School in Year 9) also talked about her fear that her lack of fluency in English would stop her from finding friends.

The intersection of language and cultural capital issues are evident within Hapsa's extract below. Hapsa recounted how she felt 'scared' and 'shy' when she first arrived in at Blackwell Street School due to not knowing English, and how misunderstandings led her into fights with other pupils ('I thought they were saying something [bad] about me'). However, in Year 9 she met and made friends with some other Somalian girls who not only befriended her, but were able to explain things about the school, teachers, lessons and other students. This intersection of both assistance in translation and the provision of knowledge (cultural capital) about the rules, regulations and everyday practices of schooling proved a key transition point for Hapsa:

> God it was too hard, I didn't know no one in this school, so I was scared and I didn't speak that much English and it was scary . . . The people was looking at you, and you go shy though . . . Before I used to be scared of people and whenever someone used to talk to me about, or how I dress or how I look, I used to fight with them, I thought they were saying something about me. . . . [Interviewer: When did that change then?] I think in Year 9, when I . . . when I came in classroom one day there was Somalian girl and . . . they help me, I used to walk around with them, they was nice to me. [Interviewer: How did they help you?] Well they used to show me all around school, everything about school they told me about and they told me all the teachers and the lessons we had . . . I used to walk around with them, even now, we are old friends now.

Summary

This chapter has discussed some of the issues pertaining to 'race', ethnicity and education among our sample of marginalised urban young people. We discussed how the students constructed complex and entangled ethnic identities that are more multifarious and trans-locational than traditional conceptualizations of hybrid or hyphenated identities might suggest. We explored constructions of racism as recounted by both minority ethnic and White young people and we outlined some of the particular issues (around trauma, cultural capital and language) that are encountered by refugee pupils.

4

'RESPONSIBLE BOYS' AND 'GLAMOROUS GIRLS'? GENDER AND SCHOOLING

Introduction

As outlined in Chapter 1, educational debates in the UK, US, Australia and New Zealand remain highly concerned with the issue of boys' 'underachievement' (Francis and Skelton, 2005; Younger et al., 2005). In the UK, such debates run alongside policy concerns to redress ongoing low progression rates into further and higher education among 'working-class' young people (Archer et al., 2003), with particular emphasis placed on increasing *male* participation rates (for example, DfES, 2003c; DfES, 2004; Social Exclusion Unit, 1999).

Yet, as previously discussed, the assumption that all girls are doing well educationally and all boys are doing badly does not stand up to scrutiny. There are complex differences in achievement and post-compulsory educational participation across social class, 'race'/ethnicity and gender (Gillborn and Mirza, 2000). Indeed, gender differences pale in comparison to the striking achievement differentials by social class and 'race'/ethnicity. Moreover, the notion of female educational 'success' has been roundly problematised in feminist writings. For instance, work has drawn attention to the emotional and psychic 'costs' of success for both middle-class and working-class girls (for example, Hey, 2003; Walkerdine et al., 2001). Likewise, research has sought to tease out the interplay of 'race'/ethnicity, class and gender within the lives of different groups of boys, to try and understand how identities and inequalities interact to render educational engagement and success more difficult for some boys (for example, Archer and Yamashita, 2003a; Martino and Pallotta-Chiarolli, 2003; Mills, 2003). Following this, in this chapter, we put forward a critical, feminist reading of the boys and girls in our study and their dis/engagement from education and schooling. We try to understand the ways in which inequalities of 'race'/ethnicity and social class position the young people in disadvantaged ways and how their espousal or taking up of particular (racialised, classed) identity discourses around masculinity and femininity (the ways in which they 'do' boy/girl) work to make certain options and routes un/desirable and un/thinkable.

Problem boys or 'responsible' young men?

Of the 30 boys that we tracked in the study, 15 were clear that they did not want to continue in education past the end of compulsory schooling (age 16) and would 'rather work'. There was considerable talk and anticipation among these boys about how they 'can't wait' to leave school and start work. As Ben (Hillside Park) said, 'I can't wait till I go and get my job, that's all.' This eagerness was evidenced by their suggestions that they would rather take a less preferred, or indeed 'any', job in order to enter the labour market, than wait for their preferred career choice to materialise. For instance, Bob (Eastleigh Central) wanted to be an electrician but was adamant that 'even if it has to be not a good job, I will get a job. I need a job.' Likewise, James (Littleton) explained: 'I have always wanted to be an electrician but the locksmith's job has come quicker than the electrician's and so I will just take that.'

The other 15 boys in the study, while often expressing similar ambitions (for example, to go into the trades) all saw FE (college) as a logical, and mostly taken-for-granted, next step. We found this distinction interesting, not least given the recent policy shifts that have rendered continuation in some form of education or training post-16 as the most viable route for today's young people. Consequently, we here explore in greater detail the views and rationales of those 15 boys who were resistant to the idea of continuing into post-16 education. Table 4.1 sets out some of the characteristics of these two groups of young men. As the table shows, there were roughly equal proportions of boys from White UK backgrounds who said they would rather work or continue into college, but it seems that boys from Black backgrounds (although not those from mixed families) were slightly more likely to envisage staying in post-compulsory education than leaving to find work. Obviously this is not a definitive finding due to the small numbers, but it supports other studies showing that Black (and minority ethnic families in general) tend to value education highly and convey to their children a clear preference for staying on (see Mirza, 1992).

There were no clear or discernible patterns in relation to achievement or aspirations – those boys who wanted to leave had neither noticeably lower patterns of attainment than those who envisaged progressing to college, nor very different sets of aspirations and both groups shared similar socio-economic backgrounds and educational attainment. Indeed, among the White UK boys in particular, there was a remarkable similarity in the ambitions across the two groups, notably to pursue careers in manual trades. Hence our interest lies in what makes 'staying on' feel like an unacceptable option for some but not for others. Are some more 'laddish'? Or are some more 'at risk'? In terms of the latter, we could find no clear differences between the two groups in terms of parental occupations or unemployment patterns, or family composition. That is, those desperate to leave education appeared no more 'at risk' than

Table 4.1 Summary of boys' statements about post-16 intentions

	Name	Ethnicity
'Rather work'	James	White UK/Jamaican
	Ben	White UK/Trinidadian
	Bob (Eastleigh Central)	White UK/Mauritian
	Darrell	Black Caribbean
	Robert	Iraqi
	Mark (Littleton)	White Irish
	David (Littleton)	White Polish
	Bob (Riverway)	White UK
	Mike (Littleton)	White UK
	Max	White UK
	Verona	White UK
	Lee	White UK
	Mike (Hillside Park)	White UK
	Nathan	White UK
	Mark (Hillside Park)	White UK
Go to FE College	Peter	Black UK
	Roger	Black Caribbean
	Germaine	Black Caribbean
	Jason	Black African
	Tyson	Mixed
	Babu	Bangladeshi
	Helal	Bangladeshi
	Dan	White UK
	Tim	White UK
	Nick	White UK
	David (Hillside Park)	White UK
	Darren	White UK
	John	White UK
	Jay	White UK
	Steven	White UK

those who planned to stay on. Neither did those boys who wanted to leave education appear to be suffering from a lack of male role models, as some proponents of the 'at risk' boys thesis might imagine. Many boys suggested that their valorisation of work was influenced by their fathers' and/or other male family members' participation in manual professions. For example, Bob (Riverway) said that he wanted to become a builder like his father and Verona (Riverway) and Dan (Riverway) both expressed an interest in working in delivery, like their fathers. Robert (Eastleigh Central) was considering becoming a mechanic like his uncle and Mike (Hillside Park) described being influenced by his stepfather, who 'does plastering and all sorts', and his uncle, a plumber and who had promised him employment. Both groups included instances of out of work parents, but across the board boys expressed distinct aspirations for future jobs, many of which came from their networks of male relatives. In other words, family unemployment had not seemed to 'kill' these boys' aspirations, nor did it prevent them from aspiring to join professions that their fathers and relatives had previously worked in.

Laddishness?

'Laddishness' is a term in both popular and academic usage associated with hedonistic young male practices that draw on aspects of popular and hegemonic masculinity such as 'having a laugh', drinking alcohol, participating in and watching sports, sexism/objectification of women and hyperheterosexuality, as epitomised in the UK by the so-called 'lads mags' *Loaded* and *Nuts* (Francis, 1999). It has been identified by various politicians over the years as a key problem preventing boys from achieving academically. For instance, MP Stephen Byers spoke out about laddishness ten years ago (see Francis, 1999), followed shortly by the then Secretary of State for Education David Blunkett: 'We face a genuine problem of underachievement among boys, particularly those from working-class families. This underachievement is linked to a laddish culture which in many areas has grown out of deprivation and a lack of both self-confidence and opportunity' (DfEE, 2000).

Performances of laddishness involve displaying anti-education, or 'anti-swot' behaviours in school, including 'playing up' in class, being cocky and not appearing to put much effort into school work. However, a question arises as to whether boys' performances of laddishness necessarily prevent, or distract, them from achieving *per se* or whether 'being laddish' is mainly aimed at managing the *appearance* of (not) working. For instance, research shows how some boys may engage in public displays of laddishness but maintain their work 'under cover' (Frosh et al., 2002) and/or still hold strongly pro-education values and beliefs (see Archer and Francis, 2007: in relation to British Chinese boys). Moreover, while laddishness is most frequently associated with working-class boys, it can also be found among middle-class and higher achieving boys (Connolly, 2004) and among girls (Jackson, 2006b). Perhaps the allure of laddishness for a range of boys can be seen in its offering of a 'win-win' scenario – boys who successfully perform laddishness can achieve peer status and approval (i.e. be seen as 'cool') and those who do not succeed academically can 'blame' it on their laddishness (Jackson, 2006b). Moreover, those who manage to also do well academically while performing laddish behaviours can pass it off as the 'effortless achievement' of the ideal learner (Archer and Francis, 2007; Mac an Ghaill, 1994).

In our study, 'anti-boffin' popular culture was raised by several teachers as an issue impacting particularly on boys' achievement:

> I think it is generally fair to say that the girls in the school behave better than the boys. I think there is pressure on boys to be macho and behave badly. I think the sort of yob culture or whatever the [news]paper defines it as is quite evident here. Boys are very keen not to be boffin or not to be seen as hard working. If they are, they don't want it to be publicly acknowledged.
>
> (Social Inclusion Manager, Hillside Park)

I think that the kind of anti-boffin culture, which the kids might call it, is strong. As it probably is in most urban areas in this country.

(Deputy Headteacher, Hillside Park)

Boys themselves also described the pressures they experienced to act 'hard' and 'tough'. In school, this often meant being loud, 'mouthy' and 'back chatting' (being confrontational and talking back to teachers). Many also talked about their dislike of school and (some) teachers. Out of school, boys described how 'acting tough' involved getting into trouble, engaging in sexual activity, vandalism, drugs, drinking and crime (such as, stealing cars). As 16-year-old Tyson (Littleton) explained, 'Like boys will act rough on the streets and muck about – climb on roofs and blah, blah, blah'. 'Looking hard' and projecting a suitably 'tough' image was also considered essential for staying safe, in the sense of not becoming a victim (although, paradoxically, 'acting tough' is more likely to lead boys into unsafe activities and dangerous/violent situations).

'Acting hard' in school not only meant not appearing to work hard, but also required boys to make public declarations about disliking school ('well if they say they don't like school then it makes them look like they're tough', David, Hillside Park) and to appear confident in their abilities. This meant that many boys did not seek help when they encountered difficulties in class and would not revise sufficiently for examinations. Verona (Riverway) described the peer pressure to misbehave in class, saying 'when you are with your mates you feel like you want to get cocky'.

However, the boys' propensity to engage in laddishness did not correlate with an intention to stay on or leave education. For instance, both Lee ('rather work', Riverway) and Roger ('stay on', Littleton) had been excluded from school and both described themselves as 'mouthy' and 'back chatty'. Peter ('stay on', Eastleigh Central) also talked of his 'attitude problem' in school and his tendency to 'get angry quick'. Likewise, Dan (Riverway) described how he and his friends would 'torment' and 'wind up' their peers and he recalled an episode in which: 'In maths, the teacher started saying stuff to me and getting on my nerves and I just switched and threw my chair on the floor and tipped over the tables and walked out.' Yet Dan was also one of the boys who not only expected to go to college but had held one of the most consistent aspirations in the study, to pursue a career in the army. David's (Hillside Park) comments suggest that perhaps there may be little or no real difference between those who say they intend to leave school and those that plan to stay on – as someone who planned to stay on, he complained that many of his male peers would try to deny that they would go to college but that this may not reflect reality, 'they probably will [stay on]. They're probably just *saying* that they won't.' However, we did find some distinguishing, or at least more prevalent, discursive tropes within the talk of those boys who professed a strong desire to leave and work rather than progress on to college – which we discuss next.

The mental-manual divide: learning versus earning

The boys who strongly claimed that they would 'rather work' constructed a rigid dichotomy between 'education' (collapsing together school, college and university) and 'work'. This opposition between 'learning and earning' has been noted in other studies as characteristic of some working-class men's resistance to post-compulsory education (Archer et al., 2001; Burke, 2006). Their anxiousness to leave was palpable:

> I don't enjoy school, I just can't wait to get on . . . I don't want anything to do with more education because I don't like it.
>
> (Mark, Hillside Park)

> I don't like learning a lot, I'd rather just go out and work.
>
> (Mark, Littleton)

> I'm sick of school. I don't want to go university I won't like it. If I leave school, I'll start work.
>
> (Robert, Eastleigh Central)

Post-compulsory education was resisted on the grounds that it would be 'like school', a view that was shared by some of their parents. For instance, Mike's (Hillside Park) mother agreed of her son that 'he's got no intentions of staying on . . . He's never liked school, never ever' but also imagined herself that further and higher education would not suit him because it would be 'like school'.

This strict division between education and work was set within a classed and gendered dualism, in which education and 'the academic' is configured as middle-class and feminine whereas work and 'the practical' are aligned with the working class and the masculine. Table 4.2 illustrates how the qualities that the boys used to characterise education/learning versus work/earning clearly reflect a gendered and classed dichotomy (illustrated by the last two, italicised rows of the table) in which the former is imputed to be middle class and feminine (Francis, 2000b) and the latter appears as working class and masculine. In other words, education and learning are rejected and resisted as inherently 'other' to the boys' sense of self (and representing all that they aspire *not* to be).

The association of academic achievement with the middle-class, feminised embodiment of the 'boffin' or 'swot' has been noted elsewhere (Francis and

Table 4.2 Gendered and classed dichotomies in boys' constructions of education and work

Education/Learning	Work/Earning
'School'	Employment
Academic, 'pen and paper'	Practical, 'hands on'
Mental	Manual
Passive	Active, 'doing'
Wasting time, 'dossing'	'Grafting', 'getting on'
Immature	Mature, 'real man'
Irresponsible masculinity	Responsible masculinity
Feminine	*Masculine*
Middle-class	*Working-class*

Note: Italics denote inferred qualities.

Skelton, 2005; Jackson, 2006b; Martino, 1999; Reay, 2002; Warrington et al., 2000; Younger et al., 1999). This dichotomy is also fuelled by the academic-vocational binary. Just like the 'lads' in Willis' landmark (1977) study, the boys here expressed a desire for the 'practical', the 'manual' and the 'hands on'. This was positioned as diametrically opposed to academic (or mental) learning in school, with 'pen and paper' activities being particularly disliked and derided. This division between the practical and the academic was underscored by a gendered and classed association of working-class masculinity as 'active', set against 'passive' femininity and middle-classness. Indeed, and drawing on popular stereotypes of masculinity, as espoused by the *boys will be boys* discourse outlined in Chapter 1, the boys were portrayed and portrayed themselves as inherently active and unable to sit still in class ('racing around and shouting and stuff', Kay, Cowick). For instance, Lee (Riverway), Bob (Eastleigh Central) and Mark (Hillside Park) were all adamant that 'the thing I don't want to do is sit behind a desk', seeking instead a job that would be 'hands on' and 'outdoors' with the potential sense of achievement derived from 'building something'. As Mark went on to explain, 'I need to do stuff that is energetic' that is 'more than just writing down . . . I just want to get out and do something'. Mark (Littleton) echoed this preference for 'hands-on' work rather than 'pen and paper'.

The boys' eagerness to leave full-time education and enter the world of work meant that most reported feeling frustrated and disillusioned with the advice that they received from Connexions and careers advisors, in which they felt that they were being strongly steered towards staying on in (further) education. Several described both resisting this advice and refusing to attend further appointments.

The binary also impels us, as Pearce and Hillman (1998: 41) suggest, to consider the incentives for leaving education (the 'pull' factors), as well as the disincentives (the 'push' factors) associated with staying on. As Bowlby and colleagues (1998: 229) emphasise, paid work can offer young people independence and social identities that 'play a major part in conferring social status and public acceptability as an adult'. Indeed, joining the workforce and earning a wage can be important symbolic and constitutive markers of adult masculinity (for example, McClelland, 1991; Nayak, 2003; Tolson, 1977). As Archer and colleagues (2001: 437) maintain, 'in British Industrial society, the achievement of manhood for working-class men has been linked inextricably with the achievement of secure skilled work, both as a source of income and social status'. International research, such as Nayak's (2006) work in the north of England, Fine and colleagues (1997) research on young White men in the US, and Connell's (1995) work in Australia reveals similar findings. As Connell (1995: 33) succinctly puts it, 'the central function of masculine ideology is to motivate men to work'.

The boys' construction of a rigid classed and gendered dichotomy between 'education/learning' and 'work/earning' rendered post-compulsory education both unthinkable and undesirable in their eyes. The other boys, however, (those who planned to continue in college) were able to adopt a more flexible view, in which FE was seen as distinct in several key ways to school: as providing a route to work, as being potentially more adult, more flexible, practical/

vocational and 'hands on' and as 'training'. In other words, they were able to construct FE in terms that fitted more closely with the right hand side of the dichotomy (Table 4.2) and hence as more congruent with their current and desired identities as working-class men. This did not mean that all versions of post-compulsory education were rendered acceptable, indeed, for many university was still configured as something 'for boffs' and 'a bunch of geeks', as two boys put it.

The 'rather work' boys' strict binary also raises questions for the lifelong learning policy agenda as they appear unable to conceive of 'work' as a potential site of 'learning'. While the boys did of course expect to learn a whole range of skills and new forms of knowledge and competencies in paid employment, it seemed that these processes were (for them) outside the formal structures of 'learning'.

The boys' counter-discourse: responsible masculinity

As discussed above, the boys who said that they would 'rather work' regarded staying on in post-compulsory education as an 'un-manly' option. Many of them described FE as being for people who lack drive and ambition, populated by those who do not know what else to do with their time. For example, Mark (Hillside Park) said: 'I think all the people who come back here . . . are a bit sad . . . Yeah because they don't do nothing. All I see them do is either they are playing football . . . or just dossing around, they don't do anything. And they can just drop out whenever they want.' In this respect, the boys produced an interesting counter-discourse to the dominant policy and educational view that would seek to position them as problematic or 'wrong' for wanting to leave school. As illustrated by Mark's comments above, these boys constructed their wish to leave school for work as 'responsible' and 'adult' compared to those 'sad' boys who stay on 'dossing around' and 'playing football'. This view draws on the learning/earning binary outlined earlier and uses it to challenge dominant discourses and assert the validity of the boys' own choices. For instance, Max (Littleton) questioned the value of university participation, describing it as a place where young people simply go to 'bang' (have sex). In this way, he asserts his own preference for work as more mature and responsible.

The boys also overwhelmingly suggested that continuing in post-compulsory education is an 'easy' option, which they juxtaposed with the more mature challenges of 'real work'. In this sense the boys were distancing themselves from the laddishness thesis, that understands such young men as selfish, lazy hedonists who are only interested in looking hard and having a laugh. Indeed, there is an interesting inversion in the boys' talk that renders HE students as the 'real' laddish layabouts, playing football, dossing around, engaging in casual sex, and so on (see Jackson and Dempster, 2009). In contrast, the boys present themselves as aspiring to be serious, hardworking, and responsible by virtue of their wish to leave education.

For many young men, the discourse of the male breadwinner also held currency and was employed to defend their aspirations for leaving education (see Archer and Yamashita, 2003a). 'Breadwinner' masculinity is employed to render further and higher education undesirable and problematic because participation is seen as delaying 'full' entry to the labour market, restricting earning power and thus as preventing young men from achieving 'authentic' adult masculinity. For these boys, good jobs were often framed as those offering the chance to earn a decent wage. For example, James (Littleton), when talking about the job he was offered in a locksmith's asserted that 'it's a good job and it's good money' and Bob (Riverway) claimed, 'I want to get a good job, get reasonable pay'. The rhetoric of 'good money' and 'a decent wage' echoes notions of working-class respectability (Skeggs, 1997) and, we argue, is central to boys' working-class habitus. Similarly to the boys in McDowell's (2003, 2007) research, they challenged the construction of the irresponsible 'yobbish' lad, perhaps hinting at their hopes and desires to escape from a subject position that has been applied to them within the context of compulsory schooling.

Many of the boys dreamed of securing a stable income, enough to get their 'own house' a 'nice car' and raise a family. Yet rather than providing a stepping stone, post-compulsory education was seen as preventing the young men from 'getting on with life', as they felt that adult life could not fully begin until they found work and were earning money. As Mark (Hillside Park) emphasised, he just could not wait to 'get on'. In this respect, the boys seemed to confound the 'at risk' discourse, asserting clear vision, aspirations, a desire to work and an eagerness to 'settle down'.

Indeed, the theme of 'responsibility' (but particularly the framing of themselves as desiring to be responsible men) appeared to be strengthened and driven by some of the boys' experiences of living in 'at risk' conditions of social inequality. Six of the 'rather work' boys were in single-parent families, most with low wages, and two (Verona, Riverway, and Robert, Eastleigh Central) had unemployed parents. The drive to find work in these cases was explained by the boys as a desire (and duty) to improve their family's situation. Indeed, several boys stated that their family was one of the most important aspects of their life. Mark (Littleton), for example, was scathing of young people who take money from their parents to buy alcohol and drugs, and was adamant that he would not damage his family in this way. He talked about enjoying working with his father, helping him build an extension on their home. Verona explained that a key motivation for wanting to start his own catering business was to encourage his dad (a single father) to go into business with him. Verona wanted to create a means to employ his dad, who had been unemployed for some time. He reminisced about when his father was working:

> I don't know if you watch a programme called [Only] Fools & Horses? Me and my dad used to get called the Trotter family because we used to go round the [local area] selling food to doors and I always said to my dad that when I'm older we are going to become millionaires and I am going to have a Ferrari and that was my ambition in life to make it big.

Such examples suggest that for some men, the behaviour they display in schools and their resistance to education may not, as popular representations might have it, be predominantly driven by asocial and hedonistic concerns, but can reflect other identities and ideals of domestic responsibility to their families (see Evans, 2006; McDowell, 2003; McDowell, 2007, for similar findings). The boys' espousal of this form of independent yet also socially embedded and connected, 'responsible' masculinity complicates any simple or straight-forward readings of their resistance to post-compulsory education. Their discourses also point to the complex task of deciding what might be the best form of support and 'intervention' for them.

But what happened next . . .? The reality of the post-school labour market

Despite the boys' attempts to defend their desire to leave education through the assertion of their identities as 'responsible men', they experienced a rude awakening when they left school and found the labour market not quite as they expected. The decline of traditional industries in the UK has meant that typical 'working-class' jobs, but especially those coded as masculine, have been transformed (Ainley, 2005; Byrne and Rogers, 1996; Nayak, 2006). Willis's (1977) work showed how working-class boys were essentially trained for the shop floor within schools, and how, with relatively secure and dependable futures awaiting them, many never saw much need to engage with school. The educational and occupational terrain has since shifted considerably. In 1977 less than 25 per cent of 16-year-olds continued in post-compulsory education (McDowell, 2003) and the types of jobs that Willis's 'lads' might have walked into – unskilled manufacturing work with relatively good rates of pay and job security – have virtually disappeared (Bynner et al., 2002; Byrne and Rogers, 1996; McDowell, 2003). In contrast, recent years have seen a creeping credential inflation accelerate into a torrent, as ever higher levels of educational qualification are required for entry into previously 'open' sectors and as drives increase to 'professionalise' low, semi-skilled and skilled areas of employment through the standardisation of qualifications and the introduction of new forms of audit, management and monitoring (see Osgood, 2006). In this context of post-industrialisation there is a growing body of work on contemporary White working-class men and their changing relationships to education and the labour market (for example, Dolby et al., 2004; McDowell, 2003; Nayak, 2003):

> Large numbers of youth are now growing up without the expectations of stable employment around which familiar models of working-class masculinity were organised. Instead they face intermittent employment and economic marginality . . . in such conditions what happens to the making of masculinity?
>
> (Connell, 1995: 94)

By the final interviews, many of the boys found that they had held unrealistic views of the labour market and their plans to find work at age 16 had not materialised. This was something that few, if any, had foreseen. They had also been unprepared for their ineligibility for mainstream state benefits, which again has closed down the available options for school-leavers who cannot find work. When we caught up with them again, several of those who had initially left school at 16 had now returned to education. Mark (Littleton), for instance, was retaking his GCSEs (to 'open a bigger door') and Ben had enrolled on a GNVQ (a vocational qualification) in Leisure and Tourism after failing to find work: 'I thought I was going to get a job, but now I know it's not that easy . . . I went down to the Job Centre in [local area] and I didn't really like anything there so I left that. I was going to wait until something pops up but nothing did.' Among the younger boys (those now entering Year 11), there was also evidence of a change of heart among some. Mark now felt he would need to go to college to do a trade apprenticeship and had begun to challenge his previous subscription to a simplistic dualism between work and education:

> I have definitely got to go to college. Because everyone is always 'oh yeah – get a job straightaway' and that is what I used to want to do, I used to want to just get a job straightaway. I spoke to my brother and he said 'just make sure you get into college at least like once a week, like get a job and college' because otherwise I could never really get a profession or something. If I want to do electrics or something I need to go to college.
>
> (Mark, Hillside Park)

Mark listened to his brother's advice about changes in the labour market and 'new' forms of apprenticeship that involve both work and college attendance (Byrne and Rogers, 1996). Among our sample of boys, social capital seemed to provide the only glimmer of hope for entering work on leaving school. Indeed, by the end of the project, of the boys in their final school year only Mike (Hillside Park) had a job lined up for when he left, as a gas fitter. This job offer had been obtained through the family network, working for a family friend. In fact, employment levels among parents at Hillside Park School were higher than at the other schools in our sample, most likely because of its location in an area of higher employment.

Thus, despite boys' attempts to assert the validity of their 'rather work' position, in reality most found this to be untenable and unfeasible. The question this leaves us with is how the boys then manage to reconcile these situations with their previously held performances of masculinity?

Glamour, boyfriends, ladettes and 'speaking my mind': young women and education

As discussed in Chapter 1, comparatively little research and policy attention has been given to the experiences of those girls who are failing, or being failed by, the educational system. In our study, girls' disengagement seemed to remain 'hidden' in two key ways. First, it was generally (though not exclusively) perceived by staff to be less pressing, or more unusual, than boys' disengagement. Secondly, girls' disengagement tended to be harder for staff to notice or spot. For example, Leah (Sikh, Cowick) was described by staff as 'quite demure', 'pleasant' and 'really quite quiet' but 'does miss a lot more school than she needs to' for unknown reasons. Leah herself explained that she often did not attend school since her father had been attacked (and seriously hurt) at work, and she now often felt scared to leave home. Melissa (Turkish, Eastleigh Central) also described how she consciously hid her disengagement from teachers by appearing to work in class, while really listening to the radio through her mobile phone: 'I never used to go to my lessons. I didn't go for six weeks and I used to hate the . . . lesson, it was just so boring and I used to sit there and didn't do nothing. I used to listen to the radio on my phone. I held a pen in my hand to pretend I am working and . . . that is like my little trick'. These forms of disengagement contrast sharply with boys' more public displays of 'laddish' masculinity, which tend to attract and demand far greater teacher attention.

Many girls in the study experienced difficult relationships with school and conversely adopted a number of common strategies for increasing their visibility and generating capital and a valued sense of self. These practices included 'speaking my mind', investments in 'glamorous femininity', heterosexuality (boyfriends) and 'ladette' femininity. However, as we now go on to discuss, these practices were problematic for girls in that they produced or reinforced social inequalities and positioned the girls as 'problematic' learners. Moreover, this created dilemmas for the girls concerned, who tried to manage their positioning as 'bad' through appeals to being 'good underneath' and through engagement in processes of transformation.

The generation of agency and visibility: 'speaking my mind' (or 'biting my tongue')

Almost a third of the whole study sample (boys and girls) described themselves as 'bad pupils' and for many, this notion of being bad was linked to engaging in bad behaviours in class. While boys tended to construct bad behaviours in terms of verbal and physical aggression and other markers of 'hard' popular masculinity, for girls, being bad in class was equated with being 'loud' and 'speaking my mind'. For instance, Jordan described herself as follows:

> Oh I'm very loud. I've quite an attitude problem, I've a lot of questions about most of the rules, I don't understand why most of the rules are necessary and what their advantage is to us . . . I'm not a, what's the word, I'm not a *star student* [Int: What do you mean by that?] Oh I'll argue with the tutors if I don't think they're right, I won't just sit there. I'd have to stand up and wave my arms around, 'no – I don't think that's right'.
> (Jordan, Blackwell Street)

Similarly, Latoya (Cowick) described herself as 'quite rude' because she always speaks out if someone gets on her nerves and Kyle (Cowick) felt she was a bad pupil because she is often late and 'a bit of a rebel . . . because if I look at the way other people see me, I can see it from their point of view'.

Jane (Hillside Park) reported challenging particular teachers who she felt lacked appropriate knowledge or experience, for instance correcting their terminology. Like numerous other girls, Jane explained this as reflecting her own independent and assertive nature: 'I've always been quite like really strong-minded and like "you have no authority over me!" kind of thing . . . I have got loads of opinions but I just have to keep quiet'. These extracts illustrate how dominant educational discourses of the ideal female pupil may be experienced as narrow and constraining by young working-class women, who find it difficult to reconcile a positive view of themselves as pupils with their own notions of assertive, strong femininity. The girls' assertions of 'loud', active and visible femininities can be understood as challenging the forms of submissive, passive femininity that are usually rewarded within schools. For boys, such behaviours may tend to be read as part of 'normal' masculinity, but they bring young women into conflict with the school because they are interpreted as deviant and undesirable aspects of femininity (for example, as problematic or aggressive rather than 'assertive'). It was notable that most of the girls who described their conflict with staff in these terms had recorded middle to higher levels of achievement at KS3. For example, Jordan, Jane and Analisa (discussed below) all recorded average to good results at KS3, but underperformed at GCSE, suggesting that their conflict with schooling was implicated in their declining attainment.

Experiences of conflict due to being 'loud' and 'speaking my mind' were particularly pronounced among minority ethnic young women. For example, Analisa (Black African, Cowick) described her conflict with teachers as follows:

> Some of my teachers would see me as a right nightmare. All my teachers probably would think I am such a bad child because when they say something that I don't think is right, I will answer back and I will tell them. . . . when the teachers get on my nerves I just cuss them, insult them and they would send me to [exclusion area].

She said 'I would describe myself as a girl that wants to be independent' and valued education as a route to this desired independence. However, her belief in her own right to self-expression drew her into conflict with teachers. She also felt regularly and unfairly picked on by teachers ('well, most of them think I am talking, but sometimes it is not me'), which seemed to be exacerbated by her friendship group with 'all the rude Black girls'. Analisa's attainment had been quite low for several years, despite being regarded by her teachers as having the potential to be an 'A student'. However, Cowick's Head of Year 11 saw her behaviour, notably being 'extremely disruptive' and 'extremely confrontational', as a key obstacle to her success.

Over the course of the project Analisa managed to push her grades up from Ds and Es (phase one), to Bs, Cs, D and E (phase two) and she ended up achieving 'mainly Cs' at GCSE, and 'screamed the school down' in delight with her C in maths. She reflected: 'I know that I was stupid I could have done better. I could have got a good set of grades if I'd been, because most teachers just say if you'd been like that in Year 10 you would have been an A student, an A/B student. And it's like why did I do it? . . . I know I would have done better, much, much better'. By the end of the study, Analisa developed a reflexive awareness of how her own temper and performance of 'loud' femininity played a part in her clashes with school ('I could get angry in a second and I do, like the things I do is horrible'). Yet studies also suggest that we need to be aware that White staff may be more likely to read the behaviour of Black girls (Mirza, 1992) and Black boys (Sewell, 1997) as aggressive and challenging – and of the resultant clash between 'other' femininities (and masculinities) and dominant school cultures and expectations.

Melissa (Turkish, Eastleigh Central) similarly described how she came into conflict with the school over the expression of her opinions, particularly when she disagreed with particular teachers or school rules. Melissa identified with an active and assertive identity, and described herself as 'loud'. She constructed this loudness as a valued aspect of Turkish femininity, which she identified with her mother ('I probably get that from her because all of her family is loud'). One of her older brothers, who 'loved' school, advised her to 'bite her tongue' and not answer teachers back, but Melissa rejected this: 'I don't want to bite my tongue, I will probably bite too hard and it comes off or something.' Melissa's comment conveys a depth of feeling among the young women regarding their desire for self-expression and their experiences of the attempted regulation and control of their femininities.

Issues of disengagement, and particularly whether young women's disengagement was confrontational or quiet, were at times framed by teachers in explicitly racialised terms – with Black girls being seen as 'louder' and more challenging than 'quieter' Asian (and to some extent Turkish) girls (see Ali, 2003; Brah, 1996; Mirza, 1992). As Brah and Minhas (1985: 15) have argued, 'Asian' girls have long been treated as a homogenous group who are labelled as 'passive' or 'docile' in the classroom and thus tend to be systematically forgotten or ignored. However, they and Shain (2003) also argue, when Asian girls are seen to challenge this stereotype and transgress expected behavioural codes they may be dealt with more severely than other students.

Girls' investment in appearance: the paradox of ('glamorous')
working-class hetero-femininities as a form of capital

Since the 1970s, feminists and sociologists of education have been drawing attention to how working-class girls engage in subcultural forms of resistance to education through performances of femininity. In particular, they showed how 'hyper-heterosexual' forms of femininity (organised around sexuality, romance, relationships with boys/men, marriage, motherhood, and so on), may be implicated within girls' resistances to schooling (for example, Griffin, 1985; McRobbie and Garber, 1976; McRobbie, 1978). Since this early pivotal work, it has been noted that many girls' and young women's aspirations and expectations have undergone various shifts in relation to issues such as marriage (Sharpe, 1994), careers and educational choices (Francis, 2000a, 2000b). These changes are set against the backdrop of a 'feminisation' of educational achievement. However, despite these developments, working-class young women continue to leave school earlier, and with fewer qualifications, than their middle-class female peers.

Heterosexuality continues to be a strong defining element within many working-class young women's constructions of femininity and their resistance to social and educational inequalities (Hey, 1997; Skeggs, 1997). For instance, it has been suggested that working-class young women's horizons of choice continue to be structured in terms of leaving school at 16 with the expectation of working locally and 'settling down' in a heterosexual relationship and having children (Arnot et al., 1999; Connolly and Healy, 2004). Connolly and Healy (2004) suggest that locality and social interrelationships structure and reinforce a hyper-heterosexual female habitus that prevents girls from aspiring or expecting beyond the local context. However, it has also been argued that investment in hyper-heterosexual femininity is not the sole preserve of working-class young women. For instance, research with primary school girls indicates that one of the most popular ways of 'doing girl' among both working-class and middle-class girls is through the performance of hyper-heterosexualised femininity (for example, Ali, 2003; Reay, 2001a; Renold, 2000).

Most of the young women in the study were substantially invested in producing heterosexual, 'desirable' and 'glamorous' femininities through manipulation of their bodies and appearance (Skeggs, 1997). 'Successful' performances brought peer status and approval and many girls visibly put considerable effort into constructing their everyday appearance, which they then displayed with obvious pride. For example, Leah (Cowick) dressed in black and off-set her outfit with gold jewellery, striking make-up and hair crafted into a detailed ringlet pattern on one side of her head. Jermina (Blackwell Street) sported braided hair and a pink look, with pink accessories: large pink ruffle, pink bowler Puma handbag, pink jacket, pink watch. Jane (Hillside Park) had ever-changing hair colours and styles between each phase of the research and described spending all of the £40 per week that she earned from babysitting on her appearance. The importance placed on these investments and performances by the young women was also highlighted in their photo-diaries. For example Nadia (Blackwell Street) took photographs of her favourite nail varnish, perfume and accessories such as her mobile phone. When discussing her photographs, Nadia spent a considerable amount of time evaluating and debating which photographs of her were 'ugly' or 'nice'.

The young women constructed their appearance/s through the manipulation of various classed, gendered and racialised symbols and through the fusion of global brands (especially Nike, see Chapter 2 and Archer et al., 2007b) with local identifications and subject positions. In this way, they performed culturally entangled (Hesse, 2000) or translocational (Anthias, 2001) femininities, which crossed boundaries of 'race'/ethnicity, social class and space (see Chapter 3). For instance, girls combined elements of Black, urban US styles (notably 'bling' fashion) with 'unisex' (although often coded as 'male') items of sportswear (such as Nike trainers or tracksuits) and hyper-feminine 'sexy' clothes, make-up and hairstyles. These performances, while constituting an identifiable heterosexual working-class feminine appearance, were also grounded within a disruption of binaries of Black/White and masculine/feminine styles (for example, teaming tracksuit trousers with high heels or trainers with 'sexy'/'glamorous' tops).

As various feminists have noted, working-class women's investment in their (heterosexual) appearance constitutes one of the few available sites for the generation of symbolic capital (Skeggs, 1997). Young women can achieve a sense of power and agency from their performances of hyper-heterosexual femininities (Hey, 1997) and even fairly young, primary school aged girls can recognise (and hence adopt) a hyper-feminine subject position that is imbued with 'status and desirability' (Renold, 2005: 40).

The young women in our study were similarly invested in the production of their personal appearance as a means for generating capital and exercising agency in their everyday lives. However, as we shall now argue, this form of capital is also paradoxical because it is implicated in positioning the girls conflictually within educational discourses and the formation and reinforcement of oppressive social relationships, rather than providing a simple release/escape from social inequalities.

Girls frequently talked about how their investments in producing a 'desirable' (heterosexual, working-class, feminine) appearance brought them into conflict with schools. For instance, they explained how they were frequently chastised for not having the 'correct' appearance and were regularly punished for wearing 'too much' or the 'wrong sort' of jewellery (for example, Jordan, Blackwell Street), dis-allowed items of clothing (for example, Yesim, Cowick), and a raft of other issues concerning their hair and make-up (for example, Jane, Hillside Park).

Staff who were interviewed also suggested that working-class girls' embodied femininities and investments in appearance were antithetical to a 'good' pupil subject position. In particular, the young women's preoccupation with 'looking the part' was constructed as a 'distraction' that mitigated against their engagement with education and schooling. For example, a Learning Mentor described how girls' admiration of pop stars like Beyoncé (the hugely successful Black American singer), can feed into a preoccupation with their appearance:

> Well, what the girls do, obviously there's people like Beyoncé, they do look up to them. . . . They're too busy focussing on looking good and whatever. They spend their time in the toilets . . . they're all doing their make-up and their hair, trying to look the part because if they don't look the part . . . they will get teased. Because this culture is you have to look good, you have to wear the right stuff. And they focus more on that than they focus on their education.
>
> (Learning Mentor, Eastleigh Central)

We suggest that the above quote illustrates how, within dominant educational discourses, working-class femininity is read (through working-class girls' appearance) as both overtly and *overly* sexual and is positioned as antithetical to educational engagement and success. While it has been popularly argued that education is (now) 'feminised' and equated with a female subject position (see Francis and Skelton, 2005: for critique), we would suggest that the 'ideal (female) pupil' is actually a specifically middle-class (and de-sexualised) subject position, which excludes many working-class girls. Working-class femininities have long been associated with (hetero)sexuality and the body, and have been positioned within dominant discourse as 'excessive', 'distasteful', 'disgusting' and thus requiring control and regulation (Skeggs, 1997). In contrast, middle-class femininity is coded as sexually restrained, 'demure' and passive – which is congruent with an idealised conception of the 'innocent school girl' (Walkerdine, 1990). Reay (2001a: 157), for instance, emphasises how middle-class girls engage in a 'delicate balancing act' between femininity and cleverness, as 'femininity has to be struggled over and sexuality sometimes renounced' in order to achieve educational success. Indeed, the high achieving middle-class 'nice girls' in Reay's (2001a) research and Renold's (2005: 64) 'square girls' were de-sexualised as 'high-achieving, hard-working, rule-following and lack[ing] any interest in popular fashion or "boys" either as friends or boyfriends'. Renold (2005) also notes in her study that when a 'good' (high achieving) middle-class girl attempted to perform a more 'sexy' (working-class) femininity, teachers judged her appearance to be 'inappropriate' (and indeed chastised her), even though the same 'look' was widely performed by working-class girls within the same school.

Furthermore, we would suggest that these examples show how constructions of the idealised female pupil are predicated upon a classed and gendered Cartesian dualism, in which the academic (configured as the 'mind') is separated off from the non-academic, as signified by the (female, working-class) body. Thus working-class 'glamorous' femininities can be understood as occupying a paradoxical space within schools – while they can accrue capital within the field of heterosexuality through the performance of desirable and desired embodied identities, they are also located within a discourse of derision that positions them as 'other' and as incompatible with educational success. Hence while some middle-class girls may also invest in 'girlie' femininities (Renold, 2005) we would suggest that middle-class girls will enjoy greater mobility and will be better able to pass across and between subject positions (to negotiate between both 'educationally successful' and 'heterosexually desirable' femininities) as compared to working-class girls.

The learning mentor's extract cited above also draws attention to how performances of femininity are regulated, not only by schools, but by female peers. The young women's investments in heterosexual femininities were not solely organised around power and pleasure, but were also bound up with anxiety and fear, as girls' inclusion or exclusion from peer groups was based upon their conformity to particular performances of style and appearance (see George, 2007; Hey, 1997). For example, numerous girls talked about their intricate negotiations around the markers of style as they tried to avoid being ridiculed, mocked and called 'a tramp' (as Lacie, Riverway, put it) for wearing the 'wrong' brand of trainers or style of clothing.

Hence we would suggest that the young women's performances of femininity can be understood as playing into/being implicated within a tyranny of conformity to both the patriarchal regulation of female (hetero)sexuality and to a fixing of the young women within disadvantaged social (class) locations. This fixing is brought about by the educational 'othering' of working-class young women's embodied subjectivities and by the social and economic implications of their investments in hyper-heterosexual femininities. In particular, various girls indicated their desire to leave school and start working as soon as possible in order to earn money to continue performing fashionable femininities (see Archer et al., 2007a).

Girls' investment in heterosexual relationships: the paradox of 'boyfriends' as a form of capital

For a number of girls, like Jane (Hillside Park), Nadira (Eastleigh Central) and Analisa (Cowick), their disengagement with schooling was also mediated by their investment in their boyfriends, which tended to manifest as a form of all-consuming hyper-heterosexuality (Renold, 2005). While boys would talk and joke about girls and girlfriends, they tended to do so at a distance, frequently denied any depth of feelings and would be embarrassed to mention their relationships. Boys also denied any impact of these relations on their educational engagement. Indeed, the impact of girlfriends on boys' engagement was usually positive. For example Babu (Bengali, Riverway) recounted how his girlfriend had helped him to reduce his cannabis smoking and engage more at school. However, among the girls, relations with boyfriends were mentioned frequently and spontaneously and tended to have a more profound and negative effect on their educational engagement. Jordan, for instance, became pregnant over the course of the project and had to leave Blackwell Street School. In this respect, the capital accrued by having a boyfriend often worked against other forms of capital – for instance depleting economic and educational capital.

A few minority ethnic girls from a range of backgrounds had 'secret' boyfriends (for example, Yesim, Turkish, Jermina and Analisa, Black African, and Nadira, Bangladeshi), who they hid from their families. While Yesim (Cowick) and Nadira (Eastleigh Central) both described wanting to hide their relationships from their male relatives, Jermina (Blackwell Street) was more concerned to hide hers from her mother. Her mother's concern in this respect centred around her fear that a boyfriend would impact negatively on her daughters' educational engagement ('She says I am young and I have to wait, and if I rush into anything now it is not going to be good for my education').

Indeed, Jermina's mother appeared to have cause for concern, as those girls who did have boyfriends seemed to experience a lowering of their aspirations and/or attainment. For instance, Jane (Hillside Park) had a previous record of above average achievement at KS3, but over the course of the research she noticeably disengaged from her peer group, and started to spend almost all her free time with her older boyfriend. In her first interview she defined herself through her girl friends as 'fun, outgoing, got a lot of friends that love me and that. Happy, I suppose'. But by the time of the third interview she had become critical of her female peers and distanced herself from them, preferring to spend all her available time with her boyfriend.

As depicted in her photo-diary, by the third interview Jane's school day revolved around her boyfriend: each morning he travelled over from the other side of the local area to drive her to school; at lunchtime they ate in the local supermarket (where he worked). Jane's evenings were also spent with him, for example making dinner or going to the cinema together.

This relationship not only filled her spare time, but also impacted on her aspirations. In phase 1 Jane wanted to go to university and had been on an open day, but by later phases she claimed to be no longer 'bothered', saying that she would prefer to find a job locally to be near her boyfriend. Her boyfriend also changed his aspirations and the couple now aligned themselves with 'known' working-class expectations of 'staying close' (Pugsley, 1998) and 'settling down' (Arnot et al., 1999; Connolly and Healy, 2004). Jane also became more gender-conservative in her aspirations over the course of the project, as she progressively disengaged from 'the scientific kind of things' in the curriculum and came to produce herself as 'an artistic person', interested in photography, art and music.

Nadira also changed her aspirations and engagement over the course of the project as a result of her relationship. In phase 1 she expressed a confident plan to go to university and pursue a professional career, but by the middle of the project she felt 'totally stuck, I don't know what to do'. Like Jane, the gendered and classed nature of her aspirations underwent a change, from her earlier masculinised and professional aspirations to business or IT to stereotypically working-class feminine aspirations towards childcare or beauty. Whereas previously in phase 1 she framed her (professional) aspirations in terms of social mobility and pleasing her Bangladeshi family, in later phases she described her sole motivation as being to marry her boyfriend: 'I don't know why I'm thinking about this at my age but I really, really, really want to get married to my boyfriend and so that is one thing I want, to end up with him.' Nadira justified her aspiration to get married as soon as possible to her boyfriend by recourse to 'Asian' cultural discourses. While her family wanted her to wait until she had been to university before getting married, Nadira positioned herself as simply wanting to conform to a 'traditional' Asian femininity – to 'get married early'. Nadira's changing priorities complicate simplistic popular assumptions regarding the restricted home lives and repression of Muslim girls by their families (see Archer, 2002; Shain, 2003) and point instead to more complex interactions between patriarchy, 'culture' and compulsory heterosexuality (Rich, 1981).

Whereas both Jane's and Nadira's investment in their boyfriends had the effect of lowering their educational aspirations, in contrast Analisa (Black African, Cowick) came to the realisation over the course of the project that she would have to leave her 'bad' boyfriend (who was heavily into drinking and drugs) if she was to progress educationally: 'I don't think I can see a future [with him] because in the future . . . it depends on how my A-levels go really because if I go to university I know myself and I think I would not like to hang around with someone that isn't on the same level as me you know. Probably I am going to be quite snobby.' Indeed, by her third interview she described actively trying to distance herself from her previous friendship group (with 'all the rude Black girls') and seeking new friendships with 'middle-class' pupils: 'I have started speaking to more of the middle-class kids in our school more, in around Year 10, and finding out what their parents did and their big houses and stuff. And that kind of made me think, like, you know, education is going to get you there, so why don't you just learn that and kind of pass?' Analisa's aspirations to social mobility indicate that she has internalised dominant discourses that position working-class femininity and relationships with working-class boyfriends and girl friends as incompatible with educational success. Thus, Analisa perceives the only path to educational success and social mobility (to get the 'big houses and stuff') as through 'escape' from her current subject position which requires her to seek out, and 'pass' into a new, 'snobby' middle-class femininity.

'Good underneath'

Unlike the boys, who were happy to portray themselves as 'hard' or 'bad' in line with their performance of popular masculinity, girls were often at pains to point out that – despite their conflict with teachers and/or school – they were 'good underneath'. One component of this 'goodness' was that girls frequently emphasised that, despite how they were seen and/or behaved, they valued education, although they often did not like school.

Like a number of young women, Melissa (Eastleigh Central) described herself as a 'bad' pupil on account of her constant conflict with teachers and school rules, but she also struggled to be seen as a 'funny' girl who is 'good underneath'. Along with a number of other loud/assertive girls, Melissa seemed to feel trapped between narrow subject positions. She argued that her 'loud' behaviours should not be equated with being an intrinsically 'bad' person, and while she professed not to care what people think, she also wished her teachers could understand her: 'If only the teachers could see how I am with my cousins, my aunts, my uncles, then they will know that I am actually a really good person. They think I hate everyone because I made a bad impression; that is what they think. I don't really care what people think, I am who I am.' As Sayer (2002: 4.15) suggests, the working classes are caught in a bind that produces 'acute inner turmoil as a result of the opposing pulls of both wanting to refuse the perceived external judgements and their criteria and wanting to measure up to them – both to reject respectability and to be respectable'. The young women were aware that they played into the cycle of conflict in various ways, but they also felt that they were unfairly picked on and that their assertiveness is punished, constrained and read negatively within school. Moreover, they appeared to be constrained by the lack of a discursive space within which to enact an acceptable 'bad girl' femininity. Young women cannot be 'lovable rogues' in the same way as boys because power geometries (Massey, 1994) operate to produce subject positions in different and unequal ways.

The young women's concern to be seen as 'good underneath' can also be understood, we suggest, as part of their struggle with a politics of recognition and moral worth. In particular, we feel that the discourse of 'good underneath' illustrates the girls' struggle to establish a sense of self-worth within the context of an education system and wider social field in which working-class, Black and female identities are derided and un/devalued. As Sayer (2002: 7.17) notes:

> the micro-politics of class, the struggles against the 'soft forms of domination' identified by Bourdieu are not only over access to existing goods but over the definition of what is good. And the 'goods' which are at stake are not merely material, consumption goods, but are much more importantly ways of living: they are about who people want to be, what they want and can expect to make of their lives.

Sayer (2002: 1.4) suggests that class identities are highly charged because they are associated with 'injustice and moral evaluation' and those living stigmatised class identities will work to produce themselves as having worth. Indeed, he argues that people's resentment about social or symbolic (class) stigmatisation is often stronger than their resentment over lack of material wealth. Hence young working-class women's investment in their appearance and relationships, as noted earlier, is not just about generating capital but also producing recognition and respectability (Skeggs, 1997). Thus we suggest that girls' emphasis on 'good underneath' illustrates both resistance and accommodation to class and gender inequalities and discourses around the 'good female pupil'.

Girls' investment in 'other' working-class hetero-femininities: the 'ladette'

Not all the girls in the study conformed to popular versions of 'glamorous' heterosexual femininity. When we first met Melissa (Eastleigh Central), she distanced herself from what she called the 'proper girlie' hyper-heterosexual femininities of her peers and produced herself instead as a 'tomboy': 'I do like PE, I do like the sports but the girls in my lesson are like "I am going to break my *nails*", proper girlie girlie. And I am like "this is a PE lesson – who cares what happens? You can brush your hair after and put your make-up on afterwards", but I am not really bothered with that.' Unlike most of the other girls, Melissa always wore trainers and baggy track suits or unisex sportswear. She also described herself as competitive and physical and enjoyed playing football with boys and being 'in your face'. While she herself did not use the terminology, in some ways Melissa might be read as typifying the 'ladette' image (Jackson, 2006a) – she described getting into trouble for smoking and drinking in school and was repeatedly excluded. She also talked with some pride of her 'loudness' and her ability to 'bunk off' (truant) from school without being detected.

Despite the continued media coverage of (middle-class) girls' supposed educational success, since the early 2000s there has been a growing moral panic in some quarters about the rise of 'problem' (predominantly working-class) girls, encapsulated in the image of the 'ladette'. As Jackson (2006b) discusses, while conceptualisations of the 'ladette' are contested, they tend to revolve around the notion that some (mostly working-class) girls are now aping popular 'laddish' masculinities by engaging in 'hard drinking', swearing, smoking, fighting, being loud, rude and sexually explicit. Indeed, the 'ladette' is even the subject of a UK make-over television show which aims to transform such young women *From Ladette to Lady* (which aired on ITV1 in 2005, 2007 and 2009) and the term has entered the *Concise Oxford English Dictionary* (Oxford Dictionaries, 2009) to denote 'a young woman who behaves in a boisterously assertive or crude manner and engages in heavy drinking sessions'.

Yet Melissa also described desperately wanting to be seen as 'intelligent', but felt unable to escape being labelled by the teachers as 'bad' due to her embodied style and appearance ('most of the teachers here have this grudge against me'). She felt trapped because 'first impressions always count and I should make a better impression'.

Melissa heavily invested in a 'Nike identity' (see Chapter 2) during the first two phases of the research, and only wore branded tracksuits and trainers. Her school did not have a policy on school uniform, but she felt that the way she dressed was negatively interpreted by teachers. She knew that she would have to 'change' in order to be seen as 'good' and to escape a life of poverty ('I have to fix up my life, you know? I don't wanna be this poor person begging on street corners or whatever'). But it was not until her mother and cousins gave her a 'make-over' one summer that Melissa felt able to transform herself and her relationship with education. As discussed elsewhere (Archer et al.,

2007a), Melissa's transformation was not merely attitudinal but was also embodied, involving a whole new style, dress and appearance, as she changed (in her words) 'into a girl'. She adopted a heteronormative femininity, wearing 'a skirt' and make-up. Melissa also enrolled at FE college and was attending full-time when we interviewed her for the last time ('now I think I will try and study hard and try and to do my best'). For Melissa, it appeared that her 'other' (ladette/Nike) performances of femininity were incompatible with her desire to be seen as a 'good girl' – both as a 'good' female educational subject and as an authentic and respectable (Turkish) young woman. Melissa was not alone in her transformation and a narrative of change/reform was common among several of the young women in the study (such as Analisa detailed earlier). Indeed, girls engaged in notably more internal regulation than boys, particularly as they approached GCSE examinations. We would argue that such examples reflect differential dominant gendered expectations for women to 'care for the self'. This can feed into wider inequalities in educational provision, as boys are positioned as in need of saving (and thus as legitimately deserving of resources in this endeavour), but 'good' girls must 'save themselves'. Indeed, it was notable that teachers, support staff and parents were dedicating far more time and energy to supporting and 'saving' disengaged boys than was the case for the young women, who blamed themselves (if anyone) for their situations.

Summary

In this chapter we have discussed how the young people's investments in, and performances of, masculinity and femininity (that is, their identities as young men and women) were implicated in their marginalisation from schooling and education. In particular, we discussed the discourses of a group of boys who wanted to leave school as soon as possible for work – the ways in which they justified this desire (such as, through appeals to 'responsible' masculinity) and how their hopes were thwarted, and the ways in which heterosexual discourses around desirable and glamorous femininity are implicated in girls' estrangement from schooling.

ASPIRATIONS AND 'THE FUTURE'

What are aspirations and why are they important?

The *Concise Oxford English Dictionary* (Oxford Dictionaries, 2009) defines an aspiration as 'a hope or an ambition'. This usefully combines the more concrete and definite aspects of 'ambition' ('a strong desire to do or achieve something') with the more tentative nature of 'hope' ('a feeling of expectation and desire for something to happen; to expect and want something to happen; to intend if possible to do something', Oxford Dictionaries, 2009). This provides a good starting point for examining the considerable diversity within urban young people's aspirations and orientations towards their future lives. Indeed, we found that their aspirations spanned a wide range: from intensely held goals and desires to looser, more nebulous interests; from 'high' or lofty ambitions to more prosaic, mundane or realistic expectations; from 'already known' and concrete expectations to fragile dreams that are constantly mediated and shaped by external constraints. Brannen and Nilsen (2007: 155) also usefully distinguish between plans, hopes and dreams, arguing that: 'as time horizons extend into the future, young people become less certain about the feasibility of their current plans. Thus the concept of "hopes" as a way of thinking ahead carries with it elements of uncertainty. By contrast, plans are more concrete and achievable.' Aspirations are not only framed in terms of educational or occupational possibilities, they can encompass all manner of dreams, desires and goals for the future. However, within educational policy and research, the overwhelming focus of attention has been on the expectations and motivations that young people hold in relation to their academic achievement and their future working lives. These educational and occupational aspirations have been given considerable prominence within government policy. Indeed, the so-called 'problem of low aspirations' is flagged up in the opening paragraph of *The Children's Plan* (DCSF, 2007) – the document setting out the government's agenda in relation to children and young people.

Policy texts have tended to assume that low rates of progression into post-compulsory education and training are the result of what has been termed a 'poverty of aspirations' among working-class and some minority ethnic young people. Hence initiatives like *Aiming High* and *Aim Higher* have been centrally concerned with 'raising' young people's aspirations as a catalyst for increasing motivation and engagement with learning. From this perspective, the fostering of 'high' aspirations (through the creation of a goal that requires educational qualifications and achievement to be attained) is assumed to translate into increased effort and motivation (and hence improved attainment) in school.

Fundamental to this approach is the assumption that many of the 'target' young people lack information and knowledge about both the range of possible future careers open to them and the routes required to reach these goals. A raft of initiatives, projects and resources have thus been created to encourage young people to both widen and raise their career expectations. For instance, a key area of policy since 1999 (and the publication of the Dearing Report on HE) has been to encourage young people to consider the benefits of going on to university (Archer et al., 2003).

Thus, we can see that young people's aspirations tend to be treated as important and as deserving of attention, and even intervention, where they are judged to be 'problematic' or 'low'. In policy and research terms they are not, as some commonsense views might suggest, simply trivial or inconsequential ideas about the future, even though they may bear little or no similarity to what actually happens later. The importance that is given to the topic of aspirations reflects the assumption that these statements of intent may provide some sort of window on the self and/or the individual's behaviour and social location. That is, the articulation of 'who I want to be' or 'what I want to do' is treated as meaningful to the extent that it represents something about the person articulating it and the context in which they live. For instance, in educational policy, low aspirations are often treated as reflecting low self-esteem, a lack of knowledge about educational and career routes and possibilities, a lack of motivation to succeed educationally and/or a family or cultural background that may not value education (see Chapter 2). Hence young people's aspirations are treated as meaningful and consequential in that they not only reflect something about the individual in question but also provide a degree of impetus and drive for current behaviours (including educational engagement) and future actions and choices (including decisions to stay in or leave education). As researchers we are therefore interested in trying to understand young people's aspirations – although policymakers and some practitioners may also be concerned with the extent to which it is possible to shape or guide young people's aspirations.

Within this treatment of aspirations we feel that it is useful to reflect on a core, underlying question regarding the conceptualisation of human agency and action: namely, the extent to which the individual operates as a rational, calculating actor who is the architect of their own destiny. The viewpoint taken on this will determine the way in which we understand and conceptualise young people's aspirations – for instance, late modern theorists such as Giddens and Beck would presumably see young people as rational actors who consciously weigh up a range of risks when making their life choices – and might well expect that young adults' choices and decisions will be structured so as to logically pursue their aspirations.

Indeed, Beck (1992) argues that we are moving from 'normal' biographies (life courses that have traditionally been powerfully shaped by social structures such as gender and social class) to 'choice' biographies, in which individual futures are actively created from vast arrays of possibilities. From this perspective we might expect to find that young people's aspirations no longer follow predictable patterns that are structured by social inequalities but are more diverse and unique. It might encourage us to assume that each young person has unfettered aspirations and are free to be whoever/whatever they want in life.

Beck's view has been strongly critiqued – not only for suggesting too simplistic a division between 'normal' and 'choice' biographies but also because choice can be an illusion that renders structural inequalities invisible. Young people's choices have been shown to be strongly inflected, shaped and constrained by identities and inequalities of gender, social class, 'race'/ethnicity and so on (for example, Brannen and Nilsen, 2007; Henderson et al., 2007; Walkerdine et al., 2001), irrespective of whether or not the young person in question is aware of this structuring presence.

In other words, aspirations are not entirely 'free' choices, even if they are presented as though they are by those expressing them. Indeed, they are influenced more by the logic of practice (Bourdieu, 1992) than rational logic. We thus understand aspirations as contextually produced, shaped by young people's identities, embodied practices and structural locations. While of course young people do exercise a degree of agency in their choices and produce their aspiration narratives as active individual actors, the nature of their aspirations, and the sorts of identity discourses and resources that they are able to draw on to construct these narratives, are inevitably inflected by the social contexts in which they live. As such, structural contexts can operate as the 'silent discourses' (Brannen and Nilsen, 2007: 158) within young people's identity work and their constructions of aspirations. Aspirations are also inevitably shaped and constrained by embodiment, that is, the ways in which a young person's body is marked by gender, social class and 'race'/ethnicity will play a role in shaping the possibilities which are seen as open, possible and desirable. Thus, while there may be no linear relation between a young person's aspirations and the future routes that they pursue, a study of their aspirations (for example, the possibilities that are closed off, what is unconsidered, what is seen as possible or desirable) might provide useful insights into the social justice context within which young people's aspirations are produced.

As we shall argue in this chapter, aspirations constitute an important site in which social inequalities not only shape young people's horizons of possibility and desirability (the sorts of things that they aspire to or resist) but are actively re/produced (the sorts of choices young people make and the routes they follow may be constitutive of social inequalities). This is not to deny that young people can exercise agency and choice in relation to their future ambitions, but rather we wish to muddy the waters, so to speak, to render the aspiration-engagement, aspiration-achievement and aspiration-choice equations more complex and entangled. For instance, we demonstrate how young people's aspirations and choices are not always rational and risk-calculating, but are grounded within emotional and identity discourses that may be contradictory and 'messy'. Hence choices, educational engagement and achievement may not necessarily follow smoothly or logically from aspirations. In particular, we will be arguing that structural inequalities are still very important influences and concerns in relation to urban young people's aspirations – with the implication being that policy projects that seek to simplistically 'raise' aspirations need to be rethought.

The chapter begins by detailing and mapping aspects of the aspirations of the young people who took part in our study. We suggest that while there is no simple picture, there were some broad patterns. We discuss the multiple and contradictory nature of aspirations, charting shifts over time. We also examine 'high' aspirations among our study participants and the fragility of these. We then move on to consider the motivating discourses underlying young people's aspirations and discuss the prevalence of discourses of 'being happy' and 'staying safe' and negotiations between 'escape' and 'staying put/ staying close'. Finally we ask: what constrained their aspirations? Here we discuss the role of habitus and capitals and the discourse of 'wait and see', a practice that involved the deferment of aspirations and choices with various implications for the young people.

The young people's aspirations

While we will be arguing that the young people's aspirations were highly complex, multiple and often contradictory, it is first worth noting that there were some broad patterns within the sample. The most immediate and striking feature being that this collection of 'at risk' young people did overwhelmingly express a range of 'respectable' and 'responsible' aspirations. This contrasts with popular and media representations of urban young people as 'aimless', hedonistic and without aspiration, destined for underachievement, educational failure, crime and a range of social problems, such as teenage pregnancy, alcohol and drug abuse. Rather, like the 'Status Zer0' youth in Williamson's (1997) study, even those occupying (or 'at risk' of occupying) the NEET category held high aspirations and, as Williamson found, many were optimistic that their lives would improve in the future. In our study, it was notable that only one of the young people, Roger (Littleton), claimed to have 'no idea' regarding his future. Roger's somewhat bleak view may have been influenced by his possession of a criminal conviction (which could well hinder his future job prospects).

As we discuss in detail below, the overwhelming majority of the young people we interviewed held at least one aspiration, but most commonly they embraced several possibilities simultaneously. These aspirations were not static but were worked on and revised over time, changing frequently between different phases of the study.

While each young person produced their aspirations in a unique way (tied to their own biographies and interests) there were clearly classed, gendered and racialised patterns across the sample. For instance, 61 per cent of young women aspired to stereotypical working-class, feminine occupations in either hair/beauty or social care work (such as, childcare, nursing). In contrast, 67 per cent of young men aspired to typical working-class, masculinised manual trades (such as, plumber, electrician, mechanic). An additional 23 per cent of young men aspired to becoming professional sportsmen (notably, footballer and boxer). Five boys and four girls said that they hoped to join the armed forces. In contrast, sixteen young people reported aspiring to what might be termed as professional careers, such as lawyer, teacher and accountant. These aspirations were strongly gendered, being cited predominantly by young women (48 per cent of girls versus 17 per cent of boys).

The following sections explore these aspects in greater depth, namely the multiple and contradictory nature of aspirations, and the shifting and contingent nature of aspirations, before moving on to consider these 'high' aspirations.

The multiple and contradictory nature of aspirations

Only three young people (all boys) expressed a single aspiration that they pursued consistently over the course of the study. These were:

Darren:	Chef
Mike (Hillside Park):	Plumbing
David (Hillside Park):	Computer programming

Sixteen other young people also expressed at least one consistent aspiration across the three interview phases, but it was held alongside several other aspirations (most of which changed between interviews). These consistent aspirations (expressed at each phase of the three phase interviews) were:

Mechanic:	Babu, Ben, Nathan, Robert
Nurse:	Jermina, Natalie
Hair and beauty:	Kay, Lacie
Teacher:	Nadira, Nadia
Electrician/plumber	Bob (Riverway), Mark (Hillside Park)
Football/lifeguard	Max
Police:	Steven
Army	Dan
Bricklayer	John

It was not always the case that these consistent aspirations represented their 'favourite' imagined future, although they did tend to be seen as the most realistic. For instance, Kay (Cowick) acknowledged hair and beauty as her most consistent and 'realistic' aspiration, although she also dreamt of being a travel rep or a dancer. Jermina (Blackwell Street) kept hairdressing as a back-up option in case she did not attain the grades required for nursing. Among boys, it was common to cite not only the consistent 'realistic' aspiration of joining a trade but to hold this alongside a 'dream' job. For instance, Robert (Eastleigh Central) dreamt of becoming a film director but recognised that mechanic was a more likely route. Likewise, John (Littleton) balanced bricklaying with becoming a professional footballer and Dan (Riverway) consistently identified the army as an aspiration but combined this with becoming a delivery driver or professional baseball player (phase one) and a police officer (phase three).

Indeed, the majority of young people in the study (not just those who expressed at least one consistent aspiration) described holding several aspirations simultaneously. These were not, as Leah's (Cowick) next quote illustrates, necessarily similar or coherent, but could be quite diverse in nature and in the routes and qualifications needed to achieve them: 'I would like to work in a bank, I don't know why. I like tills and things. When me and my cousin talk, we always say we would like to work in an airport or a bank. Or I would like to work in a good clothes shop or something like that. Or maybe a nursery, like my sister'. Yesim (Cowick) initially stated her aspirations as: pilot, modelling, management and accountancy. In phase two these had changed to: joining the police or working in business or accounting. By phase three she said she no longer liked the idea of joining the police and talked instead about studying French, psychology, tourism or fashion design at college. She was thoroughly confused by this point, lamenting 'I seriously don't know what I am going to be'.

Steven's (Eastleigh Central) stated aspirations were also highly diverse. When asked what he hoped to be in the future, he replied: 'a computer technician, a plumber and mainly a policeman'. This expression of a diverse range of interests and possibilities would seem to be an encouraging finding in response to policy concerns about the 'poverty' of aspirations among urban youth. Steven's response in particular appears to show that he considers a wide and varied range of careers as both possible and desirable. However, we would suggest that the holding of multiple aspirations among the young people also needs to be considered in terms of their negotiation of risk and whether they were also being enabled to identify, choose and follow routes that might lead to them achieving these aspirations. In particular, we would argue that while Yesim and Steven's responses might be read as typifying Beck's 'choice' biography (with choice framed as a matter of individual interest rather than the set following of socially prescribed routes), their structural locations mean that in reality not all of these options are open or possible. In other words, the choice biography may be more of a middle-class preserve.

Lee (Riverway) is a case in point. A White, working-class boy, in his first interview Lee was keen to join the army. By his second interview he had ruled this out as 'rubbish' and 'boring'. At his third interview, a year later, he aspired to becoming a professional rugby player or rugby coach, but with the 'fallback' options of mechanic and taxi driver. As Lee's mother explained, she herself had played a role in persuading Lee to ensure he had realistic aspirations alongside his dreams of becoming a professional sportsman: 'He wants to play rugby anyway and so I said "yeah, but that ain't going to be your main job, Lee. You ain't going to get signed up for England. That is not a main job, you have got to have a job". And so he is saying a taxi driver, he wants to be like his father'. As Lee and his mother realise, the world is not really Lee's oyster, rather his social, cultural and economic capital renders some routes more realistic and 'normal' than others.

There was an enormous complexity within the young people's aspirations – which often contradicted one another in terms of the routes needed to attain them. We would argue that this is not a reflection of cognitive confusion on the young people's part, but rather that the fluid and dynamic nature of their aspirations can be read as a pragmatic strategy adopted by those who are exposed to high levels of risk and uncertainty in their lives (Beck, 1992; Furlong and Cartmel, 1997). These young people did not enjoy the comparatively greater certainty and control that many middle-class young people are able to exercise – both in terms of securing 'good' examination results and enjoying a greater sense of entitlement and possibility of attaining 'higher' aspirations and financial security. Hence by keeping their options open and ensuring a range of fall-back possibilities, they might be understood as actively trying to manage the risk associated with their structural locations as working-class young people with fragile histories of educational attainment, living in impoverished urban locales and attending urban schools.

Research has suggested that middle-class young people may experience the 'world as their oyster' to the extent that different options and possibilities are predominantly excluded on the basis of personal preferences/desires rather than being seen as 'impossible' or 'not for people like me'. In contrast, working-class young people's 'choices' may be far more circumscribed according to their structural locations. However, we would also argue that the young people's structural locations and greater susceptibility to risk meant that their aspirations were necessarily more shifting and contingent. We now explore this idea further.

Shifting aspirations over time

A number of the young people talked about 'giving up' on their previous aspirations over the course of the study. In some cases, this meant revising earlier unrealistic youthful dreams of becoming a famous pop star or actor. For others, these changes resulted from the opening up of new possibilities and/or gaining new ideas and contacts. For instance, James (Littleton) expressed a constant ambition across the three interview phases to become an electrician but over the course of the project he was given an opening to work for a locksmith via a family contact which he took because it had 'come quicker'. We noted a sizeable trend in which aspirations not only changed but were *lowered* over the course of the study, particularly in the case of those expressing professional aspirations. As we now discuss, we interpret this as a classed process (and a form of symbolic violence) through which the young people came to 'know their place' (Reay, 1998).

For instance, Hapsa (Blackwell Street) suggested in her first and second interviews that she would like to become a doctor or a nurse but by her third interview she had lost confidence that either could be achieved, seeing them as 'too hard'. She was now unsure what to do. Jordan (Blackwell Street) also talked about her interest in becoming an accountant or a lawyer/solicitor but by her second interview she was pregnant and had not returned to education by the time of the phase three interviews. Jade's (Cowick) initial aspiration to become a lawyer and to work in probation shifted (in phase two) to a more traditionally gendered and classed ambition to work in a nursery. This new goal was reinforced by Connexions advice she received around the phase two interview and was more firmly cemented by her phase three interview.

The power of a young person's gendered, racialised and classed habitus to inflect or curtail their professional aspirations was also evident in Tyson's (Littleton) changing ambitions from becoming a lawyer/solicitor (in phase one) to dreaming of being a professional boxer (phase two onwards). Indeed, Tyson's identification with this ambition was reflected in his choice of pseudonym (after US boxer Mike Tyson), epitomising a popular form of Black masculinity that he felt more able to identify with (and more able to achieve) than the White, middle-class masculinity traditionally associated with the occupation of lawyer/solicitor. Likewise, Tim revised his initial interest in working in IT (phase one) to a more White, working-class masculine aspiration to work in the trades by his later interviews.

As discussed in Chapter 4, Jane (Hillside Park), Nadira (Eastleigh Central) and Melissa's (Eastleigh Central) aspirations also all shifted in distinctly gendered and classed ways over the course of the study, as the girls came to give up any professional dreams and substitute them for more 'traditional', working-class feminine roles.

As time progressed, it appeared that the young people became increasingly likely to 'learn their (gendered, classed, racialised) place' and brought their aspirational horizons more closely into line with the 'known' routes. Drawing on the work of Judith Butler (1999, 2004) we might read this conservative shift in their aspirations as reflecting their uptake of 'intelligible' gender identities (that is, versions of masculinity and femininity that are more conforming to dominant discourses). However, the intelligibility of these gendered aspirational identities were clearly classed – the young people were investing in identities and aspirations that were intelligible versions of working-class masculinity and femininity, coming to understand that middle-class versions were 'not for them' – being too risky, unattainable and/or undesirable.

'Higher' aspirations

As discussed earlier, education policy accords a significant role to the project of raising young people's aspirations. High aspirations are seen as a way to increase motivation and achievement in school and to raise participation rates in post-compulsory education. Contrary to dominant policy concerns about a widespread 'poverty of aspirations', a substantial proportion of these 'at risk' young people entertained a 'higher' (or professional) aspiration over the course of the study. Sixteen young people (30 per cent of the sample) indicated at some point during their interviews that they held 'high' aspirations to professional careers. Several of the pupils also aspired to more than one type of professional career (for example, both Sarah and Melissa, both at Eastleigh Central, mentioned wanting to be a lawyer and a doctor). Among the range of professional jobs that these young people aspired to, the most popular were:

Lawyer/solicitor: Charlene, Jade, Jason, Jordan, Latoya, Melissa, Sarah, Steven, Tyson

Accountant:	Analisa, Jordan, Yesim
Doctor:	Hapsa, Melissa, Sarah
Architect:	Jason, Nick
Teacher:	Michelle, Nadia

Commonly, these high aspirations were expressed in the earlier interviews (most commonly in phase one) and were abandoned by phase three, although there were a few exceptions. For instance, by phase three Steven (Eastleigh Central) had begun to talk about studying law at university, but his main ambition was to join the police. Analisa (Cowick) also maintained an aspiration to go to university across the three interview phases. Jason (Littleton) expressed the most consistent high aspirations in the study: in all three interviews he maintained an expectation to go to university and hoped that this might lead to a job in architecture (phase one) or law (phase three). We now spend a little time trying to understand what it was that made these young people stand out from their peers in this respect.

Jason is a Black African boy who lives with his grandmother and sees his father (a taxi driver) during the school holidays. Despite doing quite a lot of identity work as part of a process of 'doing boy' during his interviews (such as, portraying himself as aimless, undecided about his future and as being a bit of a 'lad' in relation to schoolwork), it also became clear that Jason had a habitus and set of family practices and values that expected him to stay on into further and higher education. He described his grandmother as playing an important role in this respect, clearly articulating her desire and expectation that he should continue into post-compulsory education ('she definitely wants me to carry on, definitely . . . yeah, she tells me all the time'). But the key source of motivation and inspiration appeared to come from Jason's older brother, who was studying business and accountancy at university in London. This powerful influence operated in several ways: it rendered university a 'knowable' and achievable goal for Jason; it provided him with practical knowledge and cultural capital in relation to the process of applying to university and understanding university life (for example, Jason discussed his knowledge of the loans system); and it contributed to a family habitus in which staying on was coming to be expected and normalised (in stark contrast to many of Jason's peers – most of whom he described as not carrying on). Moreover, Jason's good relations with, and high regard for his brother meant that he had access to a desirable/respected version of a Black working-class masculinity that stays on in education. Jason described his motivation to live up to his brother's example, saying '[I'm] still trying to follow in his footsteps'. Hence, Jason came to understand staying on at school as 'just the right thing to do' and continued into the sixth form, even though his GCSE grades were disappointing and all his friends left.

Jason also came to see himself as 'different' from others in his local area in terms of his belief in the value of education, which he compared to his peers who dreamt of working in the music industry:

[Int: OK and do you think that education is important or not?] Well of course it is. Well it is, in the local area now, everyone . . . knows that it is important but people generally, they've got their dreams. Everyone believe that they are gonna get their music business and then do this and then do that. If you don't do it, there is only so many people that do get into it. If you don't do it, *you ain't got nothing* to fall-back on except education.

(Jason, Littleton)

This pragmatism extended to an acknowledgement that his aspirations and future routes would not simply be a matter of choice and interest – Jason did not see the world as his oyster. Rather, he appeared to engage in a careful balancing between his interests, the expectations for him, and his knowledge of how achievable or feasible a particular goal might be: 'It's not really [a] choice that yeah, I get first pick: "I want to do that". It's, what can I do to get there?'

Jason's route into sixth form also appeared to have been facilitated by careers advice that he received between the second and third interviews. He described how (like most of his friends) he had started to pursue the idea of enrolling for a college apprenticeship to become an electrician, but had been put off this route by the careers advisor (who said it was oversubscribed). Jason also appeared to have benefited from good relations with teachers in his school, describing their help as useful (more so than Connexions support) and talking about how whenever he had any difficulties he would talk to the Head of Year.

Despite his aspirations, Jason did 'badly' (as he put it) in his GCSE examinations, achieving four grade Cs and three grade Ds. He was disappointed with these results but attributed it largely to a year of family problems ('Like, I did bad but at the same time I can't really complain after the year that I had'). However, the factors in his own personal biography provided sufficient 'push and pull' that he stayed on into sixth form, to study law, sociology, psychology and IT. In his final interview, Jason thought that he would probably try to do a law degree because 'law degree sounds kind of good', and he appeared to have found a new impetus to settle down and work hard, describing how a trip to Uganda that summer had instilled in him a new 'calm' and desire to 'stay in' and work, rather than go 'out on the street' with his friends.

As previously stated though, Jason's case was one of the exceptions. More commonly we found that the young people's espousal of high aspirations *per se* did not automatically foster any greater educational engagement or achievement. For instance, despite having initially high aspirations to become an accountant or a police officer, Kyle (Cowick) still ended up dropping out of school before her GCSEs. Likewise Jordan's (Blackwell Street) aspirations towards law did not protect her from leaving when she became a young mother.

So where did these young people's 'high' aspirations come from? The main sources of knowledge cited were television and personal experience. Indeed, the prevalence of popular television crime-based dramas (especially North American programmes) might provide some indication of why law was cited so frequently (Williams and Mendick, 2008). But personal experience was also powerful. For example, Tyson (Littleton) described how his aspiration to work in law was prompted by being helped by a solicitor when he got into trouble with the police. As we later discuss, interpersonal, 'hot' knowledge is particularly utilised in educational decision-making among working-class families and communities (Ball and Vincent, 1998). However, a lack of engagement with 'cold' (official) knowledge may make it more difficult for young people to subsequently navigate their way towards achieving these aspirations.

It was notable that each of the young people also held at least one other 'back-up' plan in case their higher aspiration did not work out. These higher aspirations tended to be held alongside a more 'realistic' or achievable 'plan B'. Girls appeared more likely to have a clearly 'achievable' plan B. In contrast, boys were more likely to either specify a single high aspiration or a fall-back option that would require a similar level of qualifications. For example: Jade (Cowick), Latoya (Cowick) and Melissa (Eastleigh Central) all aspired to legal careers, but, in recognition of the fragility of these ideals, they also said that they would be happy to work in a clothes shop, a beautician's or a hairdresser's, respectively.

The difficulty for these aspirant young women to imagine themselves out of their current contexts and to move beyond the 'known' was amply illustrated in the interviews. They tended to feel that their 'higher' dreams were unrealistic (as Jane, Hillside Park, put it, 'my goals are too far fetched'). These lofty goals were felt to be unattainable in comparison to the familiar, 'safe', known routes through hairdressing and beauty. For instance, Kemisha (Cowick) had ambitions to work in health and social care, and was being encouraged by her family in this respect. Yet (like Jermina, Blackwell Street) she also saw hairdressing as a more realistic and achievable option. Michelle (Riverway) wanted to become a textiles teacher but saw this as 'impossible', whereas hair and beauty would provide a far safer and more realistic path. Likewise, Kay (Cowick) loved the idea of working abroad as a travel representative, but said that she could not really imagine doing this job and had no idea of how to achieve it. Instead, she resigned herself to becoming a beautician, because 'I have more experience and I will know more how to do it'. Melissa underlined the distinction between her high aspiration to a professional career, and what she saw as the reality for her current level of attainment: 'Everyone wants to be a lawyer or a doctor [but] I don't think that is going to happen unless I have got A's and stuff like that.'

It was also evident that some of the young people's initial high expectations were subsequently curtailed and negatively impacted on by other people. In some cases, young women, like Jane and Nadia, were encouraged to lower their ambitions by parents who felt that they were setting their sights too high and feared that they would be disappointed. Jane's mother warned that sixth form would not 'suit' her and Nadia's father discouraged her from trying to become a lawyer:

> I was talking to my mum about it and she said, she like, she's really quite, like old fashioned with education ... Mum has said she doesn't think sixth form will suit me and I will probably get a good job if I leave school but I'm not sure.
>
> (Jane, Hillside Park)

> [Dad] said that it's going to be hard and he don't think I could do it.
>
> (Nadia, Blackwell Street)

Jane's and Nadia's comments are reminiscent of the resistance that working-class women describe experiencing in relation to going to university (see Archer et al., 2003; Lawler, 1999), being chastised for 'getting above your station'. But they may also reflect parents' genuine wishes to protect their children from the disappointment of failure and the risks that may follow from failing in a high-risk path. As Chris Mann's (1998) research suggests, the emotional support that working-class mothers offer their daughters is a crucial component within the production of academic success.

These sources of disapproval and discouragement were not limited to the home and family, however. Analisa (Cowick) and a number of other students indicated that either a teacher or an educational professional had played a role in lowering their expectations and thwarting their attempts to imagine themselves into more aspirant and successful identities: 'Well I was talking to my maths teacher and I said "yeah I'm going to LSE" and he goes yes if you get in there he will dance round this hall in woman's dress . . . so there's no chance of me going to LSE'. It was also notable that Analisa's high aspirations towards university were not entirely matched by high occupational aspirations. While she identified working in the media or becoming an accountant in phase one, by phase two this had changed to becoming a bank manager and by phase three Analisa was talking about working in a small shop or working her way up to become a department store manager – neither of which would require university. As discussed in Chapter 4, Analisa had developed an aspirational and upwardly mobile habitus, but it seemed that she might benefit from a more targeted and sustained institutional support with regard to providing the capitals that might reinforce and facilitate her dreams of mobility.

As discussed previously, various studies have highlighted how some teachers and schools may (often unwittingly) convey lower expectations for minority ethnic students. This tendency has also been noted in relation to the White working classes, who are increasingly marked in popular discourse as the 'unteachable' and the under-achieving. Of course as discussed in Chapters 6 and 7, many young people had been actively helped by teachers, advisors and mentors to develop their aspirations and engage with schooling, but there were also instances in which some students felt they had been discouraged. For instance, Lucy (Riverway) described how her confidence and aspirations to 'be someone' had been knocked by a member of staff who said that there was little point in Lucy studying a range of subjects because she was destined for failure (' "It ain't no point in you doing the rest of them subjects" '). This led Lucy to lose all hope and aspiration, leaving her feeling 'there ain't no point. I ain't going to go nowhere.'

A review of quantitative literature conducted for the DCSF by Gutman and Akerman (2008) states that while in general higher aspirations tend to translate into better outcomes later in young people's lives, this is not always the case:

> There are some groups for whom high aspirations do not lead to higher achievement. In particular, there is a gap between educational aspirations and academic achievement for young people from lower socio-economic

backgrounds and from some minority ethnic groups and a gap between occupational aspirations and career achievement for females.

(Gutman and Akerman, 2008: 2)

Gutman and Akerman refer to this discrepancy as 'the aspiration-achievement gap'. They thus suggest that high aspirations can mitigate the effects of low socio-economic status for some groups (for example, Indian, Chinese) but not others (for example, Pakistani, Bangladeshi, Black Caribbean), although they do not offer many explanations as to why this should be the case. While the review does not include qualitative research it does note a finding that has been corroborated in various qualitative studies, namely that while parents from minority ethnic backgrounds tend to hold higher aspirations for their children than White British parents, these higher aspirations do not seem to translate into enhanced life chances among minority ethnic young people. When taken together with Analisa's extract (above), it would seem that there is still considerable work to be done within schools with regard to combating forms of racism, sexism and classism.

Motivating discourses underlying young people's aspirations

'Being happy' and 'staying safe'

Across both parental and student interviews, we found that the main motivations cited in relation to young people's aspirations and futures were those of 'being happy' and 'staying safe'. The former echoes McLeod's (2007) study of mothers and daughters who articulate their key goal in life as 'being happy'. 'Being happy' was positioned as more important than dominant middle-class aspirational imperatives such as a 'career' ('a high powered job'), occupational status and 'earning lots of money'. Hence, it might be read as a challenging and/or justificatory discourse, asserting the validity and worth of non-middle-class routes and trajectories. As in McLeod's work, 'being happy' was also envisaged by parents as interlinked with 'being safe' and achieving a good (or often 'better') life for their children.

'Staying safe' comprised personal physical and emotional safety and economic security. Parents in particular were concerned that their children should find a job as a means for staying out of 'trouble'. As Mike's (Hillside Park) mother put it: 'As long as he's happy and he's not doing things he shouldn't be doing, you know? He's not going to be a brain surgeon or anything like that, [but] as long as he does alright'. The lure of what Mike's mother terms 'things he shouldn't be doing' was an ever-present threat within the young people's everyday urban environments that both parents and young people were wary of. Drug-taking, drug-dealing, gangs and crime were all recognised as risks in competition with the goal of 'getting a job' and being both happy and safe.

Alongside these concerns with young people's physical and emotional safety was the imperative of economic security. When asked whether she thought her son had any kind of hopes or dreams, Mike's mother replied: 'I don't know, it's hard to say really. Just to earn money, he's always been the same. He'll find something, he's that sort of child. He'll get on in life and he'll work hard, it will be good'. Indeed, while the young people expressed a range of occupational aspirations, they all expressed broadly similar views on their underlying desires and motivations for their futures. It was widely agreed economic security is paramount – attaining a 'good job' with 'a decent wage'. They aspired to being financially comfortable, rather than well-off (although a couple of boys dreamt of being 'rich').

While many considered financial security a potential source of personal happiness, some young people felt a tension between 'happiness' and 'safety'. As Jane (Hillside Park) explained, she 'can't be picky' by prioritising job interest over pay, but she worried about the potential dilemma if faced with a 'really well paid job' that she 'hated'. The potential tension between economic security and happiness was raised particularly in relation to working for transnational fast-food chain McDonald's. This was widely cited as the epitome of a 'bad' job (along with refuse collector and road sweeper), as the ultimate low status, low pay job that is physically demanding and undertaken in unpleasant/undesirable working conditions. Yet it was also recognised as the most accessible and immediate form of employment open to the young people (requiring no qualifications, often being locally situated and often recruiting new staff) and as relatively stable in terms of pay and conditions. It functioned as the repository of all that was undesirable and what young people did not want to be – yet it also constituted a source of security (always there, always accessible). It was a constant risk yet also a constant safety net. It thus might be read as symbolically marking the boundary of acceptability between 'being happy' and 'staying safe'.

It was perhaps unsurprising that economic well-being should feature so strongly within the young people's and parents' discourses, after all, they had either experienced economic insecurity directly or were living within communities where it was a prevalent, everyday concern. The government's policy agenda *Every Child Matters* (http://www.everychildmatters.gov.uk/aims/) sets out achieving economic well-being as one of its five central aims.

A couple of the higher achieving students at KS3 mentioned that they would value finding a job that they would enjoy or that would provide 'room for improvement' (as Jason, Littleton, put it), but these students were in the minority. For most, the more immediate demands of physical, economic and emotional well-being were just far more pressing.

'Escape' versus 'staying put/staying close'

Alongside the widespread concern to earn a 'decent wage', a number of pupils expressed clear aspirations for social mobility. Analisa (Cowick) described her desire to become 'independent' when she 'grows up'. She wanted to earn 'good money' and to escape the hard and poorly paid working lives of her parents, who do 'cleaning jobs and stuff'. Instead, Analisa aspired to a managerial position in a shop or bank. As part of her dream of escape she desired geographical mobility, to move away from her local area, which she described as 'dead end'. She felt that moving away would increase her chances of success ('I just don't want to grow up, live in Fairwick, be on the dole'). As Littleton's Head of Year

11 explained, 'a lot of them are trying to escape from that sort of background. They are trying to better themselves so that they can go on'. Analisa's comments echo those of the White working-class women discussed by Lawler (1999) and Skeggs (1997) and the ethnically diverse working-class women in Archer and Leathwood (2003), who dream of 'escape' and 'bettering themselves' through education.

However, most young people felt a sense of ambivalence about the prospect of geographical mobility and social 'escape'. Many expressed a clear desire to 'stay local' and 'keep close', which has been identified by Pugsley (1998) as a common working-class discourse. David (Hillside Park) was clear that he wanted to stay living locally, even though he described his local area as 'scummy'. Similarly, Jane (Hillside Park) said she would not like to move away and Tim (Hillside Park) emphasised 'I wouldn't move away from my family and mates'. Lucy (Riverway) was adamant that she would not want to go far from her area and she would like to study, live and work in her local community, hopefully opening her own hairdresser's.

While 'staying local' carries with it a range of benefits (such as emotional security, access to social capital) it can also restrict a young person's career options. As Max (Littleton) recounted, he was unable to find work as a lifeguard because there were no vacancies in any of the local leisure centres and he was constrained by his inability to travel further.

Melissa (Eastleigh Central) summed up her ambivalence in trying to reconcile social and geographic mobility. She felt that she would probably remain living in her local area, close to her friends and her tight-knit extended family, whom she valued greatly and who provided her with immense support. Indeed, as discussed in Chapter 4, her family had been instrumental in prompting Melissa's re-engagement with education and her FE application. However, she also admitted to dreaming of moving away to another city or another country: Melissa's ambivalence encapsulates the tension between individual, meritocratic discourses and collective discourses of responsibility, duty and interrelationship/inter-dependency. It also signals that educational and policy discourses need to be wary of assuming that all urban youth desire (or require) 'escape' or liberation from their urban contexts. Indeed, it suggests we remain mindful of how particular normalising assumptions may underpin commonsense discourses around aspirations. Notably, middle-class career trajectories tend to normalise social and geographical mobility in a way that may not be appropriate or relevant for all young people. In contrast, urban young people's aspirations were formed within powerful emotional landscapes – the contexts, bonds and relationships in which they lived necessitated a negotiation between the pulls of both 'escape' and 'staying close'.

Constraints on young people's aspirations

Classed capitals and habitus

The young people's aspirations were clearly grounded within, and shaped by, their social identities of gender, 'race'/ethnicity and social class. The cultural discourses and resources (capitals, see Chapter 2) that they had access to inflected the types and sources of information that they were able to draw on to construct their aspirations and inform their post-16 choices and routes. Their sense of what might be normal, appropriate and desirable was also shaped by their habitus, which was constituted by (and constitutive of) their social locations.

In line with the findings of Ball and Vincent (1998), young working-class people based their choices on 'hot knowledge', information that they gained through interpersonal contacts and local grapevines. They were heavily influenced by their own experiences and the experiences of family, friends and people in their local communities. Hence their aspirations were heavily skewed towards the 'known'. For example, Leah (Cowick) explained that her desire to work with children was influenced by her sister's job in a nursery. Jermina (Blackwell Street) regularly asked her aunt about her job as a nurse and Lee (Riverway) was anticipating becoming a black cab driver like his father if his dreams to become a professional sportsman did not materialise. Lucy (Riverway) aspired to become a hairdresser like the one who comes to her house to cut hair (and 'looks like she makes quite a bit money') and Dan (Riverway) explained how he had wanted to join the army 'since I was little and I've seen them on TV and that, and my granddad and my uncle have been talking about it'. Lacie (Riverway) wanted to be a beautician because: 'my stepmum does her own nails and it looks good and my aunt and that have moved to Spain and they have a salon, so I thought if I become a beautician I can go and work for them'.

The young people's aspirations were thus influenced more by discussions with family members than with official careers advisors or teachers. As Nadira (Eastleigh Central) put it, 'I'm just talking to a lot of people about – you know, family members – about what they would, like, think is good'. As Ball and Vincent (1998) explain, 'hot' knowledge from informal social networks tends to be trusted over and above 'cold', official knowledge because it is judged to be more 'real' (grounded in real life experiences) and more reliable (those offering the knowledge are not seen to have any overarching agenda, unlike the state and its institutions). It is perceived to be more impartial and thus more likely to be in 'our' interests (see Archer et al., 2003). Moreover, 'hot knowledge' was also valued for its associated social capital. Social capital generated through family contacts and networks provided young people with a variety of 'safe' and accessible (that is, possible and achievable) routes into paid employment. For example, Lacie's (Riverway) relatives provided not only information about the beauty industry but also contacts and job openings.

As outlined in Chapter 2, young people's preference for, and prioritisation of, 'the known' can be understood, through Bourdieu's concept of habitus, as providing young people with a sense of what is normal for 'people like me'. That is, the young people's working-class, urban locales helped shape what they perceived as thinkable:

[L]ocality provides more than a backdrop for young people's lives, but also the collective context that shapes values and meanings – what Bourdieu described as a 'logic of practice' (Bourdieu 1977). Individual young people are not determined by their localities, yet their options and identities are constrained or enabled by them.

(Henderson et al., 2007: 14)

These expectations, as discussed in Chapter 4, were clearly gendered and classed, with young women anticipating following paths into caring industries or hair and beauty, reflecting traditional gendered associations of femininity with altruism, care of others and cultivation of a feminine, heterosexually desirable appearance (Colley, 2003; Skeggs, 1997). The girls' motivations to become beauticians, hairdressers and/or clothes shop assistants also reflected their own interests (and competencies) in crafting their appearance. ('I like doing hair and stuff like that: I'm interested', Kemisha, Cowick). Several of the young women also explained their motivation to enter caring professions as being to 'help others' and hence do something worthwhile (Natalie, Hillside Park). As Hapsa (Blackwell Street) put it, 'I want to be a good person . . . who can help the people'.

Young men's interests in 'practical' jobs and manual trades reflected popular discourses around working-class masculinities (Archer et al., 2001). In addition, some boys dreamt of the 'ultimate' masculine job, namely being a professional footballer. Max (Littleton) was going to trials to try to get selected for a football team and dreamt of making 'big money' as a professional footballer, even hoping to reach Premiership level. His back-up plan also revolved around football, playing for a non-league team while working part-time.

For a few students, however, their everyday experiences and 'hot knowledge' had provided them with non-traditional aspirations. For instance, in her first interview Jane (Hillside Park) said that she wanted to become a mechanic because her father was one and she was interested in working at Citroen because her uncle works there. However, as noted earlier, this aspiration did not last – it became an unintelligible gender performance (Butler, 1999), that was thrown into particularly sharp relief when Jane got a boyfriend.

No boys aspired to traditionally 'feminine' jobs and none wanted to work in the care sector or hair and beauty industry. Indeed, boys were sometimes highly derisory about hair and beauty courses, laughingly calling them 'hair and booty'. These views were underpinned by homophobic discourses (as Lloyd said in a Hillside Park discussion group, 'because only poofs do it . . . I'm homophobic. I don't like em. They'll get beat up'), which are implicated in the construction of popular masculinities (Connell, 1989). However, most boys did feel that catering was an acceptable course for boys to undertake for, as another boy from Hillside Park said, 'you get a lot of geezers being top chefs you know, so that isn't bad' (several young people cited popular TV chef Jamie Oliver as influencing their aspirations in this respect).

This was not to say that the young people did not access any formal careers advice or that they rejected out of hand any careers advice that they did receive. Indeed, at least 19 young people described receiving some formal careers advice, either in the form of being assigned a Connexions personal advisor, receiving personalised (one-to-one) careers advice or participating in group careers advice sessions. Certainly, in their phase 2 interviews a number of young people reported receiving recent careers advice and this was evidenced in a 'spike' in their aspirations as particular routes were either introduced, discounted or solidified. For instance, Kemisha (Cowick) had reported wanting to become a hairdresser in phase one, but in her phase two interview she described receiving information and advice from Connexions that had made her think that she could 'do better' and now aspired to a career in health and social care. However, by her phase three interview Kemisha had returned to her original aspiration to work in hair and beauty. Thus the point we wish to make is that for these young people, their 'default' position was to trust and privilege 'hot' knowledge and local social capital and to be guided by a powerful sense of what is 'normal for people like me' that was strongly grounded within their classed, gendered and racialised everyday lives. Hence any interventions to change or 'raise' these horizons of choice/expectation may require considerable additional support to become sustainable. New or 'unintelligible' aspirations will be intrinsically fragile and precarious and will require sustained support to enable them to take root and grow.

'Wait and see': the deferment of aspirations and choice

We found that a key theme within the young people's construction and negotiation of their aspirations was a discourse that we have termed 'wait and see'. This was widely used to explain the deferment of plans, choices and decisions until some later point, particularly until after receiving their GCSE examination results. The practice of 'planning ahead' was seen as risky and as potentially wasting time and effort. As Darrell (Littleton) said, 'I just take every day as it comes'. Even those relatively higher-achieving and aspirational pupils like Jason (Littleton) preferred to take things 'one step at a time': 'I just can't think ahead for some reason. . . . It is like if I plan ahead it puts me off things, like, I just don't want to do it no more, like'.

GCSE examinations were constructed as a key boundary – until their results were known, many of the young people felt it would be futile to make firm plans or espouse definite aspirations:

> When I'm gonna leave school maybe then I am going to think about it.
>
> (David, Littleton)

> I just want to check and see what I have got in my exams.
>
> (Hapsa, Blackwell Street)

Most of those we talked to saw their future options as determined by their GCSE grades – even though in practice when they 'under-achieved' at GCSE many were able to negotiate satisfactory routes into post-16 education. Indeed, many felt that it was futile to identify subjects they might like to study post-GCSE, to consider whether they might like to go to university, or to be too prescriptive about what job path they might like to follow. They imagined that their options would be determined by their GCSE results and they felt unable or unwilling to predict what their GCSE achievement would be. A few students were not just waiting for academic results, but were also waiting to see if other possibilities worked out. For example, Max (Littleton) wanted to wait and 'see what is happening with my football first of all and then, if nobody wants me, then I will just go for a job'. Max had actually received assistance from Connexions who had found him a trades apprenticeship, but he was adamant that he would only consider this as a third place, back-up option in the event that he could not find a job or a professional football apprenticeship.

The young people's approach thus echoed Ball and colleagues' (2002b) 'contingent' educational choosers and Reay's (1998) 'never sure' working-class young people. Their choice trajectories stand in stark contrast to the 'always knowing' middle classes (Reay, 1998), who tend to follow a firm plan or route and can frequently mobilise various forms of cultural, economic and social capital to help maximise the opportunities on offer to achieve their goals (Ball, 2003).

We would hypothesise that the young people's deferment of their aspirations reflected their general lack of confidence in their own educational abilities. For them, educational failure was a constant threat and they were genuinely unsure as to how they might fare in the examinations. In some ways, the strategy of deferment enabled them to minimise the identity costs (such as, disappointment and shame) posed by the risk of failure because they were not hanging all their hopes on being able to pursue a single favoured option. It also provided a means for maximising their ability to negotiate failure, as it made them flexible to other options, enabling them to 'make do' according to the results they obtained.

However, this strategy of 'wait and see' disadvantaged the young people in various ways. It often resulted in them missing out on important information and opportunities that might have helped them to achieve their desired goals. For example, some young people were not studying the most relevant subjects for pursuing their preferred aspirations. They also tended to be disadvantaged in terms of FE entry because they ended up relying on late applications and hence found particular colleges or courses were already full.

> I don't know whether I'm going to go to sixth form or not yet. I don't really know what I'm going to do. I'm sure I'll be sorted by then.
>
> (Jane, Hillside Park)

> I haven't thought about college or university or anything. I just want to wait until I'm in Year 11 or in sixth form. I will then start talking to people about it. [Int: Why do you want to wait until then?] Because right now . . . I know I'm not going to take it seriously.
>
> (Jermina, Blackwell Street)

This deferment of choice meant that a number of young people resisted seeking advice or guidance from 'official' sources, such as Connexions. This placed them at a disadvantage because they lacked relevant knowledge, information and cultural capital about how to navigate the educational system and tended to lose out when it came to playing the aspirations 'game'.

The impact of 'wait and see' was particularly evident among those young people who we managed to track beyond Year 11. For example, Melissa (Eastleigh Central) had not applied to college during Year 11 because she did not expect to get good grades. She had not even considered that college might be an option until she brought her results home and her mother said to her

' "erm, are you going to college or something?" ' and en
apply. By this time, the childcare course that she most wa₁
every one of her local colleges and she had to choose m
She confessed: 'I *was* disappointed but now I don't really
ing media and I made like loads of new friends, so you kno
Ben (Hillside Park) had ambitions to be a mechanic and
However, he failed to complete an application for an
ended up staying on to study leisure and tourism. Indee
discourse rarely, if ever, enabled young people to fulfil their original ambitions. Rather it channelled them into more tangential and opportunistic
routes.

Summary

In this chapter we have put forward a conceptualisation of the young people's
aspirations as complex, multiply-held and often contradictory social phenomena that change over time. We have attempted to demonstrate how young
people are not always rational and risk-calculating beings when it comes to the
formation of aspirations and post-16 choices. Rather, aspirations are intrinsically grounded within emotional and identity discourses that may be contradictory and 'messy'. We argued that aspirations are closely bound up with
young people's social class, 'race'/ethnicity and gender locations and that educational engagement and achievement may not necessarily follow smoothly
or logically from 'high' aspirations. We identified key motivations underpin-
ning aspirations, namely to 'be happy' and 'stay safe' and the constraints
enacted by particular classed and gendered habitus'. Finally, we outlined the
pervasive – and pragmatic-discursive practice of 'wait and see' that characterised many of the young people's approaches to their future choices and argued
that, while pragmatic, it is also implicated in the reproduction of social
inequalities.

6

RESPECT, RECIPROCITY AND RELEVANCE: THE THREE Rs FOR URBAN SCHOOLS

Learner identities: being good and bad at school

In this chapter we explore how the young people in our research saw themselves as learners and how urban schools can support students like them. We explore not only how 'educational systems are complicit in the abuse of [young people] through "systemic violence" ', and via the 'practices and procedures that prevent children from learning' (Epp and Watkinson, 1996: 1), but also how education can intervene positively in young peoples' lives. In other words, schools can both reproduce and challenge inequalities. Our starting point is that, although the young people we worked with varied in the extent to which they saw themselves as 'good' or 'bad' students, only five of the 53 described themselves as being 'good' students and three felt they were 'middling'. The majority either described themselves as a mixture of good and bad, or simply as bad.

Interestingly, these young people's views of themselves did not correlate with their recorded levels of achievement. For example, among those who self-identified as 'good' students, their levels of achievement were average for the study sample and below the nationally expected standard for their age. For example, Dan (Riverway) confidently described himself as 'quite clever in some lessons, and intelligent . . . I'm good at designs, I'm good in PE, tech[nology], science, English and maths', despite failing to achieve a grade in KS3 English and gaining the levels expected of 9- to 11-year-olds in his other subjects. The two girls seeing themselves as 'good', Leah and Kemisha (both at Cowick), based their judgements on their behaviour rather than attainment.

Looking at students' KS3 scores, it was striking that none of those who achieved the highest levels of achievement across the sample (6s and 7s) saw themselves as 'good' students. They either described themselves in mixed terms or as 'in the middle'. Jason (Littleton) and David (Hillside Park) portrayed themselves as intelligent, but as prone to not doing homework and to being 'bad' or, as David put it, being a 'pain in the arse' in lessons. Jane (Hillside Park) was not sure that she was strong enough to progress further educationally: 'I'm not very confident about getting good like A-levels'. While she recognised that she was, uniquely among our participants, achieving well across the curriculum and 'in the top ["ability" group] for everything', she felt that her abilities varied across subjects. In particular, she suggested that because she is 'quite an artistic person', she was doing well in photography, art and music but not in science and maths. In this next quote we can see her efforts to sustain this story of herself as bad at scientific subjects despite making good progress in them: 'There are a few subjects that I'm really not quite good at . . . Like kind of the scientific kind of things like well obviously science and maths . . . I'm arty, I think, so maths and science are really bad for me but I'm still working at C level now in maths and science. I just got to try and keep that up'. (In Chapter 4 we argued that this related to her positioning within dominant discourses of heterosexuality.)

In all these examples, we can see how learner identities are not simply a reflection of attainment but are constituted from a mix of factors. In particular we can see gender in play as David attempts to maintain a role as a 'lad' (Jackson, 2006b) and Jane positions herself as able at subjects that are constructed as creative and feminine and as unable at those that are oppositionally constructed as rational and masculine (Mendick, 2006). We looked in Chapter 4 at further ways that gender played out in the identity work of the young people who described their learner identities in mixed terms. There we argued that boys commonly drew on laddish discourses that suggested they had ability, but were lazy, 'mucked about' or lacked application. While for girls, their notion of being 'bad' was linked to being 'loud' and expressing opinions, going against dominant discourses around the 'ideal (female) student'. Many young working-class, minority ethnic women appeared to experience these discourses as restrictive, creating tensions between their desires to have a positive learner identity and to see themselves as strong-minded.

Thus, judgements about young people's 'behaviour', 'ability', and fit to an imagined 'good student' influence their learner identities (see Archer and Francis, 2007). These judgements are formed within the broader discourses that we examined in earlier chapters which construct low working-class aspirations and more aspirational members of ethnic minorities, problematic lads and even more problematic ladettes, the lure of the estate, quiet Asian girls, oppositions between sciences and arts, and so on.

What comes through these young people's talk is how difficult it is to escape being and feeling 'bad' at learning. Understandably, most of those we spoke to expressed a desire to get out of their current positions. Often girls accounted for 'mixed' learner identities in terms of their attempts to change from a 'bad' student to a 'good' student. We explored in Chapter 4 how they articulated this in terms of being 'good underneath' and of attempts late in their school careers to recover this authentic goodness. For example, Nadira (Eastleigh Central) explained, 'now I am regretting it because I am so behind in coursework but like I know how I am going to catch up and I want to catch up on stuff'; Jermina (Blackwell Street) told us 'I've set myself a target, that I want to be good and all, like I want to get good things, good results in my GCSEs this year and like, I'm really trying this year to be good and not to do like what I used to do in Year 7, 8 or 9'. But these attempts at change were difficult. In Jermina's case they were in tension with her home life – as discussed in Chapter 2, she ran away from home due to violence. And, although Nadira was working hard to catch up, and was identified as capable of getting C and D grades, she expressed feelings of defeat in her last interview: 'I think it's so useless for me now cos I haven't done none of the coursework, I've done, like, one and you need like minimum two [pieces] to like get entered for the GCSE and time's running out'. Other students and their parents also expressed the idea of getting stuck in particular learner identities, some of which predated the transfer from primary to secondary school at age 11:

> I think the trouble is once you – when you come up from Year 7 if you're finding it hard and you haven't got the right sort of help or the right sort of teachers that will sort of say, 'alright we'll sit down and look at it', once you're labelled as someone who is going to say 'I can't do it' and start shouting, it just carries you through, it stays with you wherever you go.
>
> (Mike's mother, Hillside Park)

So, in this chapter we want to address the questions:

- How are schools complicit in producing and maintaining these stigmatised learner identities?
- How can they support young people's desires for change to alternative learner identities?

We look in turn at pedagogy, assessment and curriculum. We suggest that whatever is taught and however it is measured (the common preoccupations of educational policy), it is the relationships between students and teachers which make learning possible. However, these relationships are not simply negotiated between individual students and teachers, for both groups are caught within social and political structures which have particular implications for urban schools.

Pedagogy

Supporting findings from other research (for example, Bibby, 2009; McWilliam, 1999), participants repeatedly told us that teacher-student relationships are a crucial factor affecting their engagement with schooling. This extract, typical of many, shows that the relationship with even one teacher can make a difference to how 'at risk' young people feel about school:

> And because I really like my tutor I listened to her and what I want to do, yeah, is in Year 10 to work more harder and to always come to school . . . So now I come to school I do my work and whatever I have to do in school . . . I tell her everything, she's like a mother to me. And whenever I tell her, because I never lie to her or nothing, she always believes me.
>
> (Yesim, Cowick)

Teacher-student relationships like this one involve feeling trusted and listened to. They were often compared to relationships with friends and family, as in Yesim's maternal comparison. Similarly, Jermina (Blackwell Street) valued a teacher who 'is like half my mum in this school'; Nathan (Hillside Park) appreciated a teacher who 'I could talk to him, like a good mate and would give me a hand with my work and that when I needed it'; and Jane (Hillside Park) connected with a teacher who she described as 'the same as me, like really arty and I get on with her'. Interestingly, all these words were about English teachers suggesting that some subjects are more likely to create spaces for teacher-student relationships in which young people feel safe, valued, cared about and understood. That young people want these things is not surprising. As Noddings (2003: 244) puts it:

> It is not only students' rationality that must be respected; students need and want teachers to care for them as persons and to convey this care through listening and responding to their expressions of concern. . . . It matters to students whether or not they like and are liked by their teachers. The teacher as person is centrally important in teaching.

The students broadly agreed with each other and with the sentiments in this quotation in their constructions of 'good' teachers – they were those whose relationships with students were characterised by respect and reciprocity. As discussed in Chapter 2, respect has been appropriated by the government agenda for tackling anti-social behaviour (http://www.respect.gov.uk/). However, we see respect, following Sennett (2003), as about how institutions such as schools treat people – students *and* teachers – not about controlling individuals' behaviour.

The young people described good teachers as fair and measured in their discipline (not too strict or lenient) and able to maintain discipline in their classes without having to resort to 'shouting' – as Jermina (Blackwell Street) suggested, 'it would make school more fun if you had a teacher that didn't shout a lot'. Nathan's (Hillside Park) description of his new art teacher was reiterated by numerous other students as typifying the 'ideal' teacher: 'he is alright. He is a bit strict but he is good with people and we don't really mess around'. His discipline is based in his relationships with students. Students also place considerable emphasis on teachers being able to provide explanations of, and support with, the work. For example Babu (Riverway) wanted teachers to 'make more examples' and to clarify the tasks ('they write on the board and say answer the question, and they don't even explain what you have to do'). He said he likes his maths teacher because he 'teaches better and explains more stuff and helps you a lot'. Jordan (Blackwell Street) said: 'I have some really wonderful teachers that really do explain things properly and thoroughly'. For them, understanding does not come from being told, it comes from feeling that they are listened to and respected as 'able' to understand.

We can also see the desire for respect and reciprocity in the accounts of young people who described how they disengaged from lessons where they could not understand and felt marginalised or ignored. For instance, Janine (Hillside Park) described herself as 'not a very good student . . . I'm sometimes disruptive', but also described not getting the support she needed, with her teacher going 'to everyone else and by the time it's the end of the lesson, I'm still sitting there waiting to be told what to do. . . . It makes me feel, not left out, but makes me feel that I'm just not there'. This is a painful account of feeling invisible, of not being seen and recognised by the teacher. Poor behaviour makes sense as a response to this at both conscious and unconscious levels, as Lucy (Riverway discussion group) explained, 'it would be all right [if they respected us], everybody would respect them but they treat us like shit so we treat them like shit'.

In particular, relationships with teachers affected young people's perceptions of their ability to change. Steven and Verona complained that teachers seemed to be unwilling to give them a second chance:

> I was real good at school, but now the last couple of years because the teachers have all treated me like crap and that, I think, 'well go away I am not going to do anything'.
>
> (Steven, Eastleigh Central)

> I went 'can't you just give me a second chance? Because this year I really want to prove myself I can do it' and he still won't give me a chance.
>
> (Verona, Riverway)

Thus, relationships are central to what is possible in education. This raises the issue of how to create the conditions in schools to make relationships of respect and reciprocity more possible between teachers and students.

Urban schools face particular issues in developing such relationships. Schools like those in this research, with higher than average proportions of FSM students and lower attainment, make greater use of supply teachers (Hutchings et al., 2006a). Due to the temporariness of a supply teacher's presence in the school, they often have problematic relations with students. As members of staff recognised, students' engagement diminished in lessons with supply teachers due to the lack of stability and lack of time to build up good relationships:

> We have many supply teachers and kids bunking. [They] have a quick look, 'oh it's a supply' and they'll just bunk because they know the supply is not going to have any work on them, actual work. They know the supply teacher is not going to realise that he's away or whatever so they won't go. . . . Also, when you have a teacher continuously, they keep track of what you're doing because with a supply teacher nothing is actually being recorded.
>
> (Learning Mentor, Eastleigh Central)

Lee (Riverway) agreed: 'we don't do no work with supplies'. Preparing work and keeping track can indicate a teacher who cares about their students, who respects their students as worth expending time and effort on. Not only do urban schools use more supply staff on average but those supply teachers they do use are more likely to be young and/or overseas trained teachers obtained through an agency who are looking for full-time work. Hence they are often people who do not like doing supply, have less experience, do not know the school and have no access to professional development. In contrast, rural schools tend to rely on known supply teachers who can form ongoing relationships with students (Hutchings et al., 2006a). Further, urban schools tend to have higher rates of teacher turnover (Bubb and Earley, 2007; Hutchings et al., 2002) and many of our young people felt let down by this: 'With my science I haven't done any coursework because we have had about five or six different teachers for the last two years because my old science teacher she kept on getting pregnant, kept on having babies, so she left and that and we have just been stuck with supply teachers every single day for ages' (Steven, Eastleigh Central).

A broader problem with developing a relational understanding of pedagogy is that this is absent from the current technicist view of teaching and learning put forward through recent policy initiatives in England. A series of policies, including the standards for Initial Teacher Training (ITT) in England and Wales and the National Numeracy and Literacy Strategies, tells teachers *how* to teach (Moss, 2005) reducing pedagogy to a list of ingredients for effective, excellent or quality teaching. Recent policies have placed a lot of emphasis on the 'quality' of teachers and teaching (DCSF, 2009b; HM Government, 2009). As well as attempting to homogenise practice, the government has sought to improve this by raising the qualification levels of teachers: attempts are being made to develop and trial a new Masters in Teaching and Learning programme for newly qualified teachers to enrol on. This is part of a growing emphasis on continuing professional development tied to systems of accountability, such as the new 'licence to teach' which will be renewable regularly. Thus teaching becomes about the knowledge and qualifications of the teachers, for these can easily be quantitatively measured, rather than about their capacity for creating relationships with their students based on respect and reciprocity, which cannot.

While this reductive approach to pedagogy clearly affects all students and their teachers, we would argue that it has particular implications for those working in urban schools for 'when teacher competence is constructed as a technical activity, it ignores the social-political context as well as any appreciation of ethical debate' (te Riele, 2006a: 60–1). As discussed in Chapter 2, for the young people in our study there is a mismatch between home and school cultures, which means that students need opportunities to learn 'the rules of the game' in ways that acknowledge their constructed and contextual nature and so do not position the students as defective (Wrigley, 2006). This requires that teachers and students know and trust each other, can listen to each other, and can talk about social structures and inequalities. For example, we feel that it takes more than a weekly citizenship lesson to respond meaningfully to Mark's views on 'race' and immigration discussed in detail in Chapter 3 (Epstein, 1993) – that he 'hates this country' because of 'poncers coming into' it who are 'just taking over' although he 'don't mind if they are actually working' and thinks that refugee young people in his school are 'alright to talk to'. This is something that happens more often in primary schools through practices such as circle time. Here it is more possible for difficult issues to be raised because the organisation of the curriculum in primary school is such that children are taught most subjects by one teacher, and, circle time, unlike citizenship, has neither an official syllabus nor external examinations. The interlinked practices of assessment and curriculum determine much of what is possible in education and so we explore these before returning to matters of pedagogy.

Assessment

Assessment plays an increasingly important role in education. As discussed in Chapters 1 and 2, the decline of manufacturing means that few young people can expect to get a job straight from school with no qualifications; this has positioned education as vital to our, so-called, knowledge economy. Pupils and teachers are subject to ongoing measurement and surveillance, including: regular audits, inspections and, of course, national tests, the results of which are published widely in league tables (Ball, 2008; Woodrow, 2003). In 2009 the government announced plans to move from raw league tables of results, to 'school report cards' that assign scores to schools based on a range of indicators, rather than solely on examination results (DCSF, 2009b). However, while this is positive in widening the range of measurements used to evaluate schools, it simultaneously compels schools to produce all these measurements. Also, despite the move to a range of measures, examination results remain the most prominent indicator.

In an ethnography of two urban primary schools, Hall and colleagues (2004: 802) explored the messages supplied by staff in their interactions with pupils and by school and classroom structures 'about how to behave generally and about how learning should be done and who is doing it well'. They found that the actions of both teachers and learners were dominated by SATs. This constrained what teachers did in their lessons, the positions available to their pupils and, in particular, what and who were valued. They argue that SATs constructed a hierarchy of pupil, and by extension parental, worthiness, which mapped predictably to inequalities of class, 'race'/ethnicity and gender. They conclude:

> Children do not enjoy equality of respect since their worth seems to depend so much on their varying ability and willingness to achieve in SATs. The message carried by the culture in both schools and clearly delivered and received by pupils is that the major incentive for learning, for working hard to learn, for coming to school, etc. is not the satisfaction of understanding or coming to know; it is not to become a more fulfilled person; it is the reward of 'high numbers' in SATs.
>
> (Hall et al., 2004: 811)

Supporting this, Carlile (forthcoming), in her study of exclusion in a London borough, documented that those permanently excluded young people who were likely to achieve highly in examinations were the most desirable to headteachers regardless of their behaviour record. In this section we explore how this assessment driven hierarchy of value played out in the lives of the young people in our study, by analysing what they said about the practice of 'ability' grouping or setting (called 'tracking' in the US).

All the schools in the study made use of setting. This extract captures something of the valuations attached to it and their implications for learner identities.

> We have [sets] one to three and then four to six. It goes one half of the year is one, two, three and then the other half is four, five, six. And six is the top set and one is the top set. And so four and three are bum sets. I'm in the top set for maths, . . . for English and the second set for science. I prefer to be in the second set for science because the top set is like really hard. I was in the top set and I have been put down.
>
> (Mark, Hillside Park)

Mark uses the structure of setting by 'ability' to find his place and to place others: he is a set two person for science, not fitting the 'hard' top sets or the 'bum' bottom sets, but a set one person for maths and English. The language of setting, with its high and low, top and bottom, is embedded with values, and slips easily into Mark's slang term, 'bum'. These labels then transfer from the sets to the people in them. As Dylan indicates:

> I understand why they do that ranking, counter, that sets one, two, three. But I don't think they should do it like that, they have their reason to, because it puts people down because . . . people in set one usually are like people that will go round boasting or something like that going, 'ah I'm in set one. What's this? What's this question? What's this answer?' And then people in set six, like their confidence is kind of low in a way, or they're just like really random and can't be bothered with school . . . it makes you feel that ah you can never compare to people like in set one.
>
> (Dylan, Littleton discussion group)

Dylan experiences setting as producing stigmatised identities and competitive practices.

Supporting this, we, unsurprisingly, found that those young people placed in 'bottom' sets were unhappy and felt that they had been labelled as 'stupid'. For example, Jermina (Blackwell Street) states: 'In science, since Year 8, I've always been in the lower group and I feel like I am not improving at the science at all'. Yesim (Cowick) was unhappy that she had been moved from the middle to the lower set. She felt 'bad because I thought I was doing more better so I thought I would go higher but somehow I went down'. She resisted being positioned as 'stupid', saying of her new group: 'Sometimes I do feel cleverer than them ... you see what goes on in a class when the teacher asks the questions, they rarely answer and when they do answer it's always they do a mistake or get it wrong, but whenever I answer I always say it correct'. However, Yesim's resistance is based on seeing herself as in the wrong set rather than rejecting setting *per se*.

Most of the students in our research were in lower or middle sets. Although, many of those in the middle sets reported feeling comfortable with their position (for example, Bob (Riverway): 'I feel comfortable with them cos the C band's easy and the B band that I'm in is going alright at the moment'), these positionings fed into young people's constructions of their value and capability as learners and can partly explain why so few saw themselves as good at school.

Research confirms the young people's insights that teachers use different approaches with different groups based in their expectations about their 'ability' (Boaler, 1997; Houssart, 2001). Not only are different teaching methods and resources employed in different sets but different knowledge is communicated. Since setting controls access to knowledge, a student's access to particular assessments and so to the symbolic capital of qualifications is dependent on their position in the setting system – this has been called the 'rationing of education' by Gillborn and Youdell (2000). There is a wealth of research showing that systems of 'ability' grouping reproduce inequalities, with working-class and Black students far more likely to be allocated to lower sets (for example, Gillborn and Youdell, 2000; Lynch and Lodge, 2002). Young people internalise their 'ability' as part of themselves, rather than seeing it as ascribed through a social process (Reay and Wiliam, 1999). Even our earlier critic, Dylan, begins 'I understand why they do that ranking ... they have their reason'. 'Ability' grouping is part of the unchallengeable commonsense of teaching and learning, despite evidence of its damaging effects.

Indeed, the way that practices of 'ability' grouping construct powerful but fictive identities for students was carefully documented by Ball back in 1981. He carried out a compelling ethnography of 'banding' in Beachside comprehensive school, where students were organised into broad 'ability' groups that they stayed with for all their lessons. In particular, he showed that the labelling as band 2 was embedded in teachers' shared meanings, *not* dependent on specific students and produced a polarisation into pro-school and anti-school groups:

> Once established, the typification 'band 2 form' or 'band 2 pupil' merely awaits the arrival of each new cohort in the school. I am not suggesting that the 'label' of being band 2 in itself creates a 'deviant' identity and is the cause of . . . 'deviant' acts . . . But the label of being band 2 imposes certain limitations upon the sort of social identity that may be negotiated by the band 2 pupil. When persons are subjected to a process of categorization, they are subject also to the imputation of various social identities by virtue of their membership of that category. In this case, it is an identity that involves a status-evaluation and allocation to an inferior position in the status-hierarchy of the school. Band 2 forms . . . are considered to be 'not up to much academically' and most teachers find them 'unrewarding' to teach.
>
> (Ball, 1981: 36–7)

Their teachers 'tend to jump from a single cue or a small number of cues in actual, suspected or alleged behaviour, to a general picture of the "kind of person with whom one is dealing" ' (p. 37). This resonates with our data and was a key obstacle for students working to improve their reputations with teachers. As discussed in Chapters 4 and 5, between Year 9 and Year 11, Analisa (Cowick) made an 'enormous change like I've changed, my personality and stuff. I'm not rude to the teachers any more. ... Now I'm a good girl and learning and stuff'. But her teacher, who already had a clear idea of her 'ability', mocked her desire to go to a high status university saying, 'if you get in there [I] will dance round this hall in woman's dress'.

In critiquing 'ability' grouping we are not trying to deny that there are differences in what people are able to do. The problem with 'ability', as it is currently enacted in schools, is the way that the associated labels become fixed as part of people's identities. Even the very word 'ability', suggesting links to a fixed inner capacity, constructs a social issue as an individual one and a mobile condition as a fixed one. Teachers know that people's abilities can shift rapidly as a result of changes in their learning environment, teachers, motivations or personal circumstances; and that every class and every learner is a complex mixture of abilities, no single one of which will determine how well they will do on a particular day, in a particular subject. That disengagement, and the associated low attainment, is neither a uniform nor permanent state, is nicely illustrated by Babu's (Riverway) involvement in the research study. Babu was seen negatively within school. For example, his Head of Year 10 said: 'He won't go to sixth-form college; he will never go to university; he won't have a job. He's our local gangster. . . . No respect for education whatsoever; no respect for females whatsoever; out of control basically. . . . I would say, that he will be pushed off site before he gets to Year 11'. But Babu did get to Year 11, and was still in school by the time of the last interview. He developed positive relations with the White female researcher, borne out by his completion of all three interviews, the photographic diary exercise and facilitating his mother taking part in a parental interview.

Thus, we need to find a way to disrupt the jump from assessment to 'ability' seen as a fixed judgement about the person. Moving to 'all-ability' teaching is an important starting point but is not enough because of the pervasiveness of 'ability'. We also have to pay attention to the ways that educational practices routinely reify 'ability', for example, through the public reading out of test marks and the innocuous-sounding question 'hands up whoever's finished?' (Mendick, 2002). Assessment for Learning (Black and Wiliam, 1996, 1998) can help to detach assessment from hierarchies of value. Here a range of formative assessment processes is used – including peer- and self-assessment and the feeding back of comments without grades – to focus on what students need to do and to avoid comparisons between them. However, once again we want to stress that teachers and schools cannot act in isolation. Alongside this we need to see both a reduction in the amount of national testing and in what is at stake in these tests, and we need to begin to talk about the way that the organisation of learning through 'ability' reproduces inequalities in the wider society, making sure people know their place and are confined to an 'appropriate' curriculum (Young, 1961).

Curriculum

Curriculum is often presented as the solution to disengagement: if you present students with appropriate material, it is argued, they will apply themselves. Typically in these extracts teachers proposed offering students an alternative to the academic curriculum:

I mean, you know, Blair and Co want the school leaving age to be 18. I guess it just depends on what you call school. I mean if staying in school until you're 18 means sitting down in a classroom listening to teachers talking at you then it is a disaster because there is no way that a quite significant percentage of our population probably anywhere in the world can deal with that for 18 years of their life. If being at school means that you could be doing [a] level two course in motor vehicle maintenance or in trade skills, plastering, plumbing as well as making sure your English, maths and your IT are up to speed at the same time [then that might work].

(Deputy Headteacher, Hillside Park)

You bring kids in, [but if] they can't adapt to the curriculum they're going to bunk. But the government is saying that they should be doing GCSEs . . . I don't think they should.

(Head of Year 11, Eastleigh Central)

Such arguments are behind the government's introduction of vocational qualifications into compulsory education, including most recently through diplomas. In this section we critically explore these arguments drawing on the views of our young people, many of whom were enthusiastic about pursuing more practical and vocational options. However, we argue that rather than being straightforward evidence for an increased vocational curriculum, their words support a *relevant* curriculum. In this sense, we will suggest that what is taught is less important (although this does matter) than how it is taught.

On a first reading, our data support a shift to a more practical curriculum for many 'at risk' young people. Babu (Riverway) named his best lesson as the support option where 'we talk' rather than write; Kyle's (Cowick) favourite subject is textiles because there are 'lots of activities'; Lacie (Riverway) enjoys 'getting my hands dirty and the drawing' in art. These examples show how 'practical' was broadly defined, encompassing any activity that was not copy-ing notes or completing written exercises. Practical lessons offered students opportunities to get a sense of achievement: 'I'd just rather do practical stuff like every day, all day . . . Put a car in front of me, tell me what to do and I'll fix it. Put work in front of me I'll sit there and take as long as I want on it. The car I'll do it there and then because it's something that I've achieved, it's done' (Ben, Hillside Park).

Young people saw 'practical' subjects as relating directly to their aspirations, and useful for entering the labour market. For example: Germaine (Blackwell Street) explained, 'I'm doing sports science so I can be a physio[therapist] and work in a gym anything like that' and Yesim (Cowick) felt IT would be import-ant for securing 'office work'. For most of the young people, like Germaine and Yesim, their engagement with the curriculum was shaped by whether they perceived particular subjects as relevant to their current and future lives. How-ever, these judgements did not fit a simple pattern of seeing the academic as irrelevant and the practical or vocational as relevant. They shifted as students realised (or were advised) that they would need core subjects for a range of jobs and training opportunities. Bob (Riverway) for example, said: 'I'm focusing on them [English and maths] as much as other subjects because you need them grades to become an apprentice'. Parents also tended to see the value of the curriculum in terms of its perceived relevance to their children's lives. Lee's mother (Riverway) assessed his curriculum as follows: 'Japanese, no: he ain't going to go and get a job [involving that]. Science, no: because he ain't going to be a forensic scientist. English and maths he really needs because he can't walk into a job without education, that thing. History I'm not too sure but he loves, likes, history. And PE I think he wants to do that because he wants to become a coach'. This complicates the notion of reading curriculum relevance solely in terms of practical skills. We can muddy this picture further by looking at the many students who felt positively towards academic subjects.

Joe (Littleton discussion group) asserted that he liked history because 'I believe in history ... I'm really influenced by history'. Robert (Eastleigh Central) enjoyed media studies because, 'I see films in a different way than when just watching. I see how they make it and that.' Lacie (Riverway) mentioned that she had always liked maths because 'I don't find it that easy, it is the challenge that I like.' Even Dan and Lee who were disengaged from the mainstream curriculum volunteered for after-school Japanese lessons. They both enjoyed these classes, seeing them differently from other lessons and more like a hobby (although they were organised by, and held at, Riverway School). As Dan put it, 'well it is not like a lesson [and] it gets me out of the house for an hour or so'. These examples point to how many young people deemed 'at risk' or with 'fragile' learner identities can connect the academic to the everyday within subjects as diverse as Japanese, history, media and maths.

Thus, we want to propose an alternative to either an academic or a vocational curriculum: a relevant curriculum which connects to young people's lives but not in a narrowly utilitarian way, one which provides opportunities for re/engagement in learning and feelings of success. We think this is important for avoiding a two-tier education system where those 'at risk' are confined to what are seen as McDonald's qualifications (Allen and Ainley, 2007). This evocative/provocative classification of vocational qualifications is problematic. But, in England, the vocational has far less status than the academic. As exemplified in the earning/learning dichotomy discussed in Chapter 4, it is a split deeply entrenched in our class system and the division between middle-class and working-class occupations, between mental and manual; the academic/vocational divide persists despite government attempts to establish 'parity of esteem' (Leathwood and Hutchings, 2003; Willis, 1977). Vocational and practical choices also tend to be more rigidly gendered and racialised than other curriculum choices (Fuller et al., 2005). Thus it could be argued that these fix people in place earlier in life.

Pedagogy is a vital part of making curriculum relevant. Several of the young people we spoke to were involved in schemes which involved them in studying vocational skills at college, instead of school, for part of their week, and others moved onto vocational courses after Year 11. Most were positive about these experiences and for some they had been a way of re-engaging with learning. But when they spoke about college, they talked more about their relationships with the teachers, the pedagogy, than the curriculum. For example, Melissa (Eastleigh Central) said: 'I love the teachers at college I love them better than in thingy [school], erm, cos like they treat you like an adult, like a young adult. And you don't get to call them sir or miss you get to call them by their names.' Melissa described her college teachers treating her with respect, eschewing one of the artificial hierarchies of schooling: the use of first names for students but not teachers. Like the 'responsible' young men who want to get jobs rather than continue in education and the young women who value a traditional heterosexual femininity, both discussed in Chapter 4, Melissa wanted to be/feel adult. Pursuing vocational options at college and the pedagogy on offer there provided a space for this. As did, for some, moves to PRUs. For example, Max's (Littleton) time at the PRU had 'made a big difference' because of the attitude of teachers and the ethos: 'The teachers ain't so hassley and that. They ain't going mad at you all the time and like it's not that hard to get, it's not like you don't have to wear uniform. It's not that long hours really and it's all right. The teachers are alright with us.' Some students also found such spaces in school: Nadia (Blackwell Street) was chosen to be a senior student, 'like a role model for younger students', which increased her engagement: 'you have to be good at attending, behaving in school, be very good'.

This prioritising of pedagogy over curriculum is part of the earlier pattern we observed whereby young people conflated feelings about the teacher and their subject. This is something which the rigid timetabled structure of secondary schooling denies, but that is present in the structure of primary schooling (Shaw, 1995). Over and over again we found that where relationships were positive, students engaged and attended more regularly; where they were poor, students disengaged and/or truanted. As Darren put it, his engagement 'doesn't depend on the subject, it depends if I like the teacher or not. If I like the teacher, I do it.' Nadia (Blackwell Street) explained that she likes English because she really likes the teacher. She was enthusiastic enough to borrow a copy of Dickens' *A Christmas Carol* (which they had studied the previous year) to re-read. Lee's mother explained: 'I know there is a [science] teacher here that can't stand him, she disliked him straightaway and every time he walked in [the class] she would kick him out . . . He likes Mr Orange the history teacher. He worships his form teacher Mrs Jasmine; he worships her; he thinks the world of her'. Lee agreed that he worked harder for teachers who he felt shared his interests:

> They'll just sort of, like they'll speak to you about like football and stuff like that and rugby and not all boring classroom stuff. And they will, and then you sort of, once they speak about something like football or something you start to sort of settle down and do your work, you wanna do your work for that teacher. So you do your work for him so you get a good reputation.
>
> (Lee, Riverway)

This example is not unproblematic, since using football to teach can reinforce a laddish anti-school masculinity (Skelton, 2001). But it does show the importance of teachers drawing on the relationships they have with students to connect what they teach to young people's experiences.

Appelbaum's (2007) idea of popular pedagogies is useful here. He starts from the learning that young people engage in through their everyday cultural practices: in fashion, music, computer games, and so on (see also Gee, 2007; Willis, 1990). He then proposes that we organise school so that young people can use the same ways of learning. This approach changes the position of young people's cultural capital in the field of the school. 'Understanding youth cultural practices requires that we look at youth as inherently creative problem solvers, posers, solution-finders, etc. The teacher enters her/his room assuming that her/his students are already some form of mathematician, scientist, poet, architect etc.' (Appelbaum, 2007: 235). Teachers and students both know things and both learn things. The power relations between students and teachers alter as teachers act more as professional amateurs 'someone who doesn't limit themselves through their special knowledge of a discipline' (Appelbaum, 2007: 236). This would also enable teachers to cover a range of subjects and so to spend more time with students. This approach is respectful of young people and is characterised by reciprocity between students and teachers and students and students. This resonates with the methods that we suggested for bilingualism in Chapter 3, in which young people's linguistic capital is seen as an asset rather than a hindrance to their learning; an area in which they, not their teachers, are experts. It also means being honest with young people about the power relationships in which they are caught, saying, for example: 'Well, yes, this is kind of silly, but this stuff is on the tests you'll be facing, and I want you to do well' (Noddings, 1996: 615).

This approach must be accompanied by support that addresses what often motivates students' preference for practical work: their problems with literacy and so with accessing the academic curriculum.

> I hate writing. I hate it. And that is one reason why I can't stay in my lesson because it is always written work and I hate writing. . . . Every time I used to go to school I always used to get sent, sent home most of the time. Cos, I'm not gonna lie, it's mainly my fault, it is my fault cos I can't, can't put pen to paper. I just find it the most boring thing on the earth.
>
> (Peter, Eastleigh Central)

> Well we have these books and we have to read it all and then answer the questions and it is quite difficult for me to read everything when they['re] all long words and I can't read it. . . . I get annoyed because everyone else I think is cleverer or better than me at English and I get frustrated.
>
> (Lacie, Riverway)

A sizeable proportion of the young people, predominantly male, related their disengagement from aspects of the curriculum and from school itself, to difficulties with and a consequent dislike for reading and writing. Like Peter and Lacie they did not speak of this as an educational or social failure, linked to the under-resourcing of urban schools, but as a personal one. This repeats the neoliberal recasting of social problems as individual ones that we have highlighted throughout this book. The young people took this inability as evidence of their self being damaged or wrong as when Babu (Riverway) moved from 'I can't write much' to 'I ain't good at nothing' echoing the younger pupil in Reay and Wiliam's (1999) research who, when faced with the likelihood of a low test result, said 'I'll be a nothing'. This internalisation of educational failure into an aspect of the self can result in chronic disengagement, through a defensive response in which learning and education are seen as antithetical to a student's sense of being (see Chapter 2). These problems were particularly pronounced for students whose first language was not English (see Chapter 3).

One response to this might be to allow people who have literacy problems to spend much of their compulsory education engaged in activities that involve little reading and writing. However, this denies them access to powerful knowledge that is central to how we engage with the world and understand our humanity. Although vocational courses are usually taught alongside literacy and numeracy, these are often framed as basic skills and different from academic versions of English and mathematics, thus reinforcing the dominant construction of such courses as second-class routes for those not up to academic study.

Several students, like Lee (Riverway) had arrived at their secondary schools unable to read and write but had received additional support. Lee recalled: 'At the beginning it was hard and that was because I couldn't write and read properly. So I had special needs lessons and I learned properly from there.' Riverway's Babu and Bob and Blackwell Street's Jermina and Nadia all found that their engagement and achievement improved when they received extra learning support. One student, Lacie (Riverway), disliked getting support, feeling self-conscious at being singled-out and grouped together with 'the not-so-clever'. Thus we need to develop ways to offer support without stigma. Critical pedagogies offer a way forward by advocating that literacy teaching be a political act, that engages with the ways that illiteracy is a social rather than an individual failing (Freire, 1972).

Pedagogies to make a difference in urban schools

For teachers to create space for their students to be heard and valued (as we have advocated in this chapter) relies, in part, on teachers themselves feeling that they are heard and valued by others rather than being tired, stressed and overwhelmed by their situation. We have looked in earlier chapters at the psychic and social costs to students studying in schools like Blackwell Street, Cowick, Eastleigh Central, Hillside Park, Littleton and Riverway. Striving for educational success brings fear and anxiety and can demand enormous emotional work on the self. For young working-class men and women, it can be experienced as a struggle against the odds (Reay, 2002; Walkerdine et al., 2001). There are also psychic and social costs to teachers working in urban schools. In these circumstances: 'It is tempting to draw back into the safety of a system that has "worked" for generations; but safety and privilege are gained only at great cost. We must find a way for our schools to become crucibles for change. Unless we can do that, we, with our children, are trapped in a repeating violence of our own making' (Epp, 1996: 192–4). We share Epp's concern to make schools places where change happens – places that make a difference. While the relational pedagogy proposed here is not the 'magic bullet' solution, we hope that it is one of many possible starting points.

We end this chapter by comparing our approach to that of a new charity that also seeks to make a difference to urban schools. This charity, Teach First (TF), aims 'to address educational disadvantage by transforming exceptional graduates into effective, inspirational teachers and leaders in all fields' (http:// www.teachfirst.org.uk/what_is_teachfirst/our_mission). It began in London in 2003 and has since expanded to the East Midlands, West Midlands, Yorkshire and the North West of England. It takes 'top' graduates and trains them on-the-job to teach in urban schools. The TF scheme is praised and cited as a case study of good practice in the education White Paper (DCSF, 2009b). Central to TF is a model of pedagogy based on the 'inspirational teacher'. TF and their older, sister organisation Teach for America have developed an approach to teaching and learning in 'challenging' schools that conceptualises such teaching as inspiring and such learning as being inspired and becoming inspiring. The skills needed in leadership and teaching are constructed as identical: 'To be able to stand in front of people and capture their attention – as a teacher or a management consultant – you need to be intelligent, confident, and compelling' (http://www.teachfirst.org.uk/why_teachfirst/a_cut_above_the_rest). In this and similar statements from TF there is a particular construction of ideal teacher-student relationships in 'challenging' schools. Teachers and students are positioned respectively as leader and led.

Key aspects of this view of inspirational teaching are having high expectations of students and a sense of urgency in working with them. TF and Kopp, the founder of Teach for America, stress the need both for having high expectations and for 'doing whatever was necessary to reach' (Kopp, 2001: 159) them, to go 'above and beyond' (http://www.teachfirst.org.uk/what_is_ teachfirst/our_schools). This involves teachers becoming part of the lives of their students outside of school and involves them in working together outside of the normal school day. 'Urgency' follows from high expectations: 'With lofty goals for their students, who are already significantly behind, the teachers know they need to maximize every moment' (Kopp, 2001: 167). They are expected to 'inspire pupils to try harder and challenge themselves further than they ever thought possible. Your influence will extend far beyond the classroom' (http://www.teachfirst.org.uk/why_teachfirst/learn_to_lead).

This approach differs from ours in three key ways. First, it positions 'regular' teachers as not doing enough – either through inability or lack of commitment – they are not inspiring and/or do not go 'above and beyond'. The website statement that 'Teach First unashamedly expects many of its participants to become the future Ministers, CEOs, and serial entrepreneurs of our times' (http://www.teachfirst.org.uk/what_is_teachfirst/our_vision), clearly positions the majority of urban school teachers as inferior and inadequate to the task, they do not teach *first* before going onto something better, they teach *forever*. Second, it constructs TF participants, and by extension all teachers, as being in a position 'to do something about the external forces that [keep them] from ensuring [their] students' successes' (Kopp, 2001: 163). Thus, within this construction, the 'inspirational teacher' is assumed to be able to overcome structural sources of oppression, something which places a huge burden on the individual and creates risks of exhaustion and burn-out (Hutchings et al., 2006b). This draws on the same discourses as the Hollywood films we discussed in Chapter 1, where, for example, the teacher at the centre of *Freedom Writers* takes on two part-time jobs in order to purchase resources and finance excursions for her urban students. Third, the proposed inspiring teacher-student relationship constructs the teacher as a missionary/saviour and their students as those who need civilising. This image also draws on the Hollywood film discourses, where minority ethnic, working-class urban youth are saved by elite (White, middle-class) teachers. Smart and colleagues (2009) argue that, in its use of these discourses, TF reproduces middle-class privilege.

Teach First's inspiring relationships are not the reciprocal relationships that we have shown were desired by our participants. Instead we want to see a pedagogy based in the three Rs of respect, reciprocity and relevance. This acknowledges that teaching is a collective not an individual endeavour and that schools cannot do everything (and maybe cannot do very much). Students need to be in a position to engage in learning – personally, physically, emotionally – and so may need 'other' work first and alongside learning; and policy needs to create the possibilities for schooling to support urban young people.

Summary

In this chapter we have looked at how urban schools can both nurture and harm the learner identities of young people, so that they become stuck with labels such as 'at risk', 'vulnerable' and 'fragile'. Starting from what the young people had to say about teaching and learning, we argued that it is the relationships between teachers and learners that are at the centre of the learning process and that these should be characterised by *respect* and *reciprocity* and make learning *relevant* to young people. In arguing this we did *not* suggest that if only teachers would do their job right then the problems of inequality and social exclusion would disappear. Instead we have argued throughout, that relationships between teachers and learners are constrained by the social context and urban schools have structural reasons why they often struggle in comparison with other schools. We looked at some specific difficulties that urban schools have in this regard, such as in recruiting and retaining staff. We also suggested that some more general problems such as the financial constraints on supporting excluded students, the disciplinary organisation of the curriculum and the dominance of assessment have particular implications for those working in urban schools.

7

CHOICE OR COERCION?
POLICIES TO PROMOTE
EDUCATIONAL ENGAGEMENT

Int: The government have got this idea that they want half of all the
          young people who are leaving school to go to university. What do
          you think of that idea?
Darren: If you could ever get half the people in this school that are leaving to
          go to university, I'd be shocked. . . . Cos no one that I know wants
          to go to university. They want to go to college and then get a job.
Int: So why do you think it is that they don't want to go to university?
Darren: I don't know but most people won't go to university unless they're
          smart and there's not many smart people in my year.
Int: Why do you think that is?
Darren: They're just not.
Int: Do you think people think it's important to get a job?
Darren: Well no, it's just that most people want to do what they want to do,
          not go to university.

The above dialogue between Darren (Littleton) and one of our interviewers
speaks volumes about the current education policy context. In line with
Darren's observations, the majority of the young people in our research did
not want to continue into HE, and many, as we discussed in Chapter 4, wanted
even to avoid FE in order to start work and begin earning. However, in this
neoliberal global age, the decline of manufacturing in the UK and the rise of
service industries have led to more unstable working patterns and a need for a
flexible, educated workforce, for the new 'knowledge economy' (HM Government, 2009: 3): for 'brains not brawn' (Blair, 1999). We have moved from
a society defined by 'jobs for life' to one built around 'lifelong learning'
(Walkerdine et al., 2001). Within this shift, Widening Participation has become
a major focus for the New Labour Government, exemplified by the target
discussed in the extract above for 50 per cent HE participation among 18- to
30-year-olds by 2010. Education is increasingly becoming 'compulsory' for

young people: 'In the UK, if you are between 16 and 19 and not in education, employment or training (NEET), you fall into a policy category that is the focus of a range of remedial interventions' (Thomson, 2007: 43). Young people like Darren and the others in this research, are the targets of such interventions.

In this chapter we look at the young people's views on three specific initiatives which were used to encourage educational participation at the time of the study: the Education Maintenance Allowance (EMA), the Connexions Service and Learning Mentors (through the Excellence in Cities programme). These interventions involved a range of methods to support participation. While the EMA financially incentivises young people to stay on, one-to-one sessions with Connexions Personal Advisors and Excellence in Cities Learning Mentors operate less directly and work at changing the individual. We argue that what was crucial to young people's views of these different approaches was how far they viewed them as coercive and/or pathologising.

The context for our exploration is the contemporary heightened focus on the self and individual identity. Within this, subjects are seen as free to construct their personal 'choice biography' (Giddens, 1992, see Chapter 5). However, this self-making is not in conditions of our own choosing (Epstein and Johnson, 1998). Neoliberalism demands a particular type of self fit for the 'knowledge economy' – autonomous, flexible, enterprising and self-managing (Rose, 1999; Skeggs, 2004; Walkerdine et al., 2001). Individuals are expected to be or become this type of self. However, the specificity of this 'normative selfhood' is not acknowledged and so the failure to enact it is understood as the outcome of individual pathology (Allen, 2008; Lawler, 2005). Since this position is a middle-class one (Skeggs, 2004), policies directed at social inclusion are built on a deficit model of the 'socially excluded', constructing the root of the problem as within these individuals rather than as a function of the system itself (Colley and Hodkinson, 2001; Gewirtz, 2001; Whitty, 2001). In particular, 'targeted', including means-tested, interventions – as opposed to universal ones – inevitably stigmatise (Bauman, 1998). EMA and Connexions were resisted by the young people we spoke to both on these grounds and as overly directive. In contrast, Learning Mentors attracted very little resistance. However, we suggest that this latter approach is ambiguous: it furnishes students with valuable 'psychological capital' but also represents an extension of governmental power, as it re-makes working-class young people in the middle-class model of the neoliberal reflexive, individualised self.

Education Maintenance Allowance: 'bribing' the self

The Education Maintenance Allowance (EMA) started as a pilot initiative proposed in the SEU (1999) report *Bridging the Gap*. At the time of our study the scheme was being piloted and offered means-tested payments to young people who stayed on in post-16 education and training. It paid a weekly allowance, a termly retention bonus and an achievement bonus. A quantitative review conducted for the DfEE of the EMA's first year demonstrated that it 'appears to have raised participation in education' by around five percentage points (Ashworth et al., 2001: 1); and qualitative research suggested that the scheme impacted positively on participants' application and enthusiasm towards their course (Legard et al., 2001). However, this research evaluating the EMA used a broad cross-section of young people (for example, Ashworth et al., 2001; Legard et al., 2001; Maguire et al., 2001), the majority of whom were already planning to stay on. In contrast, our research, which focused on the 'at risk' group for whom the EMA was designed, produced very different findings. Most of these 'at risk' young people held strong negative views on the EMA, uniformly critiquing its application to them. They were concerned that it was 'basically bribing kids to stay on at school' (Nikolas, Littleton discussion group) and, although sold as an opportunity to earn while you learn (http:// ema.direct.gov.uk/), they did not see it that way. We read these objections as tied to their negotiations around 'respectability' (see Chapters 2 and 4), i.e. their desire to be seen as responsible and decent adults.

EMA was seen as a good idea for those who wanted to stay in education but not for 'people like us' who are part of the 'army of reluctant conscripts to post-compulsory education' (Furlong and Cartmel, 1997: 17). Mark (Hillside Park) described the EMA as 'rubbish . . . Cos if you're going to stay on at college, you shouldn't do it for the money . . . if they want the money they'll just stay on and just mess about and just wait for the money'. Similarly Lacie (Riverway) suggested: 'People that want to stay wouldn't really bother about the money but people that wouldn't normally want to stay on might just stay on just to get the money and not learn any more.' Jane (Hillside Park) supported this: 'if they're doing it just for the money, in the end, their hearts are not going to be in what they get out of it'.

We would argue that the EMA could be constructed as bribery by these young people because they positioned this payment differently to wage earnings. Since EMA is paid by the government it aligns with benefits and state dependency. There are longstanding discourses that locate unearned income with the 'undeserving poor' (Bauman, 1998) and so as incompatible with working-class 'respectability'. As we discussed in Chapter 4, many young men constructed learning in opposition to earning and sought to produce themselves as responsible and respectable through bringing home a 'decent wage'. These sentiments were also evident in conversations with young men and women about the EMA, where they objected to being paid by the government to stay in school, preferring to earn money for themselves. For example, Lee clearly rationalised:

> If you leave school, go into a job, they're going to pay you more money than £30 . . . I think people who like school would definitely stay on because like they are getting money for coming to school. But I think for bad people you are going to have to give them loads more money to stay on. . . . What is the point in saying well if you are getting like £30 a week or something and you could go and get a job that pays you like £100 a week or something?
>
> (Lee, Riverway)

Similarly Kay (Blackwell Street) connected being given money for staying in school to notions of dependency and hence viewed it as less attractive than being able to earn her own money independently. She told us: 'I don't really know what other people think but if someone was to pay me to stay in school I would say "no". I wouldn't want money to stay in school because I would want to earn it myself, if you know what I mean?' They rejected the 'charity' approach which, following Thomson (2007), we can read as 'extending dependency'. Ironically the EMA is pushing them into a dependent position despite broader demands to produce a neoliberal, autonomous, agentic and entrepreneurial self. Thus in these terms, young people who need the EMA are positioned as failing to become entrepreneurial selves. This positioning also makes their objections understandable.

However, the EMA was not uniformly resisted. Like many of the other young people, David (Hillside Park) derided the EMA as a 'bribe' in his first interview. However, in his third interview both he and his friend Harry emphasised that they would not have done their college courses (Entry to Employment) if they had not received a financial payment: 'If we never got paid I would tell them to stick their course up their backside. . . . But because we get paid, I am alright with it'. In David and Harry's case, the EMA was viewed positively and as a successful motivating factor for their post-16 participation. Indeed, David could not help smiling as he described his course as 'two years with money'. David explained its utility as the fact that 'it pays for things' and we would argue that there is a strong case to be made in favour of providing sufficient financial support to enable working-class young people to be able to 'afford' to continue in post-compulsory education (see Archer et al., 2003). The issue we have is in what form, and on what grounds, this support is provided.

EMA has now moved beyond the pilot phase, it has been deemed a success and is available nationally. A means-tested payment gives young people up to £30 a week. However, this is no longer simply a grant and bonuses. If attendance falls below certain levels, support is withdrawn. Thus, this initiative now bears the brunt of the 'rights and responsibilities' agenda (http://www.fabians.org.uk/events/speeches/ed-balls-progressive-full-text). Rights, in this case to income, are contingent on the production of a responsibilised self, in this case monitored through attendance. Even if payment is withdrawn, the proposal to raise the compulsory education age (by 2013) to 18 has been confirmed, so participation will be enforced by law and the young person will still have to remain in education or training (HM Government, 2009). This 'rights and responsibilities' approach is also evident in the 'Activity Agreements' that the government are currently piloting via Connexions PAs. NEET young people and their PAs sign agreements identifying the specific steps the young person should take to 'return to participation' and their weekly allowance is contingent on their fulfilling this agreement (HM Government, 2009: 66). Thus, support blurs into compulsion. This tension between choice and coercion was already evident in the Connexions service when we carried out our research.

The Connexions service: monitoring the self

The Connexions service was proposed in the 1999 White Paper *Learning to Succeed* (DfEE, 1999) to replace the previous Careers Service. The vision of the new service was to be *more than* the Careers Service: a one-stop-shop providing broad advice to 13- to 19-year-olds on education, training, employment, health and leisure *and* targeted one-to-one support for those designated as 'at risk', delivered through Personal Advisors (PAs). Thus the Connexions service has contradictory aims, being simultaneously universal and targeted. We would argue that the targeted service is primary since Connexions had its roots in the SEU's (1999) report which flagged up the 'problem' of 'disengaged' and 'disadvantaged' young people and their potential for social exclusion. Thus, the vision of creating a universal Connexions service for all young people appears to have been compromised by the overriding concern with 'social exclusion' – namely getting disengaged youth into the labour market, or at least on track to it (Ainley et al., 2002; Watts, 2001).

This tension was apparent in these young people's experiences. The ones who supported the principle of Widening Participation (WP) were those – mainly girls – who were already invested in going to university. For example, Nadira (Eastleigh Central) said 'I think it's a good idea because I've always wanted to go to university.' However, for the majority who never intended to enter HE, presentations, activities and excursions by Connexions and other WP initiatives (such as, videos about Oxbridge and summer courses at local universities) at best washed over them, and at worst, added to their sense of alienation and marginalisation. However, more controversial (and potentially more marginalising) than these universal aspects of Connexions, was the one-to-one targeted approach allocating PAs to those 'at risk'. As Robert (Eastleigh Central) put it: 'I just don't like them kind of things . . . they talk to you as if . . . you're not like everyone else, you need extra help or whatever'. This approach was met with resistance on similar grounds to the EMA discussed above – many young people disliked feeling compelled to 'choose' education, and wanted to make their own choices and 'do it on their own'.

Indeed, a few young people complained that Connexions, despite being sold as a holistic advice service, was too educationally directive and that PAs only focus on funnelling young people into further and higher education. As Bob (Riverway) put it, 'college courses are normally mentioned. That's just it really, just college courses'. While many students enjoyed positive relations with their PAs, a few experienced negative relations for this reason. Jason (Littleton), for instance, said that the PAs he had seen 'don't really help, they wind me up . . . everything I wanted to do they put me off doing that. So I got sort of, I stopped speaking to them after a while'. This frustration seemed to stem from students feeling that advisors were not listening to – or did not agree with – what they wanted to do and were more concerned to push an agenda. Jason wanted to do an apprenticeship but was advised against it by Connexions. They told him that the courses were over-subscribed and convinced him, instead, to stay on in the sixth form and do A-levels. Thus some felt that their choices were not valued and were 'wrong'. Colley (2003, citing Jeffs and Spence, 2000) argues that engagement mentoring, as it is currently formulated, poses the need for young people to re-invent themselves because they are 'the wrong sort of people, living in the wrong places, displaying the wrong attitudes'. These young people felt that the Connexions agenda was often not in their own interests, but for government gain. For example, Robert described

WP as a way to ensure that there are more people working 'for the government . . . in offices'.

Young people and PAs are operating in an increasingly choice driven, marketised society. Yet WP, and particularly the 50 per cent HE target, contradicts this idea of 'free choice'. It is choice, but only within a narrowly defined preset realm – that is, choice of some form of post-compulsory education. If the young person wants to get a job then this is increasingly not a choice that is available or encouraged (see Chapter 4). Indeed, following the decision to raise the compulsory education age, the government have introduced 'The September Guarantee'. This is the offer of a suitable place in learning for all young people completing compulsory education. Now, the 'choice' to choose education, really is just a matter of deciding *which* course. While we are increasingly positioned as 'free to choose', young people are in fact 'obliged to be free, to understand and enact their lives in terms of choice' (Rose, 1999: 87). We are not arguing that encouraging young people to stay on in education is necessarily a bad thing but that it is being resisted by some because of the narrowness of their possible 'choices'.

Further, Connexions constructs 'at risk' young people as dependent on others by positioning them as in need of help from PAs to make the 'correct' choices. This was rejected by our participants for similar reasons to dependence on the EMA, as young people wanted to earn for themselves, make their own choices and do it on their own. Latoya's outburst is a lively illustration of this resistance to being coerced into staying on in education. She explains how if she chose her own college course she would probably stay on and enjoy it, but if it was someone else's decision, she would not: 'If I picked it, if they didn't pick it, if I picked it and I liked it then I would stay on. But if they picked it and I didn't really like it then I won't really probably enjoy it because they picked it and I never had no choice in picking.' Although she is talking about choice of college course, this sentiment also arose around careers advice. There was a clear sense that young people wanted to make it by themselves without state-provided assistance. As discussed above, forgoing dependence in favour of 'doing it on your own' can be read as part of the young people's production of themselves as respectable (and as adept neoliberal 'choosers'). Because of Connexions' role in helping the disadvantaged, it was avoided. Mark (Littleton) said he could not be 'bothered' to seek careers advice, claiming 'I'll get my own job.' Similarly Jordan (Blackwell Street) argued: 'I'm just happy sitting back doing what I've got to do to see if I can get there myself without any help.'

As in Chapter 6, we want to emphasise that we are not blaming Connexions staff for these outcomes. Like teachers and young people, PAs are acted upon by policy. All are operating in an increasingly marketised society in which targets and performance are monitored. Thus Connexions PAs cannot be impartial advisors but are functioning within this neoliberal agenda, which focuses on employability and constructs education as central to our national competitiveness.

[E]ducation and learning have become the means, par excellence, of achieving a range of governmental objectives by aligning outcomes for the nation in a global economy ('national competitiveness'), goals for the domain of the social ('social cohesion') with the desires and aspirations of individual subjects ('creativity' and 'personal prosperity', for example). Implicit in this configuration is the 'responsible citizen', maximising their own human capital in constructing a viable and rational identity that incorporates ambition and aspiration as principal elements of self.

(Bradford and Hey, 2007: 597)

All educational institutions are under pressure to produce such citizens.

Recent policy shifts have acknowledged that, as our own and other early research showed, Connexions does indeed lack the capacity to deliver both targeted support and broader universal careers education (Ainley et al., 2002; Garrett, 2002; Watts, 2001). The recent review by The Panel for Fair Access on the Professions (2009: 74), concluded: 'that its focus on the minority of vulnerable young people is distracting it from offering proper careers advice and guidance to the majority of young people'. The panel recommended transforming careers advice in schools and colleges, by abolishing the careers advice function of the Connexions service and replacing it with a dedicated careers advisory service that starts from primary age, leaving Connexions as a residual specialist service focusing on 'at risk' and NEET young people. The government have taken this up and legislated for schools to provide impartial careers advice (HM Government, 2009). We welcome the move to the provision of impartial guidance but feel that issues remain around stigmatisation. Connexions looks set to remain for the marginalised few who are constructed as incapable of exercising the burden of freedom and need to be coerced to make the 'right' choices.

Having argued this, it is important to note that some of the young people we spoke to did have positive relationships with their PAs. For example, Darren, James and Max (all at Littleton) and David (Hillside Park) all described such relationships. David felt that his PA had been pivotal in 'getting me back into school' following an earlier exclusion. He continued to see his PA regularly, who was helpful again when he left school, securing him an EMA and a college place: 'If it wasn't for them [Connexions] I wouldn't have gone back to school and I wouldn't be at college.' As we saw in the last section, the EMA was critical to his decision to continue in education. However, his case is not unproblematic for he was, in some senses, a 'reluctant conscript' (Furlong and Cartmel, 1997: 17) to FE. In general, as we explore in detail in the next section, we found that mentoring relationships were more likely to be experienced as positive when there was less direct coercion involved.

Learning Mentors: re-making the self

With its roots in the US, youth mentoring has expanded rapidly in the UK becoming 'a central ingredient of almost every UK policy initiative for social inclusion since the Labour party were elected in 1997' (Colley, 2003: 2). While Connexions PAs are one form of mentoring, we have shown that their regulatory agenda was off-putting to many. In contrast, Learning Mentors, who were introduced into schools under the Excellence in Cities initiative to address underachievement and disengagement in urban areas, are less economically oriented and the young people spoke about them far more positively. In this section we look at what they got from these relationships. We argue that while providing valuable 'psychological capital' (Bradford and Hey, 2007), mentoring can be seen as part of a wider 'therapeutic turn' (Ecclestone and Hayes, 2009). And that this is part of a broader process of 'remaking selves' that happens not just in institutional settings but also within popular culture (Ouellete and Hay, 2008; Skeggs and Wood, 2008, see also the discussion of Analisa in Chapter 4), remaking young people into the 'good learner' and engaged student.

> Psychological capital is conceptualised here as an additional resource related to, but not identical with, cultural or social capital . . . It is constituted in practices of self-esteem, confidence and self-belief which are generated in a range of settings (the family, communities of various types, friendships and formal institutional settings like schools and youth projects) and can be transformed into resilience and the dispositions needed to cope with the exigencies of contemporary life . . . Yet there is a paradox here. By fostering psychological capital the potential reach of governmental power is also extended by increasing the capacity (and, potentially, desire) of the subject to work on self under the specific tutelage of the authority of success discourses.
>
> (Bradford and Hey, 2007: 600)

Young people who are identified as 'at risk' of disengaging from education are worked on to become reflexive and self-regulating, to control their aversions to learning. They are being engineered into the 'correct' way of being and doing – to become the agentic, enterprising self who values and pursues education and the professional and economic success it supposedly inevitably brings.

Thirteen of the young people that we interviewed had regular contact with a Learning Mentor. Most were very happy about the relationship. Charlene, Kemisha and Jade (all at Cowick), Jordan (Blackwell Street) and Tim and Ben (both at Hillside Park) all reported that they found seeing a Learning Mentor positive and useful. As we discussed in Chapter 6, teacher-student relationships were important to the young people in this study. When young people felt safe, respected, cared about and understood this had a positive impact on their engagement with education and enjoyment in school. This emotional dimension was also a factor in young people's relationships with their Learning Mentors. Tim (Hillside Park) recounted: 'She just makes me laugh and makes me feel good. She helps me with my work, she gives me advice.' Not only did Tim's mentor help him with his school work, but she also made him 'feel good'.

Charlene (Cowick), who speaks English as an Additional Language, initially discussed seeing her mentor three or four times a week. She was supported, not only with language, but by helping her deal with bullying and teasing. Charlene told us, through this experience 'I became more confident . . . I was very quiet and she brought me out and made me stronger'. Charlene's relationship with her mentor was clearly helpful in getting her through a difficult period of her life and adjusting to school. While, at the time of the interview,

Charlene did not have another mentor, she felt comfortable with this, because her previous mentor had equipped her to deal with problems: 'she has done what she had to do, and said what she had to say, and now it's on me'. Her mentoring experience was transformative and equipped her to take responsibility for her own educational success.

Jade (Blackwell Street) described how her Learning Mentor helped her to address her truancy and to gain a new perspective on her life and social relations, she told us how her mentor 'made [her] understand more'. Like other young people, Jade valued the interpersonal relationship that her mentor had generated with her, and which underpinned the success of their work together: 'I think she's really nice and she's funny . . . She knows what to say, like she says all the right things. There's nothing that she's ever said wrong and she gives good advice.' Jordan (Blackwell Street) was similarly highly positive about her Learning Mentor and his pastoral skills, and described working with him to try and catch up on her work: 'He could be having the worst day of his life and he'd still have time to sit there and listen, so. I'm not a very good one with coping with problems. I storm up to [the learning support centre] and tell [my mentor] and he sits me down and calms me down and tells me "it'll be all right, it'll be all right, we'll sort it out".'

Clearly Tim, Charlene, Jade and Jordan gained a lot from these mentoring relationships. Several authors have highlighted how in policy documents mentors are imbued with particular qualities, seen as 'social entrepreneurs' (Ainley et al., 2002) and 'people changers' possessing 'personal charisma' (Jordan, 2000, cited in Garrett, 2002: 605) and 'inspirational qualities' (Garrett, 2002: 604). These qualities are reminiscent of those ascribed to Teach First teachers in urban schools, as discussed in Chapter 6. There we argued that what the young people in our research wanted from their relationships with educational professionals was not inspiration but reciprocity. In our data, good mentors or personal advisors were seen by school staff as people who could 'relate' to young people. In the young people's words, they are 'nice' and 'funny', make you 'laugh' and 'feel good', always 'listen' and 'say all the right things'.

Although Learning Mentors clearly supported young people's educational engagement, we can also detect evidence of the language of 'therapy'. Mentors are 'helping' and 'advising' young people on 'coping' with problems, 'calming' them, giving them 'confidence', and making them 'stronger' and 'feel good'. The rise of mentoring in educational settings where the mentor is placed in a pseudo-therapeutic role and is charged with 'supporting' and 'caring' for 'vulnerable' young people can be seen as part of a wider therapeutic turn. Within this there is an increasing erosion of the boundary between public and private, and a preoccupation with emotional well-being, self-esteem and self-help (Ecclestone and Hayes, 2009; Furedi, 2004). This therapeutic approach is a particular way of narrating or 'telling' the self (Skeggs, 2004), which cultivates the neoliberal, reflexive subject. Mentors are helping young people to regulate the self in an individualised way. Through the mentoring relationship, Jade is able to understand more about herself and her relationships, Charlene takes her mentor's advice and then works on her self ('now it's on me'), and Jordan's mentor helps her to control her unruly behaviour. All these modifications and self-regulation feed into becoming a 'good student'. They support the development of the forms of psychological capital that are valued in the field of the school.

Rose's (1999) work on the governance of the self is useful here. He argues that, in the reformation of welfare provision, we see a new role for the subject to regulate and manage their own conduct. In particular, certain self-governing traits – including, agency, self-responsibility and entrepreneurship – are positioned as normative. Thus subjects come to regulate themselves in the 'correct' way, namely through participation in education and employment. This operates within a wider context of an increasing 'normalisation' of middle-class lifestyles values and attitudes (Allen, 2008): a moral project in which the self has to show itself to be proper and good, as an object to be worked on:

> [O]ne of the main processes by which the 'subject of value' can be distinguished from its constitutive limit is via the amount of labour that is made evident in its making. As a moral imperative people have to show that they are working on their own development, establishing value in their own subjectivity, extending their cultural exchange value.
>
> (Skeggs et al., 2007: 3)

One way of accruing value in the person is through investment in education. Following Skeggs, this is a middle-class mode of production of subjectivity. Those young people 'disengaged' from education, on the other hand, are depicted as not investing in the 'self', by resisting formal education.

The way in which both the problem and the solution is framed at the level of the individual (and even individual psychology) works to hide the structural relations and inequalities that play a role in both producing the young people in these unequal positions and in keeping them there (Allen, 2008). Eccelestone (2007) and Furedi (2004) make this point directly in relation to the current obsession with self-esteem, and more specifically how contemporary policies cite 'low self-esteem' and 'low aspirations' as major contributing factors to a raft of 'social problems' from unemployment, to disengagement from education (Colley and Hodkinson, 2001, 2004; Kenway and Willis, 1990). Thus, structural causes of poverty and inequality 'are frequently recast as individual ones that have no direct connection to the social realm' (Furedi, 2004: 25). We would therefore argue that there is a problem with the lack of attention to these structural causes within mentoring.

We can see that these young people clearly valued their mentoring relationships and we are not saying that they are undeserving of support. However, what we want to highlight is the pathologisation that follows from both the remedial focus and the suggestion that the self needs fixing (see also Chapter 5 in relation to aspirations). For many minority ethnic and working-class groups, their experiences of the formal education system are ones of alienation and hostility, and characterised by feelings of 'not being good enough' (Archer and Yamashita, 2003b; Gillborn and Youdell, 2000; Reay, 2001b; Willis, 1977). Constructing policies which are premised on changing people, without changing the system that generates these feelings of rejection and aversion, will be unsuccessful.

Only one young person showed any resistance to learning mentoring. Yesim (Eastleigh Central) lamented:

> Well basically you used to go to a mentor once or twice a week and speak to her about what you do in school. How would you develop your work ... and things like that. If you're late, why are you late? How can you resolve this? ... I don't really find that useful ... they're like 'why are you late to school?' It's because you woke up late or you couldn't catch a bus or if there was traffic, whatever. But they can't stop that can they?

Yesim's response expresses her irritation at the intense level of personal analysis (or perhaps even indulgence) that mentoring applies to what she saw as practical issues (missing the bus, getting stuck in traffic, and so on). However, as noted in Chapter 6, Yesim enjoyed a very close relationship with one of her teachers (who she saw as a 'mother' figure), and hence may not have needed another mentor-nurture relationship. In Yesim's reaction we can see that the individualised, therapeutic focus on work on the self can generate resistance. This can perhaps be seen, following Garrett (2002, citing Ennew, 1994), as resistance to the 'curricularisation' of the lives of young people – the extensive regulation of their private lives.

As we have seen, and in contrast to the more obviously coercive measures of EMA and Connexions PAs, Learning Mentors were very difficult to resist. We would suggest that this is because of the way that power works through them. As Foucault (1980: 119) writes:

> If power were never anything but repressive, if it never did anything but to say no, do you really think one would be brought to obey it? What makes power hold good, what makes it accepted, is simply the fact that it doesn't only weigh on us as a force that says no, but traverses and produces things, it induces pleasure, forms knowledge, produces discourse. It needs to be considered as a productive network which runs through the whole social body, much more than as a negative instance whose function is repression.

Through mentoring young people do get the skills needed to be valued in schools and recognised by others as 'good' students. They thus get feelings of pleasure and success from this. This is both helpful and insidious. It teaches young people the rules of the game but without making them aware that it is a game, even presenting the game as 'just the way it is'.

Since our research, mentoring for WP has continued to be rolled out and is further endorsed in the *New Opportunities* white paper (HM Government, 2009). The Aim Higher scheme is continuing – identifying young people from low income backgrounds even earlier, ensuring they receive a package of structured assistance across school, within which 'every such child should benefit from regular mentoring' (HM Government, 2009). It appears that the therapeutic approach to re-making 'such' selves is still deemed a successful policy strategy.

Learning Mentors, like EMA and Connexions, work at the level of the individual. Granted, there are some structural and systemic changes now being implemented. As we are writing this book, the new 14–19 diploma, as proposed in the Education and Skills white paper (DfES, 2005a), is being rolled out in England. This involves the option for young people to specialise in one (predominantly vocational) subject area combining theory and practice. In addition, the government claims to have 'rescued' apprenticeships, raising the number available to a quarter of a million, legislating, so that every 'suitably qualified' young person will have the right to an apprenticeship (HM Government, 2009: 58). We welcome the focus in these policies on changing the system, not changing individuals to fit the existing structures. However, the expression 'suitably qualified' suggests that young people will still need to have some educational credentials to access apprenticeships, which were once a route into professions for those *without* educational qualifications.

We are also concerned that these initiatives assume that people need lifelong learning – in other words, training and education for economic productivity. It is unclear whether the government's obsession with credentialising young people is indeed a necessity of the new 'knowledge economy' or how much it is driven by a socialising agenda (to 'civilise' the working classes) underpinned by a middle-class bias towards 'the professions' (with the assumption that more and higher education is always better). A study commissioned by the DCSF to '*understand* young people in jobs without training (JWT)' was designed to inform methods of 'encouraging 16 and 17 year olds in JWT into accredited learning' (www.dcsf.gov.uk/rsgateway/DB/RRP/u014612/index-.shtml). There is a huge assumption here that young people in JWT need and would prefer formal education and credentialised training, to a more informal development of skills. These young people are not in the problematic NEET category: 'at risk' of unemployment, welfare dependency and social exclusion; they have managed to secure a job, a job that inevitably needs doing. Yet the government is still investigating ways to steer them into more structured education, of which, like many of the young people in *our* research, they may well have had previous negative experiences (Quinn et al., 2008). This approach by the government appears over-meddlesome to say the least, and is tied to the obsession with measurable outcomes (see Chapter 6). It also fails to recognise that being in a job without training and being NEET are not permanent states (Quinn et al., 2008) and that 'good' education and development can be provided in less formalised ways. We would thus recommend the decoupling of advice and guidance from employability.

We acknowledge that there is a tricky line to be trodden here between choice, guidance, support and compulsion. Choice and autonomy are, of course, important (as Jane, Hillside Park, said: 'I think people's lives, people's education ... should be up to them') and we have argued that working-class values and choices are often devalued and derided by dominant society and that this inequality demands attention. However, we also believe that the pervasive neoliberal market in education is pernicious and works to structurally disadvantage working-class young people and their families through the technology of 'choice'. In this respect, we advocate measures that will change the conditions and structural relations within which young people make their choices, and that aspects of this may involve the provision of support and guidance (for example, distributing cultural, social and financial capitals more equitably across social groups). However, we argue that this should be provided in ways that meet and value a range of interests, not solely those of government and dominant societal groups.

Summary

In this chapter we have explored 'at risk' young people's opinions on key policy initiatives designed to increase their educational participation and engagement. We are not saying that encouraging young people to stay on in education is a bad thing, rather we have argued that the overt prioritisation of education for employability (over other motivations) is problematic and is often met with considerable resistance. We have demonstrated that 'at risk' young people frequently reject incentive approaches, such as EMA, and the Connexions service's attempts at monitoring and engineering their subjectivities. Learning Mentors were viewed more positively by the young people because their approach was felt to be more responsive and less coercive. However, such approaches are concerned with remaking the self and the transformations involved are not unproblematic as they often normalise particular dominant (gendered, classed and racialised) identities and practices as the 'right' ways of being.

8

CONCLUSIONS

At a Korean-run takeaway in West Baltimore, four 14-year-old African-American boys – Namond, Dukie, Randy and Michael – get ready to place an order. Namond is treating his friends using money he has earned through his new career as a drug dealer. When Dukie orders 'yakame with turkey grease', Namond and Michael start laughing. Dukie wants to know what they find funny as this is his mother's regular order. Namond exclaims, 'yo, you was really one of them at risk children, you know that, Dukie'. Michael gently explains that turkey grease 'makes the drunks, you know, throw up all that liquor they was drinkin' so they can get back to swilling that shit'.

(Burns, 2007)

In this scene from US urban drama *The Wire*, we can see something of the way that the 'at risk' label works. The young people – who all attend the same 'poor performing' school – use it ironically to make distinctions between themselves. Namond who jokingly labels Dukie 'at risk' is himself regularly excluded from school and one of a group of eight highly disruptive pupils who have been withdrawn from their regular classes and placed on a special curriculum designed to 'socialise' them. Michael, who explains to Dukie the strangeness of his food order, like Dukie himself, lives with a drug addict mother and is the main carer for his younger half-brother. We can see in this usage how the term 'at risk' draws together a collection of linked factors – educational failure, poor diet and health, economic deprivation, inadequate housing, irresponsible parenting, addiction, and so on. In this realist drama, fact and fiction blur to create an image of the 'at risk teen' that pre-exists those who become so labelled and 'imposes certain limitations upon the sort of social identity that may be negotiated by [them]' (Ball, 1981: 36–7). The term has immense productive power and its occurrence in the everyday talk of these young men indicates something of its currency.

It is because of this widespread usage that we adopted 'at risk' in this book, in the hope of intervening in the debates that circulate around it within educational research, policy and practice. But, we also chose to enclose it in inverted commas. This was to draw attention to its problematic and contested status. As in the scene from *The Wire*, the term is used to make distinctions and to 'other' those to whom it is attached. It positions their perspectives as outside the normal, on the margins, lesser. We have sought to challenge this by putting the views of 'at risk' students at the centre of this book. These young people:

> with no institutionalized 'other' that [they] may discriminate against, exploit, or oppress often have a lived experience that directly challenges the prevailing classist, sexist, racist social structure and its concomitant ideology. This lived experience may shape [their] consciousness in such a way that [their] world view differs from those who have a degree of privilege (however relative within the existing system).
>
> (hooks, 1984: 15)

We attempted to make sense of the young people's lived experiences in relation to two overarching questions:

• How can we understand the identities and educational engagement of urban, working-class London youth?
• What are the powers and possibilities of schooling and broader educational policies in these processes?

In this book we have argued that these questions are inextricably linked; how we understand the categories of 'working class', 'urban education', 'at risk' and so on, is, in part, through the discourses about them that circulate within policy, and within the broader social discourses from which policy draws. In this final chapter we draw together our key ideas under four overarching themes: responsibility, respect, difference and the urban. We also suggest some ideas for change. Schools and allied services cannot be expected to 'magic away' inequality. But the evidence suggests that schooling and education policy can not only play a role in fostering or exacerbating disengagement and non-progression, but can actually make an important difference in struggling against it.

Responsibility

Working-class children and young people in urban areas are inflected with a dual disadvantage. In the UK, on average, children in state schools in urban areas perform less well in national examinations, and accordingly these schools feature at the bottom end of government school 'league tables'. Fewer than average urban young people progress into post-16 education, including university. Obviously lower working-class post-compulsory education progression rates do matter: they impact on life chances and we see a value in trying to widen participation in the sense of making access more equitable. However, we have argued that the issue at stake is how useful and just it is to frame the problem as predominantly one of the bad choices, 'wrong' values and poor parenting practices of the working classes rather than seeing it as a more complex product of people's experiences of living subordination and multiple forms of inequality (including inequalities in the type, form and cost of HE that is accessible to different social groups, see Archer et al., 2003). Thus, the important questions here concern where we locate responsibility and what action we take as a result.

In Chapter 5 we looked at this in relation to aspirations. We argued that the problem is created not by some people having sufficiently lofty aspirations and others suffering from a poverty of aspirations, but by how aspirations are valued. The middle-class routes of university and professional careers are valued within dominant discourses as appropriate life goals. This leads, as we discussed in Chapter 7, to interventions that attempt not just to remake young people's inappropriate aspirations, but to remake their self, after the middle-class model. They are impelled to take up the opportunity to become the kind of self that aspires to the 'right' things in life, and must assume responsibility for any failure to do so. We argued that a range of counselling, mentoring and other pseudo-therapeutic approaches attempt to enact this re-engineering. These are useful to many students, giving them access to the 'psychological capital' – self-esteem, confidence and reflexivity – that 'can be transformed into resilience and the dispositions needed to cope with the exigencies of contemporary life' (Bradford and Hey, 2007: 600). However, such interventions do this by normalising classed, gendered and racialised ideas of the successful subject – 'one that calculates about itself and works upon itself in order to better itself' (du Gay, 1996: 124) – without critical reflection. Thus, the social structures and inequalities that create the need for, and form of, this mode of re-engineering are disappeared. Such approaches draw on and contribute to contemporary processes of individualisation whereby failure is rendered the fault of (or within) the individual: 'the price of being "offered" autonomy is accepting responsibility for exercising it in particular ways and for the outcomes its exercise produces. This means that individuals are more personally exposed to the costs of engaging in any activity and more dependent on their own resources for successfully carrying it out' (du Gay, 1996: 183). If people are expected to be more dependent on their own resources, then those with fewer resources – economic, cultural, social, psychological and symbolic – are more likely to fail. This failure is then read as a personal failure, as the inability to be a suitably calculating, self-actualising, aspiring individual.

We would suggest that rather than trying to impose White middle-class selfhood upon urban youth, policy interventions to 'raise' aspirations should take seriously the ways that urban young people make decisions about their future: in particular their 'wait and see' strategies and their reliance on 'hot knowledge' that we identified in Chapter 5. Support might address the 'wait and see' approach to educational decision-making by enabling young people to develop a range of options (including non-stereotypical routes) – so they know there are back-ups in place and are clear about these – and encouraging them to make early applications to colleges to help them to access their preferred course/institution.

Schools can foster 'hot knowledge' by inviting older siblings or other young people from the local area and/or of similar backgrounds to talk to small groups of students about their post-16 experiences of (the difficulty of) finding work and the requirements for securing apprenticeships and training. This introduces young people to a wide range of possibilities that are perceived by them as real and achievable by people who they see as 'like us' and who have successfully, and unsuccessfully, followed different routes. As part of this, young people should be opened up to the possibility of non-stereotypical aspirations. Alongside career guidance, work placement opportunities can be productive in this respect. Yet strong concerns are being expressed that the government is failing to do enough on this front. The Equality and Human Rights Commission (2008) argues in particular that recent DCSF guidelines on work-related training make no reference to the importance of challenging stereotypes through the offer of non-traditional placements.

At the level of national policy, we would support calls for shifting responsibility away from punitive modes of regulation and towards more productive and constructive forms of engagement. Responding in a parliamentary briefing to the Education and Skills Bill, the Equality and Human Rights Commission (2008: 3) argues that:

> [A] requirement to engage with additional education and training can only unlock potential if it adequately identifies and addresses the reasons for disengagement and underachievement. Therefore the focus of the Bill needs to shift from the process of compulsion and penalties to improving the substance, quality and equality of the post-16 offer.

Respect

The processes summarised above – whereby responsibility for social inequalities is placed on the individuals who suffer from them – create a society in which it is difficult for young people, like those in this book, to gain respect for their choices, aspirations and selves. This structural lack of respect feeds into personal and social concerns about respectability:

> Respectability is one of the most ubiquitous signifiers of class. It informs how we speak, who we speak to, how we classify others, what we study and how we know who we are (or are not). Respectability is usually the concern of those who are not seen to have it. It would not be of concern here, if the working classes (Black and White) had not consistently been classified as dangerous, polluting, threatening, revolutionary, pathological and without respect. It would not be something to desire, to prove and to achieve, if it had not been seen to be a property of 'others', those who were valued and legitimated.
>
> (Skeggs, 1997: 1)

As with responsibility, respect/ability normalises some and pathologises others, looming largest in the latter group's identity work. We explored urban working-class young people's desire for respect and their negotiations around respectability throughout the book, but particularly in Chapters 2, 4 and 6. In Chapter 2 we showed how the lack of respect within dominant discourses for urban locales, schools and selves fed into the young people's attempts to generate value through versions of style/appearance, the consumption of branded products and, in particular, to the construction of what we called 'Nike identities'. In Chapter 4, we argued that respectability took gendered forms and is evident in the young people's aspirations to perform gendered heterosexual roles as male responsible earner/provider and as female girlfriend/wife and mother/carer. Thus, many of the things which young people are chastised for within media and policy discourses – such as their attachment to consumer goods and their aspiration to manual labour or motherhood rather than education – can be understood as attempts to gain value and respectability in the absence of respect. This absence of respect can also be used to understand the White working-class racisms which we found in a few cases and discussed in Chapter 3.

Many of these strategies for gaining respectability, while important and useful to the young people in the communities where they live, can disadvantage them in the world beyond these communities. For example, we showed how such practices are implicated in making it less likely for young people to progress to post-compulsory education, especially university. In response, we would suggest that FE and HE need to be made economically viable and compatible with their consumer and wage-earner aspirations and their material needs. Participation in post-compulsory education and training needs to be made affordable and possible for all. We feel that universal services and benefits are the best way to avoid the stigmatisation that, as we showed in Chapter 7, led to resistance to means-tested measures and interventions targeted at those 'at risk'.

In Chapter 6, we suggested that one of the ways that teachers and schools can address these issues is through basing their pedagogy on relationships of respect between teachers and students. Contrary to current dominant policy discourses: 'Teaching is not simply the aggregation of effective techniques: it is a moral activity which integrates practical, cognitive, interpersonal, affective and intellectual aspects of the teacher and requires recognising those aspects of the learner too' (Povey, 1995: 264). This necessitates developing an approach where: teachers and students can get to know and trust each other; the things that young people know about and value from outside school are valued inside school (while also being treated critically); differences of social class, 'race'/ ethnicity and so on between students and between teachers and students are acknowledged as part of the classroom. The young people we spoke to suggested that even 'small' practical changes would make a difference to their lives. For example, schools could allow students to wear branded clothes and trainers as part of (or in place of) their uniform, have different kinds of food in the canteen and provide lockers so that they do not have to carry their books and equipment around all day. We are not suggesting that, for example, abolishing school uniform will magically transform students' educational engagement and achievement. Rather, the point we wish to make is that we feel it is important for all young people – but particularly those from the most stigmatised and disadvantaged backgrounds – to feel listened to and respected. Student consultation should be a mainstream, meaningful part of the running of all schools (see Arnot et al., 2004 for detailed discussion and practical suggestions for implementing change in this respect through from daily class-room practices to a whole school level). However, there are challenges for achieving this in light of punitive systems of assessment and overloaded authoritarian curricula, which need addressing at the national level (Harber and Sakade, 2009).

Difference

We have been arguing that urban young people's various ways of being should be seen as different rather than deficient and should be used to inform and contribute to policy and practice, rather than simply being the 'target'. We thus echo Gewirtz's (2001: 376–7) call for policymakers to 'develop decision-making structures and curricula which engage with and give voice to the diverse experiences and perspectives of working-class children and parents as well as their middle-class counterparts'.

We put forward an approach that tries to embrace difference rather than trying to contain it. Throughout the book, but perhaps particularly in Chapter 3, we have shown something of the complexity of urban young people's identities with their entangled positions of 'race'/ethnicity, social class, gender, sexuality, nationality, language, and so on. We indicated how attempts by educational policymakers and practitioners to capture this entanglement can lead to stereotyping. For, however diverse a range of categories of difference are involved, they are always limiting. We are not suggesting that we ignore or dismiss differences, for, as we also showed in Chapter 3, some differences do indeed make a difference – more Black than White students are permanently excluded from school each year; refugee children are more likely to struggle with the language, culture and hidden rules of schooling, and so on. But we need to find ways of working with these differences that do not fix people in these categories and that are attentive to the ways in which difference is tied to 'othering' in a mobile process that relates to broader political discourses (Said, 1995).

Conceptualisations of difference might, we suggest, be usefully broadened out beyond the popular binary (of same/different) to encompass emotional relations of difference. Brah's (1999) theorisation of *apna* ('ours'), *ajnabi* (a stranger who is not yet known but who holds the promise of connection) and *ghair* (a profound gulf of difference) can be useful in reconceptualising relations of difference. Currently we feel that urban young people tend to be positioned as *ghair* within much policy and popular discourse – as unknown, risky and dangerous/frightening 'others' who threaten society. Our hope in this book would be to facilitate a reappraisal and shift in such views, in which the young people might come to be recognised as *ajnabi*, or even *apna* and attributed a more complex humanity.

In Chapter 6 we looked at some of the problems that arise when learners get stuck in particular identities. We suggested that rather than categorise learners – as 'able' or 'unable', as 'practical' or 'academic' – we should have a relevant curriculum. This would be a curriculum which seeks not to reduce difference to binary categories but to work across a wide range of differences in linguistic, cultural and social experiences. If curriculum is understood as concerned with offering identifications (Britzman, 1995), we should look to breaking down the boundaries – making the academic practical by connecting it to young people's present and future lives and the practical academic by making available a wider range of vocational options.

In practical terms, this might mean finding new ways to connect with and value the ideas, knowledge and capabilities that such young people bring with them into schools. It would mean seeking opportunities for offering young people a clean slate rather than their having labels attached to them throughout their schooling. It might entail developing methods for supporting learners to move to more positive learner identities, perhaps by changing teachers, subjects and environments; increasing opportunities to succeed educationally; and ensuring support is sensitively handled in areas where young people are experiencing difficulties or have fallen behind. More fundamentally, however, our research suggests that the current dominant educational policy context espoused and fostered by neoliberalism is not working for everyone. As schools are increasingly pressured to become 'exam factories' operating on stretched resources, it is increasingly likely that the different needs of urban young people (such as those in this study) will go unmet.

Urban pasts, presents and futures

Ward (1990/1978), writing in the late 1970s in Britain, highlighted how the expression 'urban education' has always had connotations of deficit. More explicitly, Maguire and colleagues (2006: 11) highlight how underlying the term 'urban schools' is the assumption that such schools have always served the urban working class. Indeed, in the UK urban education has historical roots in the socialisation of the 'unruly mob' of city-dwelling working classes (see Hall, 1974). We have discussed how these ideas live on in contemporary popular cultural representations of urban youth and urban schools and in area-based policy initiatives designed to address urban problems. For instance, in Chapter 2 we saw how ideas of 'the street' and 'the estate' occupy an important role in the imaginations of students, parents and staff in urban schools.

However, much is changing in London. In 2012, the city will host the Olympic Games. Former Olympian and Chair of the London 2012 organising committee, Lord Sebastian Coe can be viewed on youtube promoting multicultural London, claiming that, with young people from 200 nations, the city's young people are more than just Londoners, 'they also represent the youth of the world'. The entangled ethnic identities that we discussed in Chapter 3 are being mobilised to sell London to the world. The Olympic dream is also being marketed as a major exercise in urban regeneration, with the Olympic Park being built on old brown field sites in the East End of London and a strong emphasis being placed on the Games' legacy.

While the approaching Olympic Games are being marketed as an exercise in hope and opportunity for urban youth, it was notable that the young people and parents in our study were generally more cautious about their futures. Feelings of anxiety about the future were palpable among both students and parents. Like the working-class women in Hebson's (2009) study, future job security was felt to be risky, rather than secure. Lee's mother was typical in this respect; she worried that in order to achieve his dreams, Lee will require resources and opportunities that are outside of her control. All she can do is love and support him as best she can: 'I don't know, I hope to God all his dreams come true: it would make my day for his dreams to come true. But he has just got to have the right person at the right time watching him for his dreams to come true. But if not, I will stick by him whatever he wants to do.'

At the time of completing this book, a change of government looks imminent. But we would suggest that, whichever political party gains power, the wider neoliberal context is likely to persist with its demand for the responsibilised self. Indeed, the power of neoliberalism lies in its globalising ability to transcend borders, party politics and contexts – it is an immense normalising presence that renders alternatives 'unthinkable'. For instance, despite the positioning of the Olympics as a collective London endeavour (we are all invoked, through the catch-phrase, to 'join in'), we are being impelled to work together *as individuals*. Indeed, the project is being marketed through the story of inspiring individuals, many of whom have transformed their disability and/or deprivation into success through aspiration, enterprise and determination. Likewise, it seems unlikely that any change of government will dramatically shift away from the 'personalisation' that litters current education policy approaches (Buckingham, 2007). The cult of the individual looks set to continue.

However, we want to emphasise that by critiquing the contemporary educational policy landscape, we are not supporting a return to the policies and practices of the past. There was no golden age. But, we would argue that discursive changes are important and we must pay attention to these changes: we need to ask what is gained, what is lost and by whom? 'If a particular ethical vocabulary is jettisoned in favour of (or simply redefined in terms of) another, then the world that vocabulary brought into being will no longer be available to us' (du Gay, 1996: 184). Within the ever-changing landscape of urban education, we want to ensure that the interests, voices and needs of those most 'at risk' do not get lost, ignored or overlooked. To this end, we hope that this book does justice to the young people, teachers and parents we interviewed.

GLOSSARY

A-level	Advanced-level: high status academic qualifications taken in England, Wales and Northern Ireland at age 18+ and the normal entry qualification for university.
ASBO	Anti-social behaviour order: ASBOs are court orders that can stop an offender going to a certain area or spending time with certain people. They can be issued to anyone over the age of 10.
Connexions	The Connexions service provides information, advice and support (including careers guidance) to young people aged 13 to 19 (and those aged up to 24 with a learning difficulty or disability), with a particular focus on supporting NEET and socially excluded young people. Local authorities are directly funded to deliver the service.
DCSF	Department for Children, Schools and Families: the name of the UK government department with responsibility for schooling 2007–present.
DfEE	Department for Education and Employment: the name of the UK government department with responsibility for schooling 1995–2001.
DfES	Department for Education and Skills: the name of the UK government department with responsibility for schooling 2001–2007.
EAL	English as an Additional Language: the current UK policy term for the learning of English by speakers of other languages.
EMA	Education Maintenance Allowance: a means-tested payment paid to young people participating in post-compulsory education.
FE	Further education: a generic term used in the UK for post-compulsory education other than that offered in universities.
FSM	Free school meals: those pupils attending school who are

	entitled to receive free school meals due to low family incomes and often used as a proxy measure for social class.
GCSE	General Certificate of Secondary Education: examination taken in England, Wales and Northern Ireland at age 16+ and the qualifications generally associated with the end of compulsory schooling.
G&T	Gifted and talented: government programme of educational activities available to those designated by their schools as 'gifted and talented'.
GNVQ	General National Vocational Qualifications: vocational qualifications offered in England and Wales between 2000 and 2007, available in a range of broad areas such as leisure and tourism and health and social care, and at three levels up to A-level equivalent.
HE	Higher education: generic term used in the UK for education undertaken at university.
IT	Information technology.
JWT	Jobs Without Training: term used for those, usually young people, in jobs with no training.
KS	Key Stage: compulsory education in the UK is organised into 4 Key Stages (KS1 – ages 5–7; KS2 – ages 7–11; KS3 – ages 11–14; KS4 – ages 14–16). Primary schooling covers Key Stages 1 and 2 and secondary schooling covers Key Stages 3 and 4.
LA	Local authority: unit of local government in the UK.
NEET	Not in education, employment or training: used in the UK for those aged 16–24.
PA	Personal advisor: Connexions staff member who provides one-to-one support to young people.
PRU	Pupil Referral Unit: a centre providing education for those aged under 16 who are judged as unable to participate in mainstream schooling.
SEN	Special educational needs: the current policy term for all pupils who have learning difficulties including behavioural problems, mental and physical disabilities.
SEU	Social Exclusion Unit: the dedicated cross-departmental government unit to tackle social exclusion, set up by the incoming New Labour government in 1997.
TDA	Training and Development Agency for Schools: overarching body responsible for the training and development of teachers and other school staff.
TF	Teach First: charity set up in 2002 to recruit 'top' graduates to teach in 'challenging' schools in London, which has since expanded to other urban areas.
WP	Widening Participation: generic term for the UK government goal both to increase the number of young people attending university and the proportion of university entrants from 'under-represented' groups.

APPENDIX 1: YOUNG PEOPLE INTERVIEWED

Table A.1

Pseudonym	Gender	Age	Self-defined ethnicity	School	Mother's occupation	Father's occupation
Amanda	female	15	N/A	Cowick	N/A	Absent
Analisa	female	16	Black African	Cowick	Unemployed	Unemployed
Babu	male	15	Bangladeshi	Riverway	Unemployed	Unemployed
Ben	male	15	UK White	Hillside Park	Office worker	Security guard
Bob	male	15	White English	Riverway	Receptionist	N/A
Bob	male	15	½ Mauritian, ½ English	Eastleigh Central	Hairdresser	Stepfather: N/A
Charlene	female	15	Zimbabwean/Black British	Cowick	Studying at college	Retired diplomat
Dan	male	15	English	Riverway	Cleaner	Driver
Darrel	male	14	Black Caribbean	Littleton	Absent	Carpenter
Darren	male	15	White British	Littleton	Supervisor of caretakers	Unemployed
David	male	15	Polish	Littleton	Unemployed	Packer
David	male	15	English	Hillside Park	Absent	Works in warehouse
Germaine	male	15	Black Caribbean	Blackwell Street	Hairdresser	Absent
Hapsa	female	14	Black African	Blackwell Street	Housewife	Deceased
Helal	male	N/A	Bangladeshi	Eastleigh Central	Not working	Not working
Jade	female	14	UK mixed race	Cowick	Unemployed	Driver
James	male	15	English mixed race	Littleton	Cleaner	Absent
Jane	female	14	White British	Hillside Park	Cook	Lorry driver
Janine	female	15	English	Hillside Park	Housewife	First flight courier
Jason	male	15	Ugandan (Black African)	Littleton	Grandmother: N/A	N/A
Jay	male	15	White UK	Riverway	Unemployed	N/A
Jermina	female	14	Black African	Blackwell Street	Factory worker	Stepfather: retired teacher
John	male	15	UK White	Littleton	Cleaner	Unemployed

Name	Gender	Age	Ethnicity	Area	Mother's occupation	Father's occupation
Jordan	female	15	White UK	Blackwell Street	Unemployed	Absent
Kay	female	14	UK White	Cowick	Grandmother: N/A	Grandfather: retired cook
Kemisha	female	14	Black UK (Caribbean)	Cowick	Unemployed	Stepfather: security guard
Kyle	female	15	English	Cowick	Unemployed	Unemployed
Lacie	female	14	White UK	Riverway	Housewife	N/A
Latoya	female	15	African	Cowick	Unemployed	Security guard
Leah	female	14	UK Sikh	Cowick	Unemployed	Unemployed
Lee	male	14	White UK	Riverway	Unemployed	Unemployed
Lucy	female	15	White English	Riverway	Secretary	Stepfather: cab driver
Mark	male	15	White Irish	Littleton	Administrator	Absent
Mark	male	14	White English	Hillside Park	Accountant at University	Works at airport
Max	male	15	White English	Littleton	Housewife	Absent
Melissa	female	15	Turkish	Eastleigh Central	Unemployed	'nothing'
Michelle	female	14	English	Riverway	Secretary	Factory worker
Mike	male	14	UK White	Littleton	Cleaner at the school	Absent
Mike	male	14	British White	Hillside Park	Deceased	Absent
Nadia	female	14	White European	Blackwell Street	Housewife	Unemployed
Nadira	female	N/A	Bengali	Eastleigh Central	Sign language assistant	Absent
Natalie	female	14	Scottish White	Hillside Park	Housewife	Absent
Nathan	male	14	British	Hillside Park	Housewife	Electrician
Nick	male	14	English White	Hillside Park	Security, parcel delivery	Works at different parcel delivery company
Peter	male	15	Black UK	Eastleigh Central	Absent	Musician
Robert	male	N/A	Iraqi	Eastleigh Central	N/A	N/A
Roger	male	15	Mixed race, Caribbean	Littleton	Works in bank	Absent
Sarah	female	15	White Moroccan	Eastleigh Central	Housewife	Unemployed
Steven	male	15	White UK	Eastleigh Central	Not working	Not working
Tim	male	14	British	Hillside Park	Receptionist	Cargo handler
Tyson	male	15	English mixed race	Littleton	Housewife	Mini cab driver
Verona	male	15	White English	Riverway	Absent	Unemployed
Yesim	female	15	Turkish	Cowick	Unemployed	Unemployed

Note: This table only contains the main study participants. Discussion group members are not listed.

APPENDIX 2: EDUCATIONAL PROFESSIONALS INTERVIEWED

Blackwell Street School

Assistant Headteacher Teacher Inclusion Manager, Black Caribbean woman
Head of Year 11 and KS4 Manager, White woman
Assistant Headteacher, in charge of KS4, Turkish man

Cowick Girls School

Head of Year 11, Australian woman
Head of Year 10, Black British woman
Connexions Advisor, White British woman

Eastleigh Central School

Head of Year 11, White woman
Learning Mentor, Turkish woman

Hillside Park School

Deputy Headteacher, White man
Head of Year 10, White man
Social Inclusion Curriculum Manager, White woman
Head of Year 11, White woman

Littleton Boys School

Connexions Advisor, Black woman
Connexions Advisor, White man
Head of Year 10, White UK man (Welsh)
Head of Year 11, White English man
Education Programmes Manager at PRU, White woman

Riverway School

Technology teacher and Head of Year 10, man (unknown ethnicity)
Head of Year 11, White man

REFERENCES

Ahmed, S. (1999) 'She'll wake up one of these days and find she's turned into a nigger': passing through hybridity. *Theory, Culture and Society* 16(2): 87–106.

Ainley, P., Barnes, T. and Momen, A. (2002) Making Connexions: a case study in contemporary social policy. *Critical Social Policy* 22(2): 376–88.

Ainley, P. (2005) 'Skills shortage' suits employers well. *Guardian*, 5 April.

Ali, S. (2003) To Be a Girl: culture and class in schools. *Gender and Education* 15(3): 269–83.

Allen, K. (2008) Young women and the performing arts: creative education, New Labour and the remaking of the young female self. Unpublished PhD thesis, Goldsmiths College, University of London.

Allen, M. and Ainley, P. (2007) *Education Make You Fick, Innit?: What's Gone Wrong with England's Schools, Colleges and Universities and How to Start Putting It Right.* London: Tufnell Press.

Anthias, F. (2001) New hybridities, old concepts: the limits of 'culture'. *Ethnic and Racial Studies* 24(4): 619–41.

Appelbaum, P. (2007) Afterword: bootleg mathematics, in E. de Freitas and K. Nolan (eds) *Opening the Research Text: Critical Insights and In(ter)ventions into Mathematics Education.* New York: Springer.

Archer, L., Pratt, S. and Phillips, D. (2001) Working class men's constructions of masculinity and negotiations of (non) participation in Higher Education. *Gender and Education* 13(4): 431–49.

Archer, L. (2002) Change, culture and tradition: British Muslim pupils talk about Muslim girls' post-16 'choices'. *Race, Ethnicity and Education* 5(4): 359–76.

Archer, L. and Francis, B. (2007) *Understanding Minority Ethnic Achievement: Race, Gender, Class and 'Success'.* Abingdon: Routledge.

Archer, L., Halsall, A. and Hollingworth, S. (2007a) Class, gender, (hetero)sexuality and schooling: working class girls' engagement with schooling and post-16 aspirations. *British Journal of Sociology of Education* 28(2): 165–80.

Archer, L., Hollingworth, S., Maylor, U., Sheibani, A. and Kowarzik, U. (2005) *Challenging Barriers to Employment for Refugees and Asylum Seekers in London.* Sussex: University of Sussex.

Archer, L., Hollingworth, S. and Halsall, A. (2007b) University's not for me – I'm a Nike person: Urban, working class young people's negotiations of 'style', identity and educational engagement. *Sociology* 4(2): 219–37.

Archer, L., Hutchings, M. and Ross, A. (2003) *Higher Education and Social Class: Issues of Exclusion and Inclusion*. London: RoutledgeFalmer.

Archer, L. and Leathwood, C. (2003) Identities, inequalities and higher education, in L. Archer, M. Hutchings and A. Ross (eds) *Higher Education and Social Class: Issues of Exclusion and Inclusion*. London: RoutledgeFalmer.

Archer, L. and Yamashita, H. (2003a) Theorising inner-city masculinities: 'race', class, gender and education. *Gender and Education* 15(2): 115–32.

Archer, L. and Yamashita, H. (2003b) 'Knowing their limits'? Identities, inequalities and inner city school leavers' post 16 aspirations. *Journal of Education Policy* 18(1): 53–69.

Arnot, M., David, M. and Weiner, G. (1999) *Closing the Gender Gap: Postwar Education and Social Change*. Cambridge: Polity Press.

Arnot, M., McIntyre, D., Pedder, D. and Reay, D. (2004) *Consultation in the Classroom: Developing Dialogue about Teaching and Learning*. Cambridge: Pearson Publishing.

Ashworth, K., Hardman, J., Liu, W., et al. (2001) *Education Maintenance Allowance: The First Year: A Quantitative Evaluation (Research Brief No 257)*. London: DfEE.

Atkinson, R. and Kintrea, K. (2004) Opportunities and despair: it's all in there. *Sociology* 38(3): 437–55.

Back, L. (1996) *New Ethnicities and Urban Culture: Racisms and Multiculture in Young Lives*. London: UCL Press.

Back, L. and Keith, M. (2004) Impurity and the emancipatory city: young people, community safety and racial danger, in L. Lees (ed.) *The Emancipatory City: Paradoxes and Possibilities*. London, Thousand Oaks, New Delhi: Sage.

Baker, C. (2006) *Foundations of Bilingual Education and Bilingualism*. Bristol: Multilingual Matters.

Ball, S.J. (1981) *Beachside Comprehensive: A Case-study of Secondary Schooling*. Cambridge: Cambridge University Press.

Ball, S.J. (1994) *Education Reform: A Critical and Post-structural Approach*. Buckingham: Open University Press.

Ball, S.J. (2003) *Class Strategies and the Educational Market: The Middle Class and Social Advantage*. London: RoutledgeFalmer.

Ball, S.J. (2006) *Education Policy and Social Class: The Selected Works of Stephen J. Ball*. Abingdon: Routledge.

Ball, S.J. (2007) *Education Plc: Understanding Private Sector Participation in Public Sector Education*. Abingdon: Routledge.

Ball, S.J. (2008) *The Education Debate*. Bristol: The Policy Press.

Ball, S.J., Davies, J., David, M. and Reay, D. (2002a) 'Classification' and 'judgement': social class and the 'cognitive structures' of choice of higher education. *British Journal of Sociology of Education* 23(1): 51–72.

Ball, S.J., Maguire, M. and Macrae, S. (2000) *Choice, Pathways and Transitions post-16*. London: RoutledgeFalmer.

Ball, S.J., Reay, D. and David, M. (2002b) 'Ethnic choosing': minority ethnic students, social class and higher education choice. *Race, Ethnicity & Education* 5(4): 333–57.

Ball, S.J. and Vincent, C. (1998) 'I heard it on the grapevine': 'hot' knowledge and school choice. *British Journal of Sociology of Education* 19(3): 377–400.

Basit, T. (1997a) *Eastern Values, Western Milieu: Identities and Aspirations of Adolescent British Muslim Girls*. Aldershot: Ashgate.

Basit, T. (1997b) 'I want more freedom but not too much': British Muslim young women's constructions of race, religion and femininity. *Gender and Education* 9(4): 425–9.

Bauman, Z. (1998) *Work, Consumerism and the New Poor*. Buckingham: Open University Press.

Beck, U. (1992) *Risk Society: Towards a New Modernity*. London: Sage.

Beck, V., Fuller, A. and Unwin, L. (2006) Increasing risk in the 'scary' world of work? Male and female resistance to crossing gender lines in apprenticeships in England and Wales. *Journal of Education and Work* 19(3): 271–89.

Bhabha, H. (2001) Locations of Culture: the post-colonial and the postmodern, in S. Malpas (ed.) *Postmodern Debates*. Basingstoke: Palgrave.

Bhabha, H. (1996) Rethinking authority: interview with Homi Bhabha. *Angelaki* 2(2): 59–65.

Bibby, T. (2009) How do pedagogic practices impact on learner identities in mathematics? A psychoanalytically framed response, in L. Black, H. Mendick and Y. Solomon (eds) *Mathematical Relationships in Education: Identities and Participation*. New York: Routledge.

Billig, M., Condor, S. and Edwards, D. (1988) *Ideological Dilemmas: A Social Psychology of Everyday Thinking*. London: Sage.

Black, P. and Wiliam, D. (1996) Assessment and classroom learning. *Assessment in Education* 5(1): 7–74.

Black, P. and Wiliam, D. (1998) *Inside the Black Box: Raising Standards Through Classroom Assessment*. London: King's College.

Blair, M. (2001a) *Why Pick on Me? School Exclusion and Black Youth*. Stoke-on-Trent: Trentham.

Blair, M. (2001b) The education of Black children: why do some schools do better than others?, in R. Majors (ed.) *Educating Our Black Children*. London: RoutledgeFalmer.

Blair, M. and Bourne, J. (1998) *Making the Difference: Teaching and Learning Strategies in Successful Multi-ethnic Schools*. London: DfEE.

Blair, T. (1999) Foreword in National Advisory Committee on Creative and Cultural Education, in *All Our Futures: Creativity, Culture and Education*. London: Department of Culture Media and Sport.

Boaler, J. (1997) *Experiencing School Mathematics: Teaching Styles, Sex and Setting*. Buckingham: Open University Press.

Bourdieu, P. (1977) *Outline of a Theory of Practice*. Cambridge: Cambridge University Press.

Bourdieu, P. (1984) *Distinction*. London: Routledge.

Bourdieu, P. (1992) *Language and Symbolic Power*. Cambridge: Polity Press.

Bourdieu, P. and Passeron, C. (1990) *Reproduction in Education, Society and Culture*. London: Sage.

Bourdieu, P. and Wacquant, L.J.D. (1992) *An Invitation to Reflexive Sociology*. Cambridge: Polity.

Bowlby, S., Lloyds Evans, S. and Mohammad, R. (1998) Becoming a paid worker: Images and Identity, in T. Skelton and G. Valentine (eds) *Cool Places: Geographies of Youth Cultures*. London: Routledge.

Bradford, S. and Hey, V. (2007) Successful subjectivities? The successification of class, ethnic and gender positions. *Journal of Education Policy* 22(6): 595–614.

Brah, A. (1996) *Cartographies of Diaspora*. London: Routledge.

Brah, A. (1999) The scent of memory: strangers, our own, and others. *Feminist Review* 61: 4–26.

Brah, A. and Minhas, R. (1985) Structural racism or cultural difference: schooling for Asian girls, in G. Weiner (ed.) *Just a Bunch of Girls: Feminist Approaches to Schooling*. Milton Keynes: Open University Press.

Brannen, J. and Nilsen, A. (2007) Young people, time horizons and planning: a response to Anderson et al. *Sociology* 41(1): 153–60.

Britzman, D. (1995) Is there a queer pedagogy? Or, stop reading straight. *Educational Theory* 45(2): online.

Brown, P. and Lauder, H. (2004) Education, globalization and economic development, in S.J. Ball (ed.) *The RoutledgeFalmer Reader in Sociology of Education*. Abingdon: RoutledgeFalmer.

Bubb, S. and Earley, P. (2007) The school workforce in London, in T. Brighouse and L. Fullick (eds) *Education in a Global City: Essays from London*. London: Institute of Education.

Buckingham, D. (2007) *Beyond Technology: Children's Learning in the Age of Digital Culture*. Cambridge: Polity.

Burke, P.J. (2006) Men accessing education: gendered aspirations. *British Educational Research Journal* 32(5): 719–34.

Burns, E. (2007) A New Day, *The Wire*, 4(11): HBO.

Butler, J. (1999) *Gender Trouble: Feminism and the Subversion of Identity*. London: Routledge.

Butler, J. (2004) *Undoing Gender*. Abington, Oxfordshire: Routledge.

Bynner, J., Elias, P., McKnight, A., Pan, H. and Pierre, G. (2002) Young people's changing routes to independence. Mimeo, Joseph Rountree Foundation/YPS, York.

Byrne, B. (2006) In search of a 'good mix'. 'Race', class, gender and practices of mothering. *Sociology* 40(6): 1001–17.

Byrne, D. (1999) *Social Exclusion*. Milton Keynes: Open University Press.

Byrne, D. and Rogers, T. (1996) Divided spaces – divided school: an exploration of the spatial relations of social division. *Sociological Research Online* 1(2): online.

Carlile, A. (forthcoming) Docile bodies or contested space? Working under the shadow of permanent exclusion. *International Journal of Inclusive Education*,

Carlile, A. (2009) 'Bitchy girls and Silly Boys': gender and exclusion from school. *International Journal of Disaffected Youth* 6(2): 30–6.

Chennault, R. E. (2006) *Hollywood Films about Schools: Where Race, Politics, and Education Intersect*. New York/Basingstoke: Palgrave Macmillan.

Cohen, P. (1972) *Sub-cultural Conflict and Working Class Community, Working Papers in Cultural Studies*. No.2. Birmingham: CCCS.

Colley, H. and Hodkinson, P. (2001) Problems with Bridging the Gap: the reversal of structure and agency in addressing social exclusion. *Critical Social Policy* 21(3): 335–59.

Colley, H. (2003) *Mentoring for Social Inclusion: A Critical Approach to Mentoring Relationships*. London: RoutledgeFalmer.

Comber, B. (1998) Problematising 'background': (re)constructing categories in education research. *Australian Educational Researcher* 25(3): 1–21.

Connell, R.W. (1989) Cool guys, swots and wimps: the inter-play of masculinity and education. *Oxford Review of Education* 15(3): 291–303.

Connell, R.W. (1995) *Masculinities*. Cambridge: Polity Press.

Connolly, P. (1998) *Racism, Gender Identities, and Young Children: Social Relations in a Multi-ethnic, Inner-city Primary School*. London: Routledge.

Connolly, P. (2004) *Boys and Schooling in the Early Years*. London: RoutledgeFalmer.

Connolly, P. and Healy, J. (2004) Symbolic violence and the neighbourhood: the educational aspirations of 7–8-year-old working class girls. *British Journal of Sociology of Education* 55(4): 511–29.

Creswell, T. (1996) *In Place/Out of Place: Geography, Ideology and Transgression*. Minnesota: University of Minnesota Press.

Daily Mail (2009) Plea to black fathers over sons. http://www.dailymail.co.uk/news/article-447493/Plea-black-fathers-sons.html (accessed 22 June 2009).

Department for Children Schools and Families (DCSF) (2007) *The Children's Plan*. London: HMSO.

Department for Children Schools and Families (DCSF) (2008) *The Extra Mile: How Schools Succeed in Raising Aspirations in Deprived Communities*. London: HMSO.

Department for Children, Schools and Families (DCSF) (2009a) *Youth Cohort Study & Longitudinal Study of Young People in England: The Activities and Experiences of 17 year olds: England 2008*. http://www.dcsf.gov.uk/rsgateway/DB/SBU/b000850/Bull01_2009textvfinal.pdf (accessed 17 June 2009).

Department for Children, Schools and Families (DCSF) (2009b) *Your Child, Your Schools, Our Future: Building a 21st Century Schools System*. London: HMSO.

Department for Education and Employment (DfEE) (1999) *Learning to Succeed: A New Framework for Post-16 Learning*. London: DfEE.

Department for Education and Employment (DfEE) (2000) Boys must improve at same rate as girls – Blunkett. Press Release, 20 August.

Department for Education and Skills (DfES) (2001) *Schools: Achieving Success: A Summary*. London: DfES.

Department for Education and Skills (DfES) (2003a) *Aiming High: Raising the Achievement of Minority Ethnic Pupils*. London: DfES.

Department for Education and Skills (DfES) (2003b) *14–19: Opportunity and Excellence*. London: DfES.

Department for Education and Skills (DfES) (2003c) *Using the National Healthy School Stand to Raise Boys' Achievement*. Wetherby: Health Development Agency.

Department for Education and Skills (DfES) (2004) *Schools Race Equality Policies: From Issues to Outcomes*. London: HMSO.

Department for Education and Skills (DfES) (2005a) *14–19 Education and Skills White Paper*. London: HMSO.

Department for Education and Skills (DfES) (2005b) *Higher Standards, Better Schools for All*. London: HMSO.

Department for Education and Skills (DfES) (2006) *Social Mobility: Narrowing Educational Social Class Attainment Gaps (supporting materials to a speech by Ruth Kelly on 26 April 2006)*. http://www.dcsf.gov.uk/rsgateway/DB/STA/t000657/index.shtml (accessed 17 June 2009).

Dick, P. K. (2000) *Minority Report*. London: Gollancz.

Dodds, A. (2009) Families 'at risk' and the Family Nurse Partnership: the intrusion of risk into social exclusion policy. *Journal of Social Policy* 38(3): 499–514.

Dolby, N., Dimitriadis, G. and Willis, P. (eds) (2004) *Learning to Labor in New Times*. New York: RoutledgeFalmer.

du Gay, P. (1996) *Consumption and Identity at Work*. London: Sage.

Ecclestone, K. (2007) Resisting images of the 'diminished self': the implications of emotional well-being and emotional engagement in education policy. *Journal of Education Policy* 22(4): 455–70.

Ecclestone, K. and Hayes, D. (2009) *The Dangerous Rise of Therapeutic Education*. Oxon: Routledge.

Epp, J.R. (1996) Postscript: making central the peripheral, in J.R. Epp and A.M. Watkinson (eds) *Systemic Violence: How Schools Hurt Children*. London: Falmer.

Epp, J.R. and Watkinson, A.M. (1996) *Systemic Violence: How Schools Hurt Children*. London: Falmer.

Epstein, D. (1993) *Changing Classroom Cultures: Anti-racism, Politics, and Schools.* Stoke-on-Trent: Trentham.

Epstein, D., Elwood, J., Hey, V. and Maw, J. (1998) *Failing Boys? Issues in Gender and Underachievement.* Buckingham: Open University Press.

Epstein, D. and Johnson, R. (1998) *Schooling Sexualities.* Buckingham: Open University Press.

Equality and Human Rights Commission (2008) *Education and Skills Bill Parliamentary Briefing.* http://www.equalityhumanrights.com/uploaded_files/briefings/educationandskillsreportbriefing211008.doc (accessed 19 August 2009).

Evans, G. (2006) *Educational Failure and Working Class White Children in Britain.* Hampshire: Palgrave Macmillan.

Evans, J., Rich, E., Davies, B. and Allwood, R. (2008) *Education, Disordered Eating and Obesity Discourse: Fat Fabrications.* Abingdon: Routledge.

Fanon, F. (1986) *Black Skin, White Masks.* London: Pluto Press.

Fine, M., Weis, L., Powell, L. and Mun Wong, L. (eds) (1997) *Off White: Readings on Race, Power and Society.* London: Routledge.

Foucault, M. (1972) *The Archaeology of Knowledge.* London: Routledge.

Foucault, M. (1980) Prison talk, in C. Gordon (ed.) *Power/Knowledge.* Harlow: Prentice Hall.

Francis, B. (1999) Lads, Lasses and (New) Labour: 14–16-year-old student' responses to the 'laddish behaviour and boys' underachievement' debate. *British Journal of Sociology of Education* 20(3): 355–71.

Francis, B. (2000a) *Boys and Girls and Achievement: Addressing the Classroom Issues.* London: RoutledgeFalmer.

Francis, B. (2000b) The gendered subject: students' preferences and discussions of gender and subject ability. *Oxford Review of Education* 26(1): 35–48.

Francis, B. (2006) Heroes or zeroes? The discursive positioning of 'underachieving boys' in English neo-liberal education policy. *Journal of Education Policy* 21(2): 187–200.

Francis, B. and Skelton, C. (2005) *Reassessing Gender and Achievement: Questioning Contemporary Key Debates.* Oxon: Routledge.

Freire, P. (1972) *Pedagogy of the Oppressed.* Harmondsworth: Penguin.

Frosh, S., Phoenix, A. and Pattman, R. (2002) *Young Masculinities: Understanding Boys in Contemporary Society.* Basingstoke: Palgrave.

Fuller, A., Beck, V. and Unwin, L. (2005) The gendered nature of apprenticeship. *Education and Training* 47(4/5): 298–311.

Furedi, F. (2004) *Therapy Culture: Cultivating Vulnerability in an Uncertain Age.* London: Routledge.

Furlong, A. and Cartmel, F. (1997) *Young People and Social Change: Individualization and Risk in Late Modernity.* Buckingham: Open University Press.

Gaine, C. (1995) *Still No Problem Here.* Stoke-on-Trent: Trentham.

Gaine, C. (2000) Anti-racist education in 'white' areas: the limits and possibilities of change. *Race, Ethnicity and Education* 3(1): 65–81.

Garcia, O. and Baker, C. (2007) *Bilingual Education: An Introductory Reader.* Bristol: Multilingual Matters.

Garrett, P. (2002) Encounters in the new welfare domains of the Third Way: social work, the Connexions agency and personal advisors. *Critical Social Policy* 22(4): 596–618.

Gee, J.P. (2007) *Good Video Games + Good Learning.* New York: Peter Lang Publishing.

George, R. (2007) *Girls in a Goldfish Bowl: Moral Regulation, Ritual and the Use of Power Among Inner City Girls.* Rotterdam: Sense.

Gewirtz, S. (2001) Cloning the Blairs: New Labour's programme for the re-socialization of working-class parents. *Journal of Education Policy* 16(4): 365–78.

Gewirtz, S., Ball, S.J. and Bowe, R. (1995) *Markets, Choice and Equity in Education*. Buckingham: Open University Press.

Giddens, A. (1990) *The Consequences of Modernity*. Cambridge: Polity Press.

Giddens, A. (1992) *Modernity and Self-Identity: Self and Society in the Late Modern Age*. Cambridge: Polity.

Gillborn, D. and Gipps, C. (1996) *Recent Research on the Achievements of Ethnic Minority Pupils: OFSTED Reviews of Research*. London: HMSO.

Gillborn, D. and Mirza, H.S. (2000) *Educational Inequality: Mapping Race, Class and Gender*. London: Ofsted.

Gillborn, D. and Rollock, N. (2009) Education, in A. Bloch and J. Solomos (eds) *Race and Ethnicity in the 21st Century*. London: Palgrave Macmillan.

Gillborn, D. and Youdell, D. (2000) *Rationing Education: Policy, Practice, Reform, and Equity*. Buckingham: Open University Press.

Gillies, V. (2005) Raising the meritocracy: parenting and the individualisation of social class. *Sociology* 39(5): 832–52.

Greater London Authority (2007) *Focus on London 2007*. Basinstoke: Palgrave Macmillan.

Gregory, E. (1996) *Making Sense of a New World: Learning to Read in a Second Language*. London: Sage.

Griffin, C. (1985) *Typical Girls*. London: Routledge.

Griffiths, M. and Troyna, B. (eds) (1995) *Antiracism, Culture and Social Justice in Education*. Stoke-on-Trent: Trentham.

Gutman, L.M. and Akerman, R. (2008) *Determinants of Aspirations, DCSF Research Brief DCSF-WBL-03-08*. London: DCSF.

Hadfield, M. and Haw, K. (2000) *The 'Voice' of Young People: Hearing, Listening, Responding*. Nottingham: School of Education, University of Nottingham.

Hall, K., Collins, J., Benjamin, S., Nind, M. and Sheehy, K. (2004) SATurated models of pupildom: assessment and inclusion/exclusion. *British Educational Research Journal* 30(6): 801–17.

Hall, S. (1974) Education and the crisis of the urban school, in J. Raynor (ed.) *Why Urban Education? Educational Studies: A Third Level Course. E351*. Milton Keynes: Open University Press.

Hall, S. (1991a) The local and the global: globalization and ethnicity, in A.D. King (ed.) *Culture, Globalization and the World-system: Contemporary Conditions for the Representation of Identity*. London: Macmillan.

Hall, S. (1991b) Old and new identities, old and new ethnicities, in A.D. King (ed.) *Culture, Globalization and the World-system*. London: Macmillan.

Hall, S., Critcher, C., Jefferson, T., Clarke, J. and Robert, B. (1978) *Policing the Crisis: Mugging, the State and Law and Order*. London: Palgrave Macmillan.

Hall, S. and Jefferson, T. (eds) (1976) *Resistance through Rituals: Youth Subcultures in Postwar Britain*. London: Hutchinson.

Harber, C. and Sakade, N. (2009) Schooling for violence and peace: how does peace education differ from 'normal' schooling? *Journal of Peace Education* 6(2): 171–87.

Harvey, D. (1973) *Social Justice and the City*. London: Edward Arnold.

Hayes, D., Mills, M., Christie, P. and Lingard, B. (2006) *Teachers & Schooling: Making a Difference*. Crows Nest, Australia: Allen & Unwin.

Haylett, C. (2001) Illegitimate subjects?: abject Whites, neo-liberal modernisation and middle class multiculturalism'. *Environment and Planning D: Society and Space* 19(3): 351–70.

Hebson, G. (2009) Renewing class analysis in studies of the workplace: a comparison of working-class and middle-class women's aspirations and identities. *Sociology* 43(1): 27–44.

HEFCE (2005) *Young Participation in Higher Education*. Bristol: HEFCE.

Henderson, S., Holland, J., McGrellis, S., Sharpe, S. and Thomson, R. (2007) *Inventing Adulthoods: A Biographical Approach to Youth Transitions*. London: Sage.

Hesse, B. (ed.) (2000) *Un/settled Multiculturalisms*. London: Zed Books.

Hey, V. (1997) *The Company she Keeps: An Ethnography of Girls' Friendship*. Buckingham: Open University Press.

Hey, V. (2003) Joining the club? Academia and working class femininities. *Gender and Education* 15(3): 319–35.

Hills, J. and Stuart, K. (2005) *A More Equal Society?: New Labour, Poverty, Inequality and Social Exclusion*. Bristol: The Policy Press.

HM Government (2009) *New Opportunities: Fair Chances for the Future*. London: HM Stationery Office.

Hollingworth, S. and Archer, L. (forthcoming) Urban schools as urban places: school reputation, children's identities and engagement with education, *Urban Studies*,

Holt, M. and Griffin, C. (2005) Students versus locals: young adults' constructions of the working class Other. *British Journal of Social Psychology* 44(2): 241–67.

Home Office (2003) *Respect and Responsibility – Taking a Stand Against Antisocial Behaviour*. London: HMSO.

hooks, b. (1984) *Feminist Theory: From Margin to Center*. Boston: South End Press.

Houssart, J. (2001) Setting tasks and setting children. *Proceedings of the British Congress of Mathematics Education 5* 21(2): 136–46.

Hughes, C. (2002) *Key Concepts in Feminist Theory and Research*. London: Sage.

Hutchings, M., James, K., Maylor, U., Menter, I. and Smart, S. (2006a) *The Recruitment, Deployment and Management of Supply Teachers in England*. London: DfES.

Hutchings, M., Maylor, U., Mendick, H., Menter, I. and Smart, S. (2006b) *An Evaluation of Innovative Approaches to Teacher Training on the Teach First Programme: Final Report to the Training and Development Agency for Schools*. London: IPSE.

Hutchings, M., Menter, I., Ross, A. and Thomson, D. (2002) Teacher supply and retention in London – key findings and implications from a study carried out in six boroughs in 1998/9, in I. Menter, M. Hutchings and A. Ross (eds) *The Crisis in Teacher Supply: Research and Strategies for Retention*. Stoke-on-Trent: Trentham.

Jackson, C. (2006a) 'Wild' girls? An exploration of 'ladette' cultures in secondary schools. *Gender and Education* 18(4): 339–60.

Jackson, C. (2006b) *Lads and Ladettes in School: Gender and a Fear of Failure*. Maidenhead: Open University Press.

Jackson, C. and Dempster, S. (2009) 'Laddish' masculinities in schools and university: exploring continuities and discontinuities. Paper presented to the 7th Gender and Education Conference, Institute of Education, University of London, March.

Kemshall, H. (2002) *Risk, Social Policy and Welfare*. Buckingham: Open University Press.

Kenner, C. (2000) *Home Pages: Literacy Links for Bilingual Children*. Stoke-on-Trent: Trentham.

Kenner, C. (2004) *Becoming Biliterate: Young Children Learning Different Writing Systems*. Stoke-on-Trent: Trentham.

Kenway, J. and Bullen, E. (2001) *Consuming Children: Education-Entertainment-Advertising*. Buckingham: Oxford University Press.

Kenway, J. and Willis, S. (1990) *Hearts and Minds: Self-esteem and the Schooling of Girls*. East Sussex, UK and PA, USA: Falmer Press.

Klein, N. (2000) *No Logo*. London: HarperCollins.

Kopp, W. (2001) *One Day, All Children . . . The Unlikely Triumph of Teach for America and What I Learned Along the Way*. New York: PublicAffairs.

Lawler, S. (1999) Getting out and getting away: women's narratives of class mobility. *Feminist Review* 63(1): 3–24.

Lawler, S. (2005) Disgusted subjects: the making of middle class identities. *The Sociological Review* 53(3): 429–46.

Leathwood, C. and Hutchings, M. (2003) Entry routes to higher education: pathways, qualifications and social class, in L. Archer, M. Hutchings and A. Ross (eds) *Higher Education and Social Class: Issues of Exclusion and Inclusion*. London: RoutledgeFalmer.

Lees, L. (ed.) (2004) *The Emancipatory City: Paradoxes and Possibilities*. London, Thousand Oaks, New Delhi: Sage.

Legard, R., Woodfield, K. and White, C. (2001) *Staying away or staying on? A qualitative evaluation of the Education Maintenance Allowance*, (Research Report RR256). Mimeo, DfEE, London.

Lucey, H. and Reay, D. (2002) A market in waste: psychic and structural dimensions of school choice policy in the UK and children's narratives of 'demonised' schools. *Discourse* 23(3): 253–66.

Lupton, D. (1999) *Risk*. London: Routledge.

Lynch, K. and Lodge, A. (2002) *Equality and Power in Schools*. London: RoutledgeFalmer.

Mac an Ghaill, M. (1994) *The Making of Men: Masculinities, Sexualities and Schooling*. Buckingham: Open University Press.

MacDonald, R. (1997) Dangerous youth and the dangerous class, in R. MacDonald (ed.) *Youth, the 'Underclass' and Social Exclusion*. London: Routledge.

MacDonald, R., Shildrick, T., Webster, C. and Simpson, D. (2005) Growing up in poor neighbourhoods: the significance of class and place in the extended transitions of 'socially excluded' young adults. *Sociology* 39(5): 873–92.

MacLure, M. (2003) *Discourse in Educational and Social Research*. Buckingham: Open University Press.

Maguire, M., Maguire, S. and Vincent, J. (2001) *Implementation of the Education Maintenance Allowance pilots: the first year*, (Research Report RR255). Mimeo, DfEE, London.

Maguire, M., Wooldridge, T. and Pratt-Adams, S. (2006) *The Urban Primary School*. Buckingham: Open University Press.

Mahony, P. and Zmroczek, C. (eds) (1997) *Class Matters: 'Working-Class' Women's Perspective on Social Class*. London: Taylor & Francis.

Majors, R. and Billson, J.M. (1992) *Cool Pose: The Dilemmas of Black Manhood in America*. New York: Lexington Books.

Mama, A. (1995) *Beyond the Masks: Race, Gender and Subjectivity*. London: Routledge.

Mann, C. (1998) The impact of working-class mothers on the educational success of their adolescent daughters at a time of social change. *British Journal of Sociology of Education* 19(2): 211–26.

Martin, P.W. (2003) Bilingual encounters in the classroom, in J.-M. Deweale, A. Housen and L. Wei (eds) *Basic Principles of Bilingualism Revisited*. Clevedon: Multilingual Matters.

Martino, W. (1999) 'Cool boys', 'party animals', 'squids' and 'poofters': interrogating the dynamics and politics of adolescent masculinities in school. *British Journal of Sociology of Education* 20(2): 239–63.

Martino, W. and Pallotta-Chiarolli, M. (2003) *So What's a Boy?* Buckingham: Open University Press.

Massey, D. (1994) *Space, Place and Gender*. Minnesota: University of Minnesota Press.

Matthews, H. and Limb, M. (1999) Defining an agenda for the geography of children. *Progress in Human Geography* 23(1): 59–88.

Mayer, C. (2008) Britain's Mean Streets, *Time Magazine*, 26 March.

Maylor, U., Read, B., Mendick, H., Ross, A. and Rollock, N. (2007) *Diversity and Citizenship in the Curriculum: Research Review*. London: Department for Education and Skills.

McClelland, K. (1991) Masculinity and the 'representative artisan' in Britain 1850–80, in M. Roper and J. Tosh (eds) *Manful Assertions*. London: Routledge.

McDowell, L. (2003) *Redundant Masculinities? Employment Change and White Working Class Youth*. London: Blackwell.

McDowell, L. (2007) Respect, respectability, deference and place: what is the problem with/for working class boys? *Geoforum* 38(2): 276–86.

McLeod, J. (2007) Generations of hope – mothers, daughters and everyday wishes for a better life, in J. McLeod and A.C. Allard (eds) *Learning from the Margins: Young Women, Social Exclusion and Education*. London: RoutledgeFalmer.

McRobbie, A. (1978) Working class girls and the culture of femininity, in Women's Studies Group of Centre for Contemporary Cultural Studies (ed.) *Women Take Issue: Aspects of Women's Subordination*. London: Hutchinson.

McRobbie, A. (2008) *The Aftermath of Feminism: Gender, Culture and Social Change*. London: Sage.

McRobbie, A. and Garber, J. (1976) Girls and subcultures, in S. Hall and T. Jefferson (eds) *Resistance Through Rituals*. London: Hutchinson.

McWilliam, E. (1999) *Pedagogical Pleasures*. New York: Peter Lang Publishing.

Mendick, H. (2002) 'Why are we doing this?': A case study of motivational practices in mathematics classes. Paper presented to the 26th Conference of the International Group for the Psychology of Mathematics Education, Norwich, England, July.

Mendick, H. (2006) *Masculinities in Mathematics*. Maidenhead: Open University Press/McGraw-Hill.

Mills, M. (2003) Shaping the boys' agenda: the backlash blockbusters. *International Journal of Inclusive Education* 7(11): 57–73.

Mirza, H.S. (1992) *Young, Female and Black*. London: Routledge.

Modood, T. (1992) *Not Easy Being British*. Stoke-on-Trent: Trentham.

Moss, G. (2005) The impact of literacy policy and performance pedagogies on primary school teacher identities. Paper presented to the C-TRIP seminar series: identity, agency and policy in teachers' professional lives, King's College London, 20 January.

Nayak, A. (2003) Last of the 'Real Geordies'?: white masculinities and the subcultural response to de-industrialization. *Environment and Planning D: Society and Space* 21(1): 7–25.

Nayak, A. (2006) Displaced masculinities: chavs, youth and class in the post-industrial city. *Sociology* 40(5): 813–31.

Noble, D. (2000) Ragga music: dis/respecting Black women and dis/reputable sexualities, in B. Hesse (ed.) *Un/Settled Multiculturalisms*. London: Zed Books.

Noddings, N. (1996) Equity and mathematics: not a simple issue. *Journal for Research in Mathematics Education* 27(5): 609–15.

Noddings, N. (2003) Is Teaching a Practice? *Journal of Philosophy of Education* 37(2): 242–51.

Osgood, J. (2006) Professionalism and performativity: the paradox facing early years practitioners. *Early Years: An International Journal of Research and Development* 26(2): 187–99.

Osler, A. and Vincent, K. (2003) *Girls and Exclusion: Rethinking the Agenda*. London: RoutledgeFalmer.

Ouellete, L. and Hay, J. (2008) *Better Living Through Reality TV: Television and Post-welfare Citizenship*. Oxford: Blackwell.

Oxford Dictionaries (2009) *The Concise Oxford English Dictionary: 11th Edition Revised*. Oxford: Oxford University Press.

Panel on Fair Access to the Professions (2009) *Unleashing Aspiration: The Final Report of the Panel on Fair Access to the Professions*. London: The Cabinet Office.

Pearce, N. and Hillman, J. (1998) *Wasted Youth: Raising Achievement and Tackling Social Exclusion*. London: IPPR.

Phoenix, A. (2000) Constructing gendered and racialized identities: young men, masculinities and educational policy, in G. Lewis, S. Gewirtz and J. Clarke (eds) *Rethinking Social Policy*. London: Sage.

Povey, H. (1995) Ways of knowing of student and beginning mathematics teachers and their relevance to becoming a teacher working for change. Unpublished PhD thesis, University of Birmingham.

Pugsley, L. (1998) 'Throwing your brains at it': higher education markets and choice, *International Studies in Sociology of Education*, 8(1): 71–90.

Quinn, J., Lawy, R. and Diment, K. (2008) *Young people in jobs without training in South West England: not just 'Dead End Kids in Dead End Jobs'*. Mimeo, Marchmont Observatory/University of Exeter.

Rattansi, A. (1992) Changing the subject: racism, culture and education, in J. Donald and A. Rattansi (eds) *'Race', Culture and Difference*. Buckingham: Open University Press.

Reay, D. (1998) 'Always knowing' and 'never being sure': familial and institutional habituses and higher education. *Journal of Educational Policy* 13(4): 519–29.

Reay, D. (2001a) 'Spice girls, "nice girls", "girlies" and "tom boys": gender discourses, girls' cultures and femininities in the primary classroom. *Gender and Education* 13(2): 153–66.

Reay, D. (2001b) Finding or losing yourself?: working-class relationships to education. *Journal of Education Policy* 16(4): 333–46.

Reay, D. (2002) Shaun's story: troubling discourses of white working class masculinities. *Gender and Education* 14(3): 221–34.

Reay, D. (2004a) 'Mostly Roughs and Toughs': social class, race and representation in inner city schooling. *Sociology* 35(4): 1005–23.

Reay, D. (2004b) Rethinking social class: qualitative perspectives on class and gender, in S. Hesse-Biber and M.L. Yaiser (eds) *Feminist Perspectives on Social Research*. Oxford: Oxford University Press.

Reay, D. (2004c) 'It's all becoming a habitus': beyond the habitual use of habitus in educational research. *British Journal of Sociology of Education* 25(4): 431–44.

Reay, D. (2006) The zombie stalking English schools: social class and educational inequality. *British Journal of Educational Studies* 54(3): 288–307.

Reay, D., Crozier, G., James, D., et al. (2008) Re-invigorating democracy? White middle class identities and comprehensive schooling. *Sociological Review* 56(2): 238–55.

Reay, D., David, M.E. and Ball, S.J. (2005) *Degrees of Choice: Social Class, Race and Gender in Higher Education*. Stoke-on-Trent: Trentham.

Reay, D., Hollingworth, S., Williams, K., Crozier, G., Jamieson, F., James, D. and

Phoebe, B. (2007) A darker shade of pale?: Whiteness, the middle classes and multi-ethnic inner city schooling. *Sociology* 41(6): 1041–60.

Reay, D. and Lucey, H. (2000) 'I don't really like it here, but I don't want to be anywhere else': children and inner-city council estates. *Antipode* 32(4): 410–28.

Reay, D. and Wiliam, D. (1999) 'I'll be a nothing': structure, agency and the construction of identity through assessment, *British Educational Research Journal*, 25(3): 343–54.

Renold, E. (2000) 'Coming out': gender, (hetero)sexuality and the primary school. *Gender and Education* 12(3): 309–26.

Renold, E. (2005) *Girls, Boys and Junior Sexualities: Exploring Children's Gender and Sexual Relations in the Primary School*. London: RoutledgeFalmer.

Rethinking Schools Online (2002/2003) *Special Collection on Bilingual Education*. http://www.rethinkingschools.org/special_reports/bilingual/Bili172.shtml (accessed 15 August 2009).

Rich, A. (1981) *Compulsory Heterosexuality and Lesbian Existence*. London: Onlywomen Press.

Rollock, N. (2009) Educational policy and the impact of the Lawrence Inquiry: the view from another sector, in N. Hall, J. Grieve and S.P. Savage (eds) *Policing and the Legacy of Lawrence*. Cullompton, Devon: Willan Publishing.

Rose, N. (1999) *Governing the Soul*. London: Free Association Books.

Rudduck, J., Chaplain, R. and Wallace, G. (1996) Reviewing the conditions of learning in school, in J. Rudduck, R. Chaplain and G. Wallace (eds) *School Improvement: What can Pupils Tell Us?* London: David Fulton.

Rutter, J. (1999) *Refugee Children in the UK*. Buckingham: Open University Press.

Said, E.W. (1995) *Orientalism: Western Conceptions of the Orient*. London: Penguin.

Sayer, A. (2002) What are you worth? Why class is an embarrassing subject. *Sociological Research Online*, 7(3): online.

Scott, J. (1992) 'Experience', in J. Butler and J. Scott (eds) *Feminists Theorize the Political*. New York: Routledge.

Sennett, R. (2003) *Respect: The Formation of Character in an Age of Inequality*. London: Penguin.

Sewell, T. (1997) *Black Masculinities and Schooling*. Stoke-on-Trent: Trentham.

Shain, F. (2003) *The Schooling and Identity of Asian Girls*. Stoke-on-Trent: Trentham.

Sharpe, S. (1994) *Just Like a Girl, 2nd edn*. Harmondsworth: Penguin.

Shaw, J. (1995) *Education, Gender and Anxiety*. London: Taylor & Francis.

Sibley, D. (1995) *Geographies of Exclusion*. London: Routledge.

Skeggs, B. (1997) *Formations of Class and Gender*. London: Sage.

Skeggs, B. (2004) *Class, Self, Culture*. London and New York: Routledge.

Skeggs, B., Wood, H. and Thumin, N. (2007) Making class through moral extension on reality TV, http://www8.umu.se/medfak/cgf/bev%20warwick%20with%20 edits%20_2_.pdf (accessed 17 August 2009).

Skeggs, B. and Wood, H. (2008) The labour of transformation and circuits of value 'around' reality television. *Continuum: Journal of Media & Cultural Studies* 22(4): 559–72.

Skelton, C. (2001) *Schooling the Boys: Masculinities and Primary Education*. Buckingham: Open University Press.

Smart, S., Hutchings, M., Maylor, U., Mendick, H. and Menter, I. (2009) Processes of middle-class reproduction in a graduate employment scheme. *Journal of Education and Work* 22(1): 35–53.

Smith, G., Smith, T. and Smith, T. (2007) Whatever happened to EPAs? Part 2: Educational Priority Areas – 40 years on. *Forum* 49(1&2): 141–56.

Sneddon, R. (2000) Language and literacy: children's experiences in multilingual environments. *International Journal of Bilingual Education and Bilingualism* 3(4): 265–82.

Social Exclusion Unit (SEU) (1999) *Bridging the Gap: New Opportunities for 16–18-year-olds not in education, employment or training.* London: SEU.

Sofer, A. (2007) Global city school systems, in T. Brighouse and L. Fullick (eds) *Education in a Global City: Essays from London.* London: Institute of Education.

Sutton Trust (2009) *London the Capital of Private Tuition.* http://www.suttontrust.com/news.asp#a059 (accessed 22 June 2009).

te Riele, K. (2006a) Schooling practices for marginalized students – practice-with-hope. *International Journal of Inclusive Education* 10(1): 59–74.

te Riele, K. (2006b) Youth 'at risk': further marginalizing the marginalized? *Journal of Education Policy* 21(2): 129–45.

Thomson, R. (2007) Inventing adulthoods: a bigraphical approach to understanding young lives, in J. McLeod and A. Allard (eds) *Learning from the Margins: Young Women, Social Exclusion and Education.* Abingdon: Routledge.

Tolson, A. (1977) *The Limits of Masculinity.* London: Tavistock.

Tyler, I. (2006) Chav scum: the filthy politics of social class in contemporary Britain, *M/C Journal* 9(5): online.

Wacquant, L. (1996) Red belt, black belt: racial division, class inequality and the state in the French urban periphery and the American ghetto, in E. Minione (ed.) *Urban Poverty and the Underclass.* Oxford: Blackwell.

Walkerdine, V. (1984) Developmental psychology and the child-centred pedagogy: the insertion of Piaget into early education, in J. Henriques, W. Hollway, C. Urwin, C. Venn and V. Walkerdine (eds) *Changing the Subject: Psychology, Social Regulation and Subjectivity.* London: Methuen.

Walkerdine, V. (1988) *The Mastery of Reason: Cognitive Development and the Production of Rationality.* London: Routledge.

Walkerdine, V. (1990) *Schoolgirl Fictions.* London: Verso.

Walkerdine, V. (2003) Reclassifying upward mobility: femininity and the neo-liberal subject. *Gender and Education* 15(3): 237–48.

Walkerdine, V., Lucey, H. and Melody, J. (2001) *Growing Up Girl: Psychosocial Explorations of Gender and Class.* Basingstoke: Palgrave.

Ward, C. (1990/1978) *The Child in the City: New Edition.* London: Bedford Square Press.

Wark, P. (2007) *Lost White Boys.* http://women.timesonline.co.uk/tol/life_and_style/women/families/article2870677.ece (accessed 5 August 2009).

Warrington, M. (2005) Mirage in the desert? Access to educational opportunities in an area of social exclusion. *Antipode* 37(4): 796–816.

Warrington, M., Younger, M. and Williams, J. (2000) Student attitudes, image and the gender gap. *Gender and Education* 26(3): 393–407.

Watson, S. (2006) *City Publics: The (Dis)enchantments of Urban Encounters.* London and New York: Routledge.

Watt, P. and Stenson, K. (1998) The Street: 'it's a bit dodgy around there': safety danger, ethnicity and young people's use of public space, in T. Skelton and G. Valentine (eds) *Cool Places: Geographies of Youth Cultures.* London: Routledge.

Watts, A.G. (2001) Career guidance and social exclusion: a cautionary tale. *British Journal of Guidance and Counselling* 29(2): 157–76.

Watts, M. and Bridges, D. (2006) The value of non-participation in higher education. *Journal of Education Policy* 21(3): 267–90.

Weedon, C. (1997) *Feminist Practice and Poststructuralist Theory.* Oxford: Basil Blackwell.

Wetherell, M. and Potter, J. (1992) *Mapping the Language of Racism: Discourse and the Legitimation of Exploitation.* New York: Columbia University Press.

Whitty, G. (2001) Education, social class and social exclusion. *Journal of Education Policy* 16(4): 287–95.

Williams, K. and Hollingworth, S. (2006) 'Keeping my kids real': white middle-class parents, multiculturalism and inner city schools. Paper presented to the British Educational Research Association Conference, University of Warwick, 3–5 September.

Williams, K. and Mendick, H. (2008) 'You're hired': the intersections of class, race and gender in young people' constructions of work in television. Paper presented to the British Educational Research Association, Edinburgh, September.

Williamson, H. (1997) *Youth and Policy: Contexts and Consequences.* Aldershot: Ashgate.

Willis, P. (1977) *Learning to Labour: How Working Class Kids Get Working Class Jobs.* London: Gower Publishing.

Willis, P. (1990) *Common Culture: Symbolic Work at Play in the Everyday Cultures of the Young.* Buckingham: Open University Press.

Woodrow, D. (2003) *Mathematics, Mathematics Education and Economic Conditions.* http://www.esri.mmu.ac.uk/respapers/papers-pdf/Paper%20-%20maths,%20 maths%20ed%20&%20economics.pdf (accessed 30 July 2009).

Wright, C. (1987a) The relations between teachers and Afro-Caribbean pupils, in G. Weiner and M. Arnot (eds) *Gender Under Scrutiny.* Milton Keynes: Open University Press.

Wright, C. (1987b) Black students – white teachers, in B. Troyna (ed.) *Racial Inequality in Education.* London: Allen & Unwin.

Wrigley, T. (2006) *Another School is Possible.* London and Stoke-on-Trent: Bookmarks and Trentham.

Young, M. (1961) *The Rise of the Meritocracy 1870–2033: An Essay on Education and Equality.* Harmondsworth: Penguin.

Young, M. (1999) Some reflections on the concepts of social exclusion and inclusion: beyond the Third Way, in A. Hayton (ed.) *Tackling Disaffection and Social Exclusion: Education Perspectives and Policies.* London: Kogan Page.

Younger, M., Warrington, M. and Williams, K. (1999) The gender gap and classroom interactions: reality and rhetoric? *British Journal of Sociology of Education* 20(3): 325–41.

Younger, M., Warrington, M. and McLellan, R. (2005) *Raising Boys' Achievements in Secondary Schools: Issues, Dilemmas and Opportunities.* Maidenhead: Open University Press/McGraw-Hill.

Yuval-Davis, N. (1997) Ethnicity, gender relations and multiculturalism, in P. Werbner and T. Modood (eds) *Debating Cultural Hybridity: Multicultural Identities and the Politics of Anti-racism.* London: Zed Books.

INDEX

Related books from Open University Press
Purchase from www.openup.co.uk or order through your local bookseller

IMPROVING URBAN SCHOOLS
LEADERSHIP AND COLLABORATION
Mel Ainscow and Mel West (eds)

The improvement of urban schools is one of the major challenges facing practitioners and policy-makers today. Issues related to poverty create particular difficulties in urban schools, and the emphasis on market-led improvement strategies has tended to add to these challenges. In addition, strategies for 'raising standards', as measured by aggregate test and examination results, can result in marginalisation or exclusion of some groups of learners.

Drawing on research evidence, *Improving Urban Schools* addresses the question of how primary and secondary urban schools can be improved in a more inclusive way. The authors argue that urban schools and their communities have within them expertise that tends to be overlooked, and latent creativity that should be mobilised to move thinking and progress forward. They show that new approaches to leadership, various forms of collaborative school-to-school partnerships, and major changes in national policy development are needed to make use of this untapped energy.

The book includes vivid accounts of these activities to shed light on what really happens in urban schools, and presents practical strategies for school leaders and practitioners who want to make a difference in urban schools.

Contributors
Mel Ainscow, Alan Dyson, Samantha Fox, Helen Gunter, Andy Howes, Andrew Morley, Maria Nicolaidou, Jacqui Stanford, Dave Tweddle, Mel West.

Contents
Notes on contributors – Series preface – Editors' preface – Preface – The challenge of urban school improvement – The experience of failure in urban primary schools – The development of leadership capacity in a school facing challenging circumstances – Leading developments in practice: Barriers and possibilities – Achieving sustainable improvements in urban schools – Confounding stereotypes: Risk, resilience and achievement in urban schools – Moving practice forward at the district level – Supporting schools in difficult circumstances: The role of school to school cooperation – Moving leadership practice in schools forward – Collaboration with a city-wide purpose: Making paths for sustainable educational improvement – Beyond the school gates: Context, disadvantage and 'urban schools' – Drawing out the lessons: Leadership and collaboration – References – Index.

2006   180pp
978–0–335–21911–7 (Paperback)   978–0–335–21912–4 (Hardback)

CHILDREN, FAMILIES AND COMMUNITIES
CREATING AND SUSTAINING INTEGRATED SERVICES

Pat Broadhead, Chrissy Meleady and Marco Delgado

This book draws on the work of Sheffield Children's Centre, a well-known community cooperative which is recognized worldwide for its cutting edge approach and models of good practice that have emerged from community participation.

Gaining an insight into the work of the Centre contributes to a better understanding of the challenges, issues, difficulties and opportunities which confront integrated services for children and families. The authors illustrate how, through working closely with the local community and through hearing the voices of children and adults, service provision for children and families can meet needs and change lives.

The book:

- Looks at the alternative approach of Sheffield Children's Centre, where multi-professional working has grown through common principles and aspirations rather than through policy imperative and legislation
- Details innovative practices and approaches to holistic work with children and families
- Explores the challenges and celebrations of working with a wide range of children, families and communities both in the UK and internationally

Children, Families and Communities is ideal for researchers, policy makers, practitioners and students training to work with children and families from a range of disciplines such as education, health and social services, including those pursuing the NPQICL (National Professional Qualification for Integrated Centre Leadership) qualification and the EYPs (Early Years Professional Status).

Contents

Introduction – Acknowledgements – Foreword – Series Editor's Preface – The evolution of Sheffield Children's Centre; developing a project identity – Valuing children means valuing families – A community co-operative; growing and sustaining the services and the tensions in being a cutting-edge provider – Diversity as a cornerstone of centre development – International networks and global justice – a reciprocal highway for ongoing evolution – From cradle to grave for children, families and communities; understanding the holistic dynamic.

2007   136pp
978–0–335–22093–9 (Paperback)   978–0–335–22094–6 (Hardback)

THE URBAN PRIMARY SCHOOL

Meg Maguire, Tim Wooldridge and Simon Pratt-Adams

This book offers an in-depth understanding of the unique challenges and contributions of urban primary schools. The authors set urban education in the wider social context of structural disadvantage, poverty, oppression and exclusion, and reassert some critical urban educational concerns.

Recognising that practice needs to be informed by theory, they provide a strong theoretical framework alongside contemporary ethnographic data.

Drawing on their extensive experience in urban primary schools, as well as numerous case studies, the authors present a fresh and stimulating view of urban primary schools which will inspire education professionals and academics alike.

The Urban Primary School is essential reading for teachers and trainee teachers in urban primary schools, as well as for students of education, policy-makers, parents and school governors.

Contents
Series Editor's Foreword – Acknowledgements – Preface – Contextualising the Urban – Urban Primary Schools and Urban Children – Teachers – Headteachers – Parents Supporting Diversity – Social Class – Learning in the City – Social Justice – A USA Perspective – Understanding the Urban Primary School – Bibliography

2006   208pp
978–0–335- 20176–1 (Paperback) 978–0–335- 20177–8 (Hardback)

REFUGEE CHILDREN IN THE UK
Jill Rutter

Asylum migration causes intense media and political debate. However, little attention has been paid to how forced migrants can rebuild their lives in the UK or elsewhere.

This timely book analyzes the social policies that impact on refugee children's education, and:

- Provides the background to the migration of refugees
- Explores how dominant discourses about trauma homogenise and label a very diverse group of children
- Examines how policy towards refugees is made, and how it relates to practice
- Offers alternative visions for refugee settlement

Drawing on case studies of the experiences of refugee children, *Refugee Children in the UK* brings a much-needed insight into the needs of refugee children. It is valuable reading for academics, policy makers, students of education, sociology and social policy as well as education, health and social work professionals.

Contents
Setting the Scene – An Introduction – Who are refugee children? – Theoretical and research perspectives on refugee children – UK responses to refugee children – Learning from history: Responses to refugees 1900–89 – Modern asylum policy and its impact on children – How UK children view the refugee in their midst – National educational policy and the role of local authorities – School practices – Community case studies – The elusiveness of integration: The educational experiences of Congolese refugee children – The Somalis: Cultures of survival – Success stories: The Southern Sudanese – New visions for refugee children.

2006   248pp
978–0–335–21373–3 (Paperback)   978–0–335–21374–0 (Hardback)